*Praise for Other Girls Like Me . . .*

"*Other Girls Like Me* is funny and sad, powerful and inspirational, especially in these times that are calling for all of us to become activists. And Stephanie Davies can write. Her prose is lyrical, even at times mesmerizing." — Beverly Donofrio, *Riding in Cars with Boys*

"*Other Girls Like Me* is about women being concerned about the horrors in our world and being willing to protest and take nonviolent direct action—which is a very good thing. I do hope that lots of people read it and are inspired to take action themselves!" — Angie Zelter, Founder, Extinction Rebellion Peace

"*Other Girls Like Me* is a lyrical, fluent and elegant read—it is also funny and poignant in equal measure. In the pre Greta Thunberg era, this personal account of one young woman's journey into activism is captivating and compelling—and a salient reminder of how the power and solidarity of communities of people with shared values can shape and change our lives—for good!" — Ann Limb, Chair of The Scout Association, #1 2019 OUTstanding List of LGBT+ Public Sector Executives

# OTHER GIRLS LIKE ME

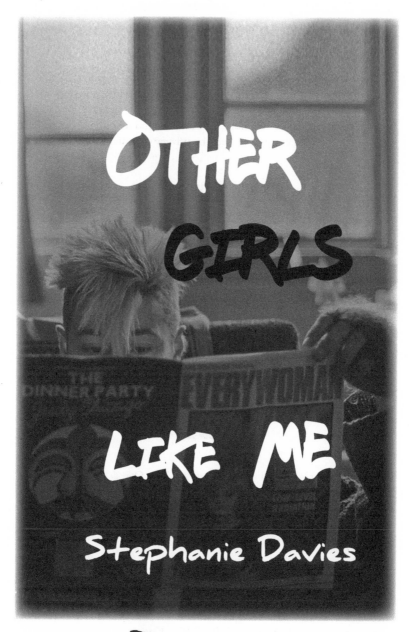

# OTHER GIRLS LIKE ME

## Stephanie Davies

BInk *Bink Books*

Bedazzled Ink Publishing Company • Fairfield, California

978-1-949290-38-7 paperback

Cover Photograph © Ming de Nasty 1985

Cover Design
by

"Happy Xmas (War is Over)" by John Lennon and Yoko Ono © Yoko Ono Lennon. Published by Lenono Music/Ono Music. Used by Permission.
"(I'm Not A) Real Woman" – Lyrics © Vi Subversa 1984. Used by Permission.

Bink Books
a division of
Bedazzled Ink Publishing Company
Fairfield, California
http://www.bedazzledink.com

*For my sister*
*Kate Brennan (1958-2017)*
*My greatest ally, biggest champion, closest friend*

*and my father*
*Robert Campbell Davies (1927-1984)*
*My hero, despite everything*

"I would not creep along the coast, but steer
Out in mid-sea, by guidance of the stars."
*George Eliot*


"WAR IS OVER (IF YOU WANT IT)"
*John Lennon and Yoko Ono*

# Chapter One

## "FREE NELSON MANDELA" THE SPECIALS

A CHILDHOOD IN St. Mary Bourne—an English village of thatched roof cottages winding along the banks of the Bourne River with its swaying water weeds, frogspawn, and fluttering ducks—was a childhood filled with wonders. I waded through fresh waters as the river rose anew from its barren bed each spring; swung across the river on tyres attached to ropes on summer nights; warmed my hands at autumn bonfires on golden evenings; and rolled in deep snow banks in the winter.

My family of six lived at the edge of the village, behind the flint schoolhouse adjacent to the primary school that my three siblings and I attended. There were eleven pupils in my year, with funny last names like Bone and Strange and Gibbons. We arrived in this peculiar land from the industrial north when I was six, my sister Kate was nine, my brother, Robert, four, with baby Sarah arriving not long after we did, bundled out of the ambulance one November afternoon and bustled into the bright kitchen for us to peer at in curiosity. People thought our Northern accents strange, but we soon lost them and became posh instead, never catching the lilting Hampshire accent that was so different from any I had ever heard.

Everything was different here. No lorries or buses rumbled past our front door, but instead there were fields and birds and horses wherever I looked, accompanied by the soothing sound of wood pigeons, hidden in trees. I lost myself in books and played classical guitar in the privacy of my attic bedroom, its slanted skylight revealing the stars, moon, and clouds in the changing sky. One evening at dusk, I watched spellbound from my bedroom window as two steaming bulls locked horns on the hill behind our house, the air visible from their flaring nostrils as they snorted and pounded the ground, dust flying. My father had landed a new job in what seemed like paradise.

But just fifteen miles away, a stretch of ancient common land, with jumping deer, bounding rabbits, and soaring kestrels, had been turned into an air force base that was soon to house the deadliest weapons ever held on our green and pleasant land: American cruise missiles, poised to strike against the Soviet Union. The first tiny signs came to us like the first buds of flowers in spring—first one American military family, then another, rented out cottages in the village; first one news piece, then another, announced the mounting support of our Prime Minister Margaret Thatcher for the United States President Ronald Reagan's build up to war.

St. Mary Bourne may have seemed like an unlikely breeding ground for an activist. But by the time the cruise missiles arrived, I was ready for them.

I BECAME AN activist—though not a feminist—with the blessings of the patriarchy—or at least of my father. I was fifteen and eating a bowl of cornflakes at the breakfast table one rainy, misty morning, when my father stood up abruptly and handed me *The Guardian* newspaper he'd just finished reading. He knew that, like him, I loved to follow current events, but his face was paler and more drawn than usual.

"Brace yourself," he said.

On the front page was a photograph of a teenager, his body bloody and limp, in the arms of a young man wearing denim dungarees who was racing toward the camera, desperate to find help. The dead boy's wailing sister, in the crisp white-collared dress and dark blazer of her school uniform, ran at his side, her arms spread out in horror, her face contorted in despair. Her brother's name was Hector Pieterson, and he had been shot dead by the police in the township of Soweto, South Africa, for taking part in a peaceful student protest against the enforced use of the white man's language, Afrikaans, in the classroom.

My father returned to the kitchen wearing his leather biker jacket, two helmets under his arm, and asked if I wanted a lift. I loved riding to school on the back of his BMW 750—along St. Mary Bourne's village road, which wound along the banks of the river and past our three churches, which my family never attended, and three pubs, which we did, often. We sailed past the watercress beds and under the

Victorian viaduct that strode across the outskirts of the village, then onto the single-track road that took us all the way to the market town of Whitchurch. I peered at the rolling hills over the high hedgerows filled with birds' nests and flowers, the two of us leaning as one, almost flat to the ground with every curve. He normally pointed out rabbits hopping across the meadows, reminding me of those in *Watership Down* who crossed our village on their journey to find a new home. But today the rabbits went unnoticed.

When we arrived, I quickly hurried away from him. I didn't want to bring attention to the fact that I was the headmaster's daughter.

At school that day, I could think and talk of nothing but Hector's photograph, which none of my classmates had seen. That night, my father and I sat riveted to the BBC six o'clock news in the living room of our 1960s bungalow, skipping the children's program, *The Magic Roundabout*, which made my father chortle, because today was not a day to smile. The story was the very first one, and the broadcast devoted most of its half hour to it. It turned out that Hector had been shot in the head and that at least one other child had been killed. There appeared to be many more deaths, the newscaster told us, as protests erupted around the country and police waded in to crowds of children with batons, hoses, and bullets. Hector's image flashed over and over on the screen.

"I'm going to give an assembly about this tomorrow," my father said, and I was happy, because maybe now I wouldn't be the only one in school who was paying attention; now they'd know what I was talking about. "I'll read something by Gandhi and Malcolm X."

Their books were on my shelves, alongside Che's *Guerrilla War*, *The Lord of the Rings*, and *The Last Unicorn*, so I ran upstairs to my attic bedroom to find them and came back down to hand them to him, feeling important, a small part of a historic moment. My father didn't do religious assemblies, because he was not religious and didn't think religion belonged in schools, but by law he had to offer them. So he used assemblies to talk about social justice, poverty, war, bullying, and kindness. He quoted from Dr. Martin Luther King, Jr., Bishop Desmond Tutu, George Orwell. I hung onto his every word. It was to please him that I called my dog Che, after the Cuban revolutionary Che Guevara.

A proud socialist in the conservative county of Hampshire, my father was nicknamed locally the Red Head because his school was the first comprehensive in the county, accepting all children no matter their background, academic status, or parental wealth. He called our school Testbourne, for the River Bourne in our village, and the River Test in Whitchurch, famous for its trout. A strong critic of the traditional grammar school system, which weeded out children with higher grades at the age of eleven for a superior education, my dad's school offered mixed ability classes, taught domestic science to boys and woodwork to girls, and had an egalitarian uniform of school sweatshirts with skirts or jeans. Interviewed by the *Hampshire Chronicle,* my father talked as much about the importance of the caretakers as he did the teachers. He was a true man of the people, at the helm of an educational experiment that believed all children deserved the same quality education. He was my hero.

He was my hero even though a few years earlier I'd been furious with him because he wouldn't support me playing football at school—my favourite thing—because I was a girl. I so wanted to understand his socialist utopia, I yearned to have a place in the society he dreamed up with his progressive friends over pints of beer in the village pub, spurred on by the revolutionaries, writers, and "angry young men" they hero-worshipped.

At home, my father quoted from Marx and Engels, and told us about the Bay of Pigs, when the bullying United States threatened the tiny island of Cuba, where Fidel Castro was creating a new, just world in which everyone had the right to housing, education, and health care. He told us how he'd stayed up until dawn night after night during the Cuban Missile Crisis, chain-smoking and drinking whiskey at the kitchen table in our small semi-detached home on the edge of a dual carriageway in Stafford, wracked with worry that a nuclear war would break out in the world he had just brought my older sister, Kate, and me into.

Kate said that he was indoctrinating us, that we should have more freedom to develop our own ideas. I was a bit caught because I wanted to agree with everything my pretty and clever sister said so that perhaps she would start to like me, but I actually agreed with everything my father said. When he gave me a book of anti-war poetry, I devoured its terrifying, traumatizing pages about children killed in Vietnam, boy soldiers slaughtered in the trenches in World War I, the cruelty of man against man.

That evening, as my father flicked through the books looking for a good reading for the next day's school assembly, I sat down on the sofa with its polyester mustard covers that clashed marvellously with our red and orange swirling carpet and the curtains' bold blue and green flowers—the same sofa my father lay on to listen to classical music after a day at school—or sometimes he lay down on the floor, in chronic pain from his bad back. Then he closed the door to us all, lost in a world we could not reach. Once, when I was seven, I stood at the frosted glass door to the living room in floods of tears.

"What's wrong?" he asked, opening the door and looking down at me.

"This music is all about death," I said.

He took me into the room, sat me beside him, and placed my hand in his. We weren't the kind of family who touched much, and this intimacy felt strange but soothing.

"This is Sibelius's second symphony," he said. "He's describing the magic of the countryside coming back to life as winter turns to spring. Listen to those strings."

I listened.

"That's the sound of the streams unfreezing and flowing down the mountainside again. If you listen to the music really carefully, you can hear the birds finding their song and furry animals creeping out from their winter hibernation. You see, it's a celebration. Not sad at all." I nodded as he handed me the large handkerchief he always kept in his trouser pocket, and I blew my nose.

After that, every so often, I quietly opened the door to the living room as he lay there, eyes closed, and sat beside him so he would make up happy stories of animals rejoicing that the hunter was dead, or the long winter ended, to go with the music I still thought of as sad. I didn't understand that it was my father who was sad.

Sitting opposite him now as he paged through the books looking for a reading, I could hear the angry clunking of pots and pans as my mother prepared the evening meal—what we called tea, because we were from the North with our proud working-class roots, and not dinner like our wealthy neighbours, the Macnamaras. I was sure what the Macnamaras served was dramatically different, too. They probably had grilled trout, fresh from Whitchurch, new potatoes glistening in real butter, watercress from the village beds, and elegant glasses of red wine. We had egg and chips, steak and kidney pie, or baked beans or tinned tomatoes on toast, with a pot of strong tea always sitting centre stage. Right then, my mother was no doubt squashing wasps on the windowpane with her thumb, with no fear of getting stung, as they buzzed lazily into the kitchen to their doom.

Over the days that followed, Hector and his sister were never far from my mind. I wondered if Hector and his sister ever played football together, like I did with my brother, Robert, my closest friend and ally in the family. I wondered if they could afford a football, if there was even room in the narrow, crowded township streets I'd seen over and over again on the television to play anything at all. I kept the horrific front-page photograph in a large brown envelope in my attic bedroom and looked at it every morning before I went to school and every evening before I went to bed. I wondered what it would be like if suddenly I had to take all my classes in German or Chinese, the way the children in Soweto were forced to learn their classes in Afrikaans.

I re-read the chapter in Angela Davis's autobiography where she stood up for herself in a shoe shop in Birmingham, Alabama, where black people were normally served at the back of the shop, out of sight. This time, she spoke French with her sister, pretending to be from Martinique, and got the kind of treatment normally reserved for whites because she was perceived to be an exotic foreigner. My heart always beat just a little bit faster when I got to the moment she exposed the shopkeeper for being a racist. I flicked through George Jackson's *Soledad Brother*, unable to comprehend how an eighteen-year-old could receive a sentence of one year to life for allegedly stealing seventy dollars from a petrol station, devastated that he was shot dead by prison guards at the terrifying sounding San Quentin State Prison. I felt lucky that such books sat in pride of place on my parents' bookshelves, by authors that nobody at school seemed to have heard of, including the teachers.

I immersed myself in the daily news accounts about the Soweto Uprising, where the death toll was rising dramatically each day. I learned that in South Africa, like in the south of the United States until the 1960s, black families couldn't eat at the same restaurants, sit on the same buses, study at the same universities, or go to the same beaches as white people. They couldn't vote. They couldn't travel freely and had to carry an ID card at all times. Many were forced to live at the edges of large cities or close to diamond or gold mines so they could work as maids, factory workers, or miners; others were banished to so-called "homelands" in rural areas with no running water or electricity. Somehow, and I wondered how, some made it to university and got degrees, like Nelson Mandela, a lawyer serving a life sentence on Robben Island, where he had to break stones in a dusty quarry on a daily basis and endure beatings. Yet he still managed to lead the resistance movement, the African National Congress, offering hope and a sense of justice to millions in Africa and one teenage girl in a small village in England. I carefully copied down his closing remarks from his trial in 1966 and blue tacked them to the wall next to my bed:

> I have cherished the ideal of a democratic and free society in which all persons live together in harmony and with equal opportunities. It is an ideal which I hope to live for and to achieve. But if needs be, it is an ideal for which I am prepared to die.

I was determined to avenge Hector's death and help bring apartheid to its knees and was amazed when my mother found someone in our village who knew firsthand about apartheid.

At a cocktail party in the neighbouring hamlet of Binley, my parents had just accepted their first glasses of white wine when the host, an elderly man with a handlebar moustache and houndstooth jacket, asked my father if he liked to hunt foxes.

"Absolutely not." My father didn't miss a beat. "As Oscar Wilde said, 'Hunting is the unspeakable in the pursuit of the uneatable.'"

"You're absolutely right," came a woman's voice from behind my mother. "Foxes are such dear little souls."

The voice belonged to Cluny, a white South African who had recently retired to Stoke, the next village along the valley, and who was a lifelong crusader against apartheid. She was delighted to learn from my mother about my obsession with the Soweto Uprising, and invited me for tea.

So began a summer of Sunday mornings of cycling excitedly along to Cluny's white stone cottage to dunk biscuits in milky coffee as we sat on stuffed Queen Anne chairs in her exotic living room, filled with photographs of South Africa and books about African tribes. She told me stories of life under apartheid and her move to London where she became an outspoken critic of the South African regime and joined the famous Bishop Trevor Huddleston on demonstrations. She supplied me with all kinds of ammunition—books by Doris Lessing, articles by Nelson Mandela, a subscription to *Anti-Apartheid News*—so that when the autumn term arrived I was ready. Armed with disinvestment petitions for my fellow students and teachers to sign, I started with Mr. Floyd, the new curly-haired Physical Education (PE) teacher, who had just come back from a three-week holiday in South Africa. He refused.

"Things aren't so bad there," he said, patronizingly, smiling as he leaned against the tennis court fence, his face and muscular arms and legs still bearing traces of the tan he had acquired in the country that killed Hector. "You'd have to be there to see for yourself."

"Didn't you even hear about the Soweto Uprising?" I exclaimed. "It happened just before you went."

I stormed off, petition in hand, and at home over the tea table, I was furious when I told my dad about the encounter.

"You should sack him," I said in conclusion.

He smiled. "I can't sack someone for not sharing my political views, unfortunately. But I can refuse to promote him if you like."

"Yes!" I said triumphant.

Then I noticed the slight crease at the edges of his hazel eyes and realized he was teasing me. But I also knew that he was proud of me as I was of him.

The following Sunday, I told Cluny what my teacher had said.

"I'm not surprised, Steph," she said. "It was only when I got to London that I began to realize how absolutely dreadful everything was back home. But we were so cloistered, we had no idea what was really going on. There are always people who are quite happy living with their eyes closed to what is going on for those less fortunate around them."

Later, when I was living at the women's peace camp at Greenham Common, I would think about the inequities perpetrated against women and how the men in our world were not so different from the privileged classes in Cluny's—so accustomed to the iniquities they were blind to the injustices. Not that women and girls were beaten or killed for who we were, not publicly anyway, not en masse, not as part of a government agenda. But I was to learn at Women's Aid about the silent, behind the scenes, domestic murders and abuses of women and girls, and find a vocabulary to describe the deep misogyny that ran through everything around me as I grew up—TV shows, literature, politics, sports. And to see how easy it was for so many to do nothing, to see nothing, to reside numbly in the status quo.

I always thought my father was different. For as long as I could remember, he'd taught me to take the side of the underdog—the local football team playing the First Division giant; the miners standing up to the government's union-busting policies; black Americans struggling for their civil rights. I had never thought about women and girls as a group in need of emancipation. He'd never talked about that, and I knew he had my best interests at heart. When he or my mother ever mentioned the word "feminist," I got the impression that feminists were all American, unshaved, and too loud. It was only when I became a feminist myself, in the muddy fields surrounding an American nuclear base, that I began to understand why he didn't take my side against injustices I felt so very deeply—like the time the school policy barred girls from going on a school trip to Wembley.

Robert and I had been kicking a football back and forth to each other since he was four and I was five and a half. I was obsessed with football, but I had never seen a live match, with its floodlights, singing, and swaying of the crowd. So when I was eleven and my school arranged a trip to watch England play West Germany at Wembley I couldn't contain my excitement. I'd been swapping football cards for years with Robert, and now I was going to see the players in person! Robert and I watched Match of the Day together every Saturday night; I joined him at the recreation ground to play evening matches with his friends, and was even picked for his boy scout team when they needed more "men." I played in my wellington boots, because I was a girl, and my parents didn't want to buy me football boots. It made it harder to run, but I ran as best I could, and I knew my brother was proud of me anyway, even of the time I tripped my opponent over as he headed toward the goal, so adamant was I to stop him scoring. Robert's approval was all that mattered—that, and getting to play the beautiful game. I supported Manchester United, partly because it was the biggest team closest to Accrington, the Lancashire mill town my father was from. But mainly it was because Robert did. He hero-worshipped Georgie Best, its handsome Northern Irish whiskey-drinking poster boy, as well as Bobby Charlton, with his famous comb-over and gentlemanly demeanour, who captained England when we beat West Germany in the World Cup in 1966. To show my support, I wore a long red and white scarf and matching bobble hat in the winter as I rode the Macnamaras' Shetland pony, Winky, through the village, or ran through the bluebell woods with Che, my constant, happy friend who slept on my chest as a puppy and who was always at my side. Now, I was going to Wembley! Robert still had a year to go before he attended Testbourne, but I planned to ask my dad if he could make an exception and let Robert come along.

I was outside performing cartwheels when my mother called, "Stephanie! Your tea will go cold," through the kitchen window in a much stronger Lancashire accent than the slight accent she had—which meant she was in a good mood and probably pretending to be a worker in a Northern chippie—to make my dad laugh.

I did one last cartwheel and ran breathlessly into the kitchen, where Robert was already seated at the Formica table, a steaming pot of tea in the centre. "Guess what?" I barged past my mother and plopped myself next to him. "I'm going to see England play West Germany. Dad, can Robert come, too?"

"Sorry, Steph," my dad said, taking his place at the head of the table. "It's boys only."

I felt punched in the heart. "Boys only? Why boys only? I want to go."

"Girls only want to go so they can be near the boys." He winked at my mother, who was at the stove slopping portions of stewed apple, pork, and mashed potato onto the plates.

"That's such rubbish. And you know how much I love football. It's not fair," I said, my heart racing with indignation. How could my egalitarian father be saying such things?

"She looks so beautiful when she pouts her lips like that, doesn't she?" He winked at my mother.

I looked across the kitchen table and tried to catch the eye of Kate, my hero, who hadn't had the time of day for me since I'd started school and no longer needed to sit at the small desks she used to line up in the garage for me and my friends, while she stood in front of a blackboard, chalk in hand, teaching us what she had learned that day in school. Today, as always, she was remote and unreachable, locked in her own world, humming a tune to herself, her long curled hair swaying as she moved her head back and forth, quietly practising for her next play at Andover Grammar. Little Sarah, focused on trying to keep her food on her fork as she ate, was too young to understand what was going on.

After doing the washing up, Robert and I went out together quietly and kicked the ball to each other on the football pitch. He said nothing. He didn't need to; I knew he understood.

"It's your school," I said to my father the next morning over breakfast, unable to stop myself even though I'd decided not to speak to him today. "Why can't you just change the rules and let girls go?"

"Sorry, love, the Wembley football trip is for boys." He put *The Guardian* down, took off his black-rimmed reading glasses, and looked directly at me. "Because the boys are the ones who play football. The girls go to Wembley to watch hockey. Because the girls play hockey."

I snorted derisively. "Nobody cares about hockey. It's not even on the telly."

My father stood up from the table, pushing back his chair. "Do you want a lift to school?"

"No," I flung over my shoulder as I grabbed my bag and ran out of the back door, vowing not to go anywhere near this second-class school trip to watch a bunch of women I had never heard of play a game nobody was interested in. And a few minutes later, marching to the school bus stop, another vow occurred to me: I would create a girls' football league at Testbourne. All we needed was forty-four girls, eleven from each house—Kestrel, Hawk, Eagle, and Merlin.

I invited my new best friend, Bridget, to stay over that weekend, and it took no convincing at all for her to agree to help. Bridget was fearless, with thick blond hair, mischievous blue eyes, and a wicked giggle. She always made me feel adventurous, courageous, and free. We crept out of the house at dawn on Saturday morning to avoid my operatic mother who could explode into fits of shouting at any moment—for leaving a shoe in the wrong place or walking in a slouch, at our next-door neighbour she called Hammer Happy Harris for banging on the vintage car he was constructing in his garage.

Once Bridget and I had made it safely down the driveway to the road, our voices rose from whispers to excited squeals as we discussed our new league. We walked a distance across fields of wet grass sparkling with dew and along the winding village road, wondering who in her house, Hawk, and who in mine, Kestrel, would agree to play. Then Bridget stopped suddenly and said, "What if we lie down here and listen for cars?" She promptly lay flat on her back in the middle of the road.

We hadn't seen a car the whole time we'd been walking, so I felt pretty confident we wouldn't get run over as I lay down next to her. She was giggling, putting her ear flat to the road, listening for vibrations. I lay nervously next to her, the cold tarmac pressed against my warm cheek, imagining something horrible would occur. Nothing bad happened, but it would the next time I found myself lying flat on my face on the ground years later, ordered to lie at the feet of men with guns inside the military base at Greenham Common. I would remember this moment in the road then and wish that Bridget, with her courage and feistiness, were with me.

Back at school the next week, Bridget and I got to work recruiting our classmates, and before we knew it we had four football teams. Over the next two weeks, we played lunchtime matches against each other, each refereed by one of the older boys. Then we picked a team of the best players, which included me in midfield and Bridget on the wing, to play the boys. It was an exciting day, despite the rain; some of the older boys came out to watch, as well as a few teachers, one of whom refereed. I looked up hopefully every now and then to see if my dad had come, but he never appeared. We lost by one goal—a great accomplishment, considering most of the girls had only just started to learn the sport. I was proud, and back home when I told my dad, he said he was proud of me. But he still wouldn't put football on the curriculum for girls.

"It's not up to me," he said. "It's up to the PE teachers."

I tore out of the house, flew across the fields, and leapt over the wooden stiles, leaving astonished cows in my wake. I climbed the tallest tree at the recreation ground, the one that even the boys dared not mount. It was considered too dangerous, and I thought of how angry my mother would be—she'd already cut down my favourite tree at the end of our driveway because she was fed up of calling me in to tea only to find me high up in its branches, waving down at her. I rose up, dangled my legs over the highest branch, and surveyed the upturned faces of the boys far beneath me. My heart racing, my mind in a fury, I dared them to join me. I vowed to myself that one day I would show my dad that girls were just as good as boys. If not better. I didn't know that this football business was just one of many disappointments to come; I'd yet to realize that my father just wasn't going to see it my way no matter how hard I tried. He really did see girls in a different light, and I really was, in his mind, destined to be a wife, and because he thought I looked like Brigitte Bardot, a sex kitten, and because I was good at languages, a bilingual secretary.

But he was dead wrong. I would never be a secretary. I would have a secretary.

# Chapter Two
## "IT'S DIFFERENT FOR GIRLS" JOE JACKSON

AND THEN I sprouted breasts.

Small as they were, they seemed to exist to be commented on, admired, imitated, or alluded to in knowing asides by male teachers and boys, while in the wider world, radio DJs, TV presenters, artists, and cartoonists never seemed happier than when breasts were in the picture. The canned laughter got louder as a woman's boobs came too close to the face of one of TV's *Likely Lads*; Benny Hill surrounded himself with buxom, giggling, scantily-dressed women; and even our family's favourite show, *Monty Python's Flying Circus*, liked low cut dresses on its real women, whose breasts seemed just bursting to get out, while the male actors mimicking us wore unduly large protrusions under their too-tight sweaters.

I tried on my first training bra at the age of twelve. It was blue and flowery, a hand-me-down from our next-door neighbour's daughter. Looking in my full-length mirror at the growing up body staring back at me, I quite liked the warm fuzz of dark hair appearing under my arms and between my legs. I read in a popular book of the time, *The Naked Ape*, that alarm of this new hair growth was the reason pubescent girls didn't like spiders—I certainly didn't, calling my mother on many a night to free me from the huge harvest spiders attracted to my warm attic room—and I wondered if boys didn't get hair like we did, since apparently they weren't afraid of spiders. Boys seemed to get a better deal all round, and whenever I could I insisted on wearing boys' clothes, never happier than the day our local Bobby mistook me for a boy in my floppy camouflage hat covered with badges and patches—of the real Che Guevara, a peace sign, the Newbury air show, a smiley face, a panda. But alone in my room, I ran my hands over my new curves every now and then and cupped my hand over my mouth and moved my head from side to side to imagine what it was like to kiss a boy, which surely would happen soon now that I was becoming a teenager. I thought of asking Kate, being so pretty, with her long thick hair, freckles, and green owl-like eyes, how she managed with all the extra attention to her burgeoning womanhood. She wore makeup and real bras, and curled her hair with big hair rollers every night so that it fell in the mornings like a dark waterfall around her pale, delicate face. I felt curious and slightly envious when I heard her giggle as I peered through the living room window to watch her kiss a boyfriend goodbye on the front porch. But I knew deep down that Kate would never fully understand, because she didn't like to play football as I did, so it wouldn't matter to her that breasts were the reason girls couldn't play football, in case the ball hit us and hurt us. Breasts, this puberty thing, got in the way of how I wanted to be treated—like a boy. I did my best to be like Theo, the cropped-haired tomboy who lived in the next village over and wore jeans, a parka, and big boots, but no amount of baggy clothing could hide the fact that underneath it all I had some curves. And so I endured wolf whistles and strange clucking noises from men, with whom my father, subtly, seemed to be in collusion.

HE CALLED ME into the kitchen one warm July afternoon, not long after I'd turned thirteen. I'd been heading excitedly out of the door to play on roller skates with friends at the village recreation ground.

"I've just been chatting with Mark," he said, pouring himself some tea.

Mark Pendleton-Brown was my father's best friend in the village, a frightfully posh psychologist with wild white hair and a tall wife with short blond hair who wore smocks and jeans and no makeup.

"Mark always expected you to turn out to be a beauty," my dad continued as he stirred his cup of tea, and he seemed to be proud.

I squirmed uncomfortably, feeling suddenly self-conscious and exposed. I just wanted to get going and try out my new skates.

"He's going to be looking out for you as you walk past his house today," he added. "He wants to know if, now that you're a young woman, you've turned out the way he expected."

I said nothing and skulked out of the house, deflated, my skates dangling at my side.

I considered walking along the footpath that meandered through cow pastures and wheat fields to the recreation ground to avoid going past Mark's cottage on the village street. But I wanted to try out my new skates; we were going to have some races, and I needed a bit of practice so that I could win. But what if I skated past Mark's house on my new skates and fell; I'd look ridiculous. So I took my skates in hand and walked along the village road. As I walked by Mark's white cottage, with its black beams and yellow thatch, I expected to see him in the garden overflowing with purple, red, white, and yellow flowers, with his wife at his side. I wondered if she knew what he'd said about me. I glanced covertly from under my fringe to see whether he was looking, but I didn't see him. I felt sick to my stomach, and a slight tinge of indignation fluttered in my chest. As soon as I was past, I bent down, put on my skates, and raced to the rec, past the village hall with its memories of Christmas pantomimes, where one year I had played a petal in the War of the Roses, the next, an elf, and, most recently, the devil. But the roller skate races with my friends were overshadowed by thoughts about whether Mark had seen me or not, what he thought, and whether he was on the phone to my dad at that very moment giving his judgment.

As I skated back to the house along St. Mary Bourne's main road, any triumph I felt at winning the races was interrupted by a rapid succession of unwelcome images. My mother saying that men didn't need me to be clever, just sexy, that I'd better be careful how much hockey and tennis I played because my legs would get too muscular, and didn't I want them to be slender and attractive, like Kate's? My father's "art" book filled with photographs of unclothed young women climbing stairs, lying on sofas, smiling coyly, nakedly, at the camera. And random newsflashes about women who had been raped or assaulted, which noted that what the victim was wearing—a short skirt or tight jeans—made her too sexy for men to resist.

I was confused. I was angry. But I didn't understand why. Feminism hadn't yet reached St. Mary Bourne, except in the nascent form of one indignant teenager, who didn't yet have the vocabulary or the understanding to put into words what she felt. I wanted to turn to my father, but he seemed to be part of the problem.

At breakfast the next morning, my father didn't mention Mark, and I wondered if it was because he didn't want to disappoint me. Did my father's middle-aged, white-haired, pot-bellied friend not find his teenage daughter attractive after all?

Mr. Mandell did. He was the tall, balding teacher who grabbed my soft face at a fifth form party in a darkened drama classroom, Gary Glitter blaring in the background. He pushed me against a wall and stuck his oversize tongue down my throat, his scratchy face rubbing against my cheek, his probing tongue making me gag. I was ashamed and disgusted and I told no one, though I saw Mr. Floyd, the PE teacher who wouldn't sign my petition, watching, and smirking. I didn't even tell my father, who surely had the power to sack Mr. Mandell. But would he? And could I have even found the words to describe the sickening gulf in my stomach mingled with a confusing pride at being chosen by a grown, albeit repulsive man, for such an adult act?

When my parents gave me a pair of suspenders and stockings for my sixteenth birthday it seemed normal, yet the only time I wore short skirts was for hockey—and then I was carrying a stick.

BY THE TIME I reached Cricklade Sixth Form College in Andover, I was a passionate hockey player. It was the only outdoor winter sport allowed to girls, and I'd given up hope of ever playing football, though I still kicked a ball around with Robert whenever I could and avidly watched Match of the Day on weekends. I'd been captain of Testbourne's school hockey team for five years and played midfield for our county of Hampshire, but when I joined Cricklade's hockey team, my father gave me an ultimatum: "Now that you're sixteen, we're stopping your allowance. So if you want to get clothes or any extras, it has to come out of your own pocket."

"This is like *Catch 22*," I said, citing my father's favourite book. "Hampshire matches are always on Saturdays. That's the only time I could work."

My father shook his head. "You have to learn to pay your way. It's up to you. You can play hockey for Cricklade. But if you want to play for Hampshire, too, don't expect a clothes allowance from us."

My favourite outfit was a pair of skin-tight jeans and a blue oversize sweater, and I thought for a moment how I could go for a year in this one outfit. I tried it out, but it didn't last long, because if I wanted a boyfriend, if I wanted to be someone, I'd need money for clothes and makeup and drinks at the pub. So I settled for a Saturday cashier job at W. H. Smiths, wistfully looking out of the window as I handed people change for pens, newspapers, or magazines, all the while imagining myself running around a muddy field slamming a hockey ball with a stick. I was keenly aware when my brother, Robert, left secondary school two years later that no word was mentioned about him giving up his Saturday football to work in a shop.

I may not have been able to play football, but I did manage to attract the captain of Cricklade College's football team. I first noticed him when he pushed in front of me on the lunch queue, his blue-green eyes flashing at me as he turned around to smile, his brown curls flouncing. Soon we were an item. I liked that his eyes changed from blue to green, depending on the light. I liked that people compared him to Paul Newman, I liked having someone's strong hand to hold, and the quick hello and goodbye kisses in the college hallways that showed the other students I was worth something. And Martin liked that I could hold my own in a conversation about football, unlike most girls, and he seemed interested when I talked about apartheid. He introduced me to punk rock and smoking pot and was proud when I embraced both as heartily as he did. I didn't really want to have sex with him, though, but he made it clear that if I didn't I'd lose him, so a month after turning seventeen, I asked my family doctor to put me on the pill. Late one afternoon, in his bedroom at his family's modern home on a cul-de-sac in Andover, Martin lay heavily on top of me. Leonard Cohen's *Suzanne* droned softly in the background, filling me with a sad melancholy. It hurt and there was blood and he seemed satisfied.

After that, whatever chance he could get, we had sex, which I endured while he enjoyed. Sometimes he took me by the hand and down to the river to have sex before we went to the pub in Abbots Ann, where I stood silently behind him as he laughed and chatted with his footballing friends, who leered conspiratorially at me from behind their pint glasses. Whenever we stayed at his parents' house, I left the bedroom assigned to me and tiptoed down the cream carpeted staircase as though I had no choice, feeling dread, wondering what unpleasant acts he was conjuring up for me, wondering if he read pornography—because how else did he get such degrading ideas? Or was this what sex was, what everyone else did, and I just had to get used to it?

I'd once told my mother I wished I were funny and entertaining like my older sister, Kate, and she responded, "Oh don't worry, you don't have to say anything. You're the kind of girl men just like to look at." I wondered then and I wondered when I was with Martin, if this really was all that girls like me could hope for. With the money I'd earned by giving up playing hockey for Hampshire, I bought halter neck tops and flowery skirts and wore heels for the first time, but Martin didn't approve of most of my outfits, saying they were too sexy, too revealing, and he didn't like me wearing makeup except when I was with him. He seemed to like me better in jeans and a Testbourne rugby shirt.

He mostly wanted me to watch him play football or cricket for his village team on Sunday afternoons or to stand in muddy fields and watch him ride his motorbike through fields or woods in a nature-destroying motorcycle sport called trials riding. He never once showed up to watch one of my hockey matches for Cricklade, or later, for Bath University. And I never asked him to, though I secretly wished he would just turn up and see me play my best match ever and be impressed. But that wasn't what boyfriends did—it was girlfriends who were supposed to stand on the sidelines admiringly.

He also didn't want me to have male friends, play my guitar, or listen to soul music. One of the first albums I ever bought was Stevie Wonder's *Songs in the Key of Life*.

"Why do you listen to that kind of music?" he asked. "It's just sexy, it's just you asking men to look at you."

Martin said he knew how men thought because he had two brothers and lots of footballing friends and that he was just trying to protect me. He said that men should always protect their women and that I was too naïve to be left alone with them. Nothing in the media seemed to contradict what he said. Our most famous children's TV presenters, Jimmy Saville and Rolf Harris, were found out, far too late, to be paedophiles preying upon young girls, so perhaps he had a point, up to a point. But it didn't sit right. I missed my male friends from Testbourne—the ones who became my main friends after Bridget moved away, because no girl could ever replace her—as one by one I stopped returning their phone calls. We'd only laughed and gossiped, and none of them had ever made a pass at me. Martin said it was just a matter of time.

LUCKILY, WHEN I went to Bath University to study French and Russian, he went to a university in London, where he couldn't stop me from doing what I wanted. I listened to Stevie Wonder and Earth Wind and Fire and Chaka Khan, played my guitar, and wore tight trousers and sometimes makeup when I went out dancing with my best friend, Fran. And as long as Martin was not visiting, I threw myself into whatever the student anti-apartheid group was doing. I joined sit-ins in the administrative offices to call for disinvestment in South Africa; I stood on picket lines in front of Barclays Bank every week because it was the major bank in South Africa and we didn't want it to prop up the regime anymore; I attended national marches in London to call for an end to apartheid and listened to Tony Benn, Julie Christie, Michael Foot, and other inspiring speakers call us to action. I met two real-life anti-apartheid exiles living in Bath and became friends with their doe-eyed and passionate daughter, Hannah, who helped me concoct a brilliant idea to support the anti-apartheid struggle, which I presented in the form of a motion to Bath University's Students' Union.

It was the first time I had addressed a large crowd of people—there must have been a hundred students in the room, and I didn't dare look up as I made my way to the stage in case it made me even more nervous. My hand shook and my voice faltered as I took the microphone.

"So many of us play Space Invaders," I said. "Have you ever wondered what happens to the thousands of pounds the game generates every year? Or what we could do with it? Why not send it to the African National Congress school in Tanzania for South African children who don't have access to education?"

I mustered the courage to look around the room, and people seemed to be listening. A few were nodding. Students were sitting on chairs lined up in rows, leaning against walls, or sitting, legs dangling, on tables at the edge of the room. My anti-apartheid friends were all sitting together at the front—including students from Zimbabwe, Palestine, and Iraq, as well as from the United Kingdom. They were all smiling enthusiastically.

We'd done our research and had at least one university administrator on our side. We felt pretty confident this would pass—and I was elated to be doing my part for the struggle.

"Black South Africans are denied their human rights, including the right to education," I said, and any nervousness fell from me like a cloak. I couldn't save Hector and all the children killed in the Soweto Uprising, but I could make sure our Students' Union sent thousands of easily gained pounds to the school to help other Hectors, other students.

"We all know apartheid is evil," I said in conclusion, "and now we have a chance to do something about it. By supporting the school, we'll be supporting the future leaders of a new South Africa. One where everyone can vote, go to school, and be treated with respect. And it takes no effort on our part. We just continue playing our space invaders."

Half the room broke out in applause. My face felt hot and I knew it must be flushed red. I didn't care. I rushed over to my anti-apartheid friends, who patted me on the back, congratulated me, hugged me.

Then the incoming Students' Union president stood up. She was skinny and serious, wearing steel-rimmed glasses, her mousy brown hair pulled back tightly in a ponytail.

"If this vote goes through," she said. "Then I will step down. The ANC school is a training ground for guerrillas."

My friends and I booed in unison. I knew this was not true—and even if it were, how else were the people of South Africa to gain their freedom? And wasn't she running on a left-wing Labour ticket?

The vote was lost, and I was devastated—and I was devastated again when in its coverage of the event, the *Students' Union News* talked more about the motion of my hips as I walked to the podium than the motion to bring justice to the children of South Africa. I called Martin in floods of tears.

"Why are you *really* crying?" he asked as I sobbed in the damp-smelling red telephone box. "You can't be upset about that stupid school. It's got to be something else. Or someone else."

It did occur to me that my boyfriend preferred cross-examining me over possible imaginary flirtations to hearing what I believed in. But Martin was the first person I had ever slept with and that seemed to have created a glue between us I couldn't unstick. This is what sex and love were like, I thought. Even when he began to call me a bitch on a holiday together in Greece when I let slip that I had played guitar with a male friend and gone riding in his sports car back at university. Martin stopped speaking to me for two agonizing days, then when he finally spoke, he called me a whore and ordered me not to speak to any other men. He declared he now had to keep a closer eye on me and might finish with me anyway, depending on how I behaved.

Then he called me more ugly names whenever we had sex, and when he was done he turned his back to me.

After I returned from Greece, I listened constantly to KC and the Sunshine Band's "Please Don't Go," choking back tears, distraught at the thought of Martin leaving me. It didn't occur to me to question whether I might not want to stay with him.

I was so upset I told my mother. I was nineteen and just about to start my second year at university. She was driving me back to Bath after the summer holiday, and I told her how I was no longer allowed to talk to boys, play my guitar, listen to the music I liked, or wear the clothes I chose. I hadn't said so much to her in years—ever since she had given away my beloved dog, Che, soon after Bridget left, leaving me friendless and bereft—and I felt suddenly vulnerable and hopeful.

My mother's eyes were on the road, looking straight ahead. Finally, she said, "You're like a prisoner. And Martin has the key."

A chink of light entered my heart.

And then she asked how my friend Fran was and moved on to tell me animatedly about my sister Kate's wonderful boyfriend, how handsome and kind and caring he was.

I slumped back into my seat and stared numbly at the English countryside racing past, the lyrics of "Please Don't Go" playing louder than ever in my head.


I DID NOT give Martin quite all of the power because I could be sneaky.

Fran and I bought the same suede ankle boots, in different colours, and I bought a pair of black shiny skin-tight trousers. I wore them with a big, loose, green and red stripey T-shirt to go out dancing with Fran, with whom I shared a room, and sometimes clothes. I wore them when Peter Gabriel performed at the university, and we all sang along in rapture to "Solsbury Hill," inspired by the real Solsbury Hill just outside Bath. I wore them to university discos, dancing late into the night with Fran to Earth Wind and Fire, Joe Jackson, the Beat, the Specials, and our hometown Graduate, which later became Tears for Fears, whom we once saw live in a small club, dancing close enough to the band we could have touched them.

Then he found the trousers. It was on one of his usual visits to Bath, with Fran staying over at her boyfriend's so that Martin and I could sleep together in our room. It was Sunday morning, the day he was set to leave. I was still in bed and he was getting dressed when he noticed them hanging in the wardrobe. I was groggily drinking coffee from a white mug with the words "End Apartheid!" emblazoned on its side. He lifted the shiny trousers up between his thumb and forefinger, frowning as if they were filthy and smelled foul, and glared at me, dangling them in front of my face. My heart pounded and my mouth was dry.

"What are these?"

"Trousers."

"They don't look like trousers."

"Well they are. I just got them."

As soon as the words left my mouth, I panicked. What if Fran had taken photos of me wearing them? What if he found the photos and realized I'd had the trousers longer than I admitted?

"When do you wear these?"

"When I go dancing."

"Why?"

"They're comfortable. I like the way they feel."

"Put them on."

"Now?"

"Yes."

"Why? I'm in bed. I'm hardly awake. I can wear them next time you come if you want."

"I want to see them now."

I climbed out of bed and squeezed into them. They were as tight and shiny as the bottom half of a suit you'd wear to deep-sea dive.

"You look like a slut," he said. "Take them off. And get rid of them."

"But I wear them with a big baggy top," I pleaded. "Nobody can see my bum."

I pointed to the long oversized shirt I wore in bed. "It looks pretty much like this, how I wear them."

"I don't believe you. I don't want to see these again."

I pulled my favourite trousers off with difficulty and hung them back in the wardrobe, stroking them goodbye as I did so. I was afraid these trousers might be the catalyst to end the relationship that I was unfathomably and inextricably bound to. My mother called Martin my jailor. But he was also judge and jury and I was constantly in the dock, pleading to be seen for who I really was.

I loved the narrow silhouette those trousers gave my skinny legs, the daring of the ankle boots, the softness against my skin. They made me feel like dancing, and I didn't want to let them go. But he'd ask me how I got rid of them, he'd check, he wouldn't forget. It wasn't worth the lying and hiding and worrying to keep them, so one day soon after, I gave my lovely shiny black trousers to Fran, and, while she tried them on, I stared distractedly for a moment at the huge *Gone with the Wind* poster on our wall, depicting Margaret Thatcher as Scarlett O' Hara in the arms of Ronald Reagan as Rhett Butler, an ominous nuclear mushroom behind them. Then we went out to a university disco and I watched her, enviously, as we danced together to her favourite dancing song, Chrissie Hynde's "Brass in Pocket." Fran was smaller than me and people thought she looked like Debbie Harry, and to me she really did as she gyrated in front of me in her new shiny black trousers, mouthing the lyrics with her perfectly formed lips:

Cause I gonna make you see
There's nobody else here, no one like me.

# Chapter Three

## "SOMEONE SAVED MY LIFE TONIGHT" ELTON JOHN

AND THEN I was saved from Martin when, at the age of twenty, for my third year of university, I spent a magical nine months abroad, far, far away, in a small French town called Riberac—where people didn't ask me who my father or my boyfriend was, and I got my first inkling that I might be enough just as I was.

Riberac was in the lush countryside of the Dordogne, where neat rows of grapevines adorned rolling hills surrounded by dense forests at the edges of deep, crystal clear lakes and slow, winding rivers; where the roofs in the cobblestone villages were red and the stone houses white; where the church bells chimed every hour of every long, luxurious day.

I worked as the English "assistante" at a large secondary school, where the headmaster's name, Monsieur Folie Desjardins, translated into Mr. Garden Madness, but nobody else seemed to think this was funny. During the day I taught twelve-year-olds English, and spent my evenings with a group of older students, young men with dreamy long hair who played guitars and smoked Gitanes in thin, trembling fingers. They were interested in my views on politics and current affairs, and I soon discovered that they were all socialists or communists, because this was France where these were normal things to be. We listened to David Bowie and Crass and the Cure late into the night, and in the afternoon, too, because once a week, I was ostensibly teaching them English. Tall, curly-haired Frank, never far from his guitar, and skinny, intellectual, chain-smoking Christophe, both a year younger than me, were the only ones who showed up. They introduced me to the ballads of Jacques Brel, the rock of Johnny Halliday, the films of Catherine Deneuve, and one day they invited me to see Frank Zappa in concert in Bordeaux, a large city seventy miles away. I readily agreed, even though I had no idea who Frank Zappa was.

I took the bus to Bordeaux with them, Thierry, a handsome martial arts expert with waist-length black hair, and skinny Nico, who skipped energetically before us like an elf from *The Hobbit* as he led us to the small flat on a narrow backstreet he shared with his pretty, dark-haired girlfriend. As we sat in a circle on the floor and passed round the strongest joint I had ever smoked, I watched as Nico and his girlfriend talked animatedly, fascinated by their French gestures, a pout here, a shrug there, and by the African prints on the wall, by their freedom. It was the middle of the day and the muted sounds of voices, cars, and mopeds on the street streamed through the window on the dust-flecked beams of sunshine. We ate soft cheese and thin slices of ham on warm baguettes, accompanied by a red table wine that tasted better than any wine I had ever had even though it was the cheapest you could find at ten francs a bottle. Then suddenly everyone was getting up, and I clambered up to follow them, wondering why we were leaving the girlfriend behind but not finding the words to ask. I noticed the cobblestones, the sunshine, the unshaven men in black berets cycling past with long baguettes sticking out of their baskets, and Christophe's nervous laughter as Nico opened the door on the wrong side of the car, forgetting he was the one driving.

"My God, we will never make it there alive." Christophe laughed and I laughed too, focusing every ounce of my consciousness on getting to the orange Renault without tripping over the uneven cobblestones.

Nico flipped the front seat forward so that I could squeeze into the back after Christophe and Frank. There was hardly room for me, so I sat across their laps, and we were all elbows and knees and laughter. Thierry was the only sober one among us because he did not do drugs or alcohol, but for some reason I did not understand, he sat in the passenger seat. Nico banged a cassette into the cassette player and loud French rock blared out of our open car windows. I had never felt so free as off we went, bumping along the tree-lined cobblestone streets bustling with normal people doing normal afternoon things like shopping and eating on café patios, while I was in a car on the way to an American concert with four handsome and crazy French men.

The concert was dark and smoke filled in contrast to the bright sunshine outside. When Frank Zappa appeared with his thick black moustache to prance electronically around the stage, we danced and yelled with the rest of the crowd, the sweet smell of pot floating in a cloud in the darkness above us. The whole concert seemed to last just five minutes, and for three of those minutes I had one arm around Christophe and one arm around Nico, whom I was snogging enthusiastically. Back in the car, we rolled the windows down to let in the warm evening air. Christophe appeared to be sulking, while Nico acted as if nothing had happened, chattering fantastically as always, irrespective of whether any of us said anything back. He was bursting with frenetic energy. and I fantasized about him leaving his girlfriend and me never leaving France, moving instead into his adorable flat and never seeing Martin again, my whole life transformed with just one brief marijuana-induced embrace. But then we arrived back at his flat and his girlfriend kissed him on the lips and me on both cheeks. Everything felt exciting, dangerous, and liberating, and I didn't want any of it to ever end.

That night I slept on Christophe's living room sofa in his small flat, nestled between warehouses on a quiet street at the edge of town. We woke up late and shared a breakfast of coffee and croissants before driving with Thierry and Frank back to Riberac, where their friend Pierre had planned a bonfire at a nearby lake. I hadn't met Pierre yet, who was a kind of local hero to my friends even though—or perhaps because—he worked at the town's abattoir. I was curious to find out why he was so special.

It was late afternoon by the time we arrived, and Pierre was sitting on a tall wooden stool at the bar of Riberac's main café on the high street. His thick black hair reached down to his shoulders, and I noticed gaps in his nicotine-stained teeth when he stood up to kiss each of us three times on the cheeks. Back on his stool, he picked up two cubes of white sugar between his thick, dirt-engrained forefinger and thumb and placed them carefully one by one into the doll's house size espresso cup before him. Christophe called to the bartender for four more espressos.

"When it was my turn to do military service," Pierre said, vigorously stirring his coffee as we sat on either side of him, "I drank twenty-one cups of these in one go." He pointed at the espresso.

Thierry, Frank, and Christophe shook their heads, smiling in admiration. They had heard this story before, Christophe told me later, but never tired of hearing it.

"Imagine how I was shaking. I didn't sleep for three nights, I drank twenty-one cups every single day. By the time I got to the interview I was crazed and my heart rate was suicidal." He leapt up from his seat and did a disjointed dance, like a puppet being jerked here and there by a giant invisible puppet master. He was shaking and laughing, and my friends and the bartender laughed, too.

I turned to Christophe and furrowed my eyebrows in puzzlement.

"To avoid military service," Christophe explained. "All young men have to do military service in France."

"Have you?" I asked, horrified at the thought of this gentle pacifist holding a gun.

"Not yet," he said. "But after university . . ."

He shrugged his shoulders, put his head to one side, and pouted his lips in another French gesture that said so much more than words ever could.

"When I got there," Pierre continued, sitting down, "I acted crazy. You know, muttering to myself, jumping at every sound, shaking, pacing. It was easy to do because I did feel crazy from no sleep, no food, and so much coffee. And it worked. They didn't send me to play their dirty war games. No guns in these hands." He looked down at his callused, thick hands.

"Bravo!" Christophe, Thierry, and Frank cried in unison.

The bartender applauded.

"That's incredible," I said, my eyes widening as his impressive act of principle sank in.

"Yes, and that is why these boys will graduate university in Bordeaux," he said, pointing at Christophe, Frank, and Thierry. "And why I am at the local abattoir. No military service, no university, no nothing when you get yourself certified mentally unfit."

Watching them talk earnestly about politics, I imagined my father at their age, smoking cigarettes and drinking pints with his friends at the local pub, putting the world to rights. Pierre talked with the rolling guttural r's of Perigord and felt even more dangerously exciting than my new friends because he was living his principles with no care for the consequences. I volunteered to drive with him to the lake because I was fascinated by his courage and apparent lack of concern for his future and because I thought he was probably the coolest person I had ever met. He drove at ninety miles an hour along winding single-track roads slicing through the lush countryside, and I laughed as I was flung into his arm and then back to the window with every turn. When we reached the lake deep in the forest, Christophe and Frank were already there, collecting wood and building the bonfire, while Thierry was in the woods, practising martial arts moves. I sat on a log and watched surreptitiously as he removed his shirt to reveal a muscular, hairless body, his long black hair flowing down his perfectly formed back.

Pierre had brought some food to heat up on the bonfire, and it turned out to be a pile of tiny birds, complete with their wings and beaks, whose bones cracked in your teeth as you chewed them. I could not bring myself to eat them even though I was not a vegetarian yet. I watched as the others crunched on them, pulling small pieces of charred bones or meat from between their teeth, then flicking them into the fire. I put small bites of baguette into my mouth, followed by a swig of red wine from the communal bottle so that I could feel its dark redness seep into every corner of the bread before I chewed and swallowed. The sun set a red glow in the pale sky over the still, blue lake and I sighed. Nothing could be more liberating than this.

I was gazing into the bonfire when Pierre patted my arm and pointed upwards. We stared together at the stars slowly emerging one by one and the moon rising over the distant edge of the lake.

"This is my university," he said.

Soon, both moon and stars were reflected on the smooth surface of the lake, and I walked to its edge, mesmerized by the silence, the darkness, and the sweet earthy scents carried on the warm breeze. Thierry joined me, and we walked along the shore together without speaking, the laughter and chatter of our friends disappearing in the distance behind us, the sound of the water lapping at the shore keeping us company.

"I have never been this happy, I don't think," I said at last. "Martin is coming next week and I am worried . . . because . . . he doesn't like me to have male friends, and I love being with you all. I am not sure what to do. I feel so free here."

Thierry stopped and I stopped too, and turned to him. Our bonfire was a small glowing shimmer in the distance behind him. He took my face in his strong hands and I stared into his dark eyes in the moonlight.

"You are a beautiful person, Stephanie," he said. "Never let anyone take your freedom away from you."

It was as though the moon and stars had entered me with their light and promise and hope.

TWO DAYS LATER, my colleague Marie-Rose invited me to dinner at her parents' home. She was a petite English teacher with wistful eyes, who wore perfect makeup in a way only French women can, and even though she wore the highest of high heels, she still only reached my shoulder. I was wearing jeans and a T-shirt, and I felt too tall and underdressed as we wandered around her parents' homestead visiting the loose chickens and ducks and caged rabbits that would soon become family meals. It was evening and the soft clucking of the hens was comforting as the lights of her parents' stone house beckoned us to dinner. We strolled back to the kitchen with its heavy wooden table and flagstone floor and ate a leisurely dinner of rabbit in cream sauce, asparagus, and garlic encrusted potatoes, washed down with an earthy St. Emilion. Her parents asked me about my professional aspirations, how I liked France, and who I would vote for if I lived here. They did not ask me once whether I had a boyfriend, and I was glad because Martin was coming soon and I didn't want to think about it.

When it was time for bed, Marie-Rose led me into a small bedroom with flowered wallpaper. A double bed stood in the middle of the room.

"Thank you," I said.

I was about to say goodnight, when she said, "I hope you don't mind sharing?"

"Of course not," I said, and my heart took off as if I were running.

Marie-Rose disappeared into the adjoining bathroom and I quickly put on the oversize T-shirt I slept in and a clean pair of knickers, even though these were the ones I had brought for the next day. When she came back she was wearing a long white nightgown tied loosely at her collarbone. I tried not to look, but I was intrigued by the contours of her body under the nightgown, and my eyes drifted to her upper body more often than I thought they should. I felt a slipping of control, a melting of senses as we lay face to face, and she told me the story of a recently failed romance.

"He's an idiot not to want to be with you," I said.

She smiled, "Thank you, Stephanie, you are so sweet."

Marie-Rose reached out her hand and stroked my face. Her hand was soft, and I wanted to lean my head against it and move my pillow closer to her and breathe in deeply. I wanted to stroke her sad face, too. Instead I became rigid, terrified of the proximity of this magnificent French woman with her soft lips, huge eyes, and delicate frame, unnerved by the delicious melting feeling that was washing over me.

Just before we at last fell asleep, I turned my back to her and clung onto the edge of the bed.

MARTIN ARRIVED THE next day. My heart dropped when I saw his muscular silhouette descend from the bus in Riberac. His blue-green eyes looked me up and down before arriving at mine, and I looked away over his shoulder, smiling at a group of teenage boys, pretending to know them. Martin was no doubt wondering why I was wearing combat pants tucked into ankle boots, with my tight T-shirt probably revealing too much. He leaned over to kiss me on the lips, and I recoiled before I could stop myself, offering him my cheek instead. I allowed a brief, awkward hug, then he picked up his backpack and slung it over his shoulder. I led him up the hill toward the school and my flat, my feet heavier with each step.

The night he was to meet my new friends, we walked hand-in-hand the twenty minutes into town, and must have looked like a happy couple. If only the people we passed knew the effort it was taking me not to pull my hand away from his. We stopped in front of the pastry shop, and I took the opportunity to let go by pointing out the must-have custard tarts with fresh strawberries crowded elegantly on their surface. We passed the butcher's, the shoe shop, and the newsagents, before arriving at the café, where a cloud of thick cigarette smoke hovered above my friends, like a bubble in a cartoon waiting for words. They beckoned us over, jumping up to kiss me the customary three times and to shake Martin's hand.

"How are you?" Thierry whispered as he kissed me in greeting.

I saw the stars and the moon in his limitless eyes.

"OK," I said, and I hoped that he heard what I was thinking. *Things are horrible, thank you for asking.* My friends were all drinking bright green menthe out of tall glasses and smoking Gitanes. I ordered some menthe for Martin and me, too, because he had never tried its sweet sticky taste before. It was like drinking chewing gum, I told him. Christophe and Pierre were in the middle of an animated conversation about the British invasion of the Falklands.

"Congratulations," Christophe said, lifting his glass as we sat down.

Martin put his arm around my shoulder and I flinched.

"For what?" I said.

"You seem to be winning the war," Christophe said and laughed.

I mock hit him, dislodging Martin's arm. "That's not something to celebrate."

I turned to Martin and saw that he was sulking. I imagined he felt left out because he didn't understand what we were saying, so I began to translate. He brushed me away with a shake of the hand.

"I thought you were teaching them English," he said, and when I told my new friends this they laughed out loud, because by now our English class had dwindled down to just Christophe, and he and I spent the entire time talking animatedly in French about politics and music as we smoked joints and drank French herbal teas called tisanes in the middle of the afternoon in my flat. I couldn't tell Martin this, though, and so I begged them to try out their English on him, but they just smiled while he glowered.

'They are talking about the Falklands," I said to Martin. "They are teasing me and congratulating me. How are things at home?"

"Jingoistic," he said and told me about the photograph on the front page of *The Sun* with its headline "Gotcha!" after the British forces sank an Argentinian ship, killing hundreds.

I turned to my friends and translated, doing my best to bridge the gap. Martin slipped his arm back around my shoulder as I spoke, just like he did when he was chatting with his football mates in the pub back in England. Only this time it was my friends we were with, they were not leering, and it was me who was talking. I felt weighted down and failed to come up with a good reason for shrugging his arm off again without hurting his feelings.

BACK AT THE flat, as soon as the door closed behind us, Martin turned to me, hissing, "What's wrong with you?" gripping his hands into fists, shaking with rage.

I pushed past him and made my way to the balcony and sat down. I pulled out some cigarette papers and tobacco from my jeans pocket to make a roll-up.

He followed me. "I leave you alone for five minutes and you surround yourself with men." He was standing over me, too close. I could smell the menthe and cigarettes on his breath. "Stupid, long-haired, French men at that."

"They're not stupid." I lit the roll-up, took a drag, and looked up at him defiantly. "I like them. And I'm sick of you telling me who I can be friends with."

He looked startled. "It's for your own good. You are so fucking innocent, don't you see the way they look at you?"

"For God's sake," I yelled, my voice ricocheting back to me from the school buildings opposite. "Not everyone thinks like you do. Just shut up and leave me alone!" My voice rose with each word, and I got up to join it.

He stood up too, blocking the sliding balcony doorway with his arm. I mustered all my strength and pushed him against the wall. "Get out of my way! Stop telling me what to do!" And I slapped him across the face.

He stepped back, and I squeezed myself under his arm and ran out of the front door. He watched me from the balcony doorway, holding his palm against his red, surprised cheek.

It was almost midnight. I ran down the dark hill into town and marched around the empty streets, my heart pounding, my head filling with random images: Pierre dancing in the café; Thierry holding my face at the lake; Marie-Rose's soft body in the bed next to mine; the brief and liberating snog with Nico; Christophe's smile as we turned up the volume to David Bowie in our so-called English class; Martin's arm in the café circling my neck like a noose.

I wondered if my neighbours—teachers and school administrators—had heard our argument. I muttered to myself in French, "I won't put up with it any more, I won't put up with it anymore," and disturbed the occasional stray cat as I wandered past shuttered stone houses. I seemed to be the only person awake at this hour. Not even a car passed as I walked by the dark church, along the high street with its shuttered storefronts and dim streetlights, and through the pitch-black market place. My mind was so clouded I didn't notice the stars and the moon, though they were surely there to help me find my way.

When at last I walked through the door, Martin was pacing anxiously, smoking a roll-up. "You've been gone three hours." He stubbed out the cigarette. He looked worried, and I was happy to see that one cheek was still pinker than the other. "Anything could have happened."

"Well, it didn't, did it?" I looked past him to the balcony, wishing he would step out there and jump. "I am perfectly capable of taking care of myself."

He looked at me gingerly. "Let's go to sleep and talk in the morning."

I was more than happy not to speak to him, so I turned and flounced into my bedroom and fell fully clothed onto the double mattress on the floor. He crept in quietly next to me, and for the second time in a week I slept with my back to someone who was sharing my bed, though this time it was because I didn't want to accidentally touch, not because I did. Listening to him breathe nervously next to me, I started to feel powerful. Tomorrow I would tell him I needed more freedom. Tomorrow I would tell him if he didn't change, I'd leave.

Over coffee and croissants the next morning, I said, "I am going to keep my male friends, and there is nothing you can do about it. I lost all my good male friends in England because of you. I'm not going to lose my French friends too. OK?"

He nodded quietly.

"And you need to treat me with more respect. You have to stop calling me names. You have to let me breathe. I need to breathe."

"I haven't seen you for so long," he said. "I just don't want to lose you, that's all. I arrive and I haven't seen you for months and you are all laughing and joking with a whole group of new friends and I don't see how I fit in."

I took a deep breath. He looked young and lost and his eyes were red, and I realized he had been crying. I wondered what it would be like if I didn't understand a word anyone was saying around me, if I went home to find him surrounded by a group of new exciting female friends, if he could tell that I really didn't want him here. And my heart softened.

THE LIBERATING DAYS of France came to an end long before I was ready, and I came home to England for my final year at university. Martin had developed a new almost-respect for me and spent the next year trying to change. He came on a peace march with me. He got his ear pierced. He even read the feminist books I was discovering. The first I ever read was the most disturbing and radical of them all: Andrea Dworkin's *Pornography*, a horrible book full of descriptions of extreme and violent pornography, and with the apparent premise that all men want to subjugate and kill women. I shrank in horror at the descriptions of images of women tied down onto car bonnets, legs and arms splayed, eyes bound, a gun pointing at their genitals; women handcuffed, beaten, or maimed, all with their mouths open invitingly, legs open unwillingly, eyes wild with terror, a man or weapon hovering threateningly in the foreground. This was all new to me and I was sick to my stomach. The pornography on my father's—on the family—shelves consisted of semi-naked nubile young women looking demure and innocent, or some French cartoon books featuring a sexy young woman whose clothes were always flying off, whose cleavage was always in view, and who seemed to take enjoyment in her varied sexual antics.

I started to look at my father differently, at Martin differently. I left Dworkin's *Pornography* out on the coffee table in the living room on a visit home from university in the hopes that my father would read it and we could have an argument, but when he picked it up, he flicked through it, put it down, and didn't say a word.

Martin, meanwhile, had been doing his best to be a "new man." He stopped calling me names in bed and started to explore the notion of non-competitive sports theory on his sports course at his university in London. But he still didn't come to watch me play hockey for Bath University and still sulked if I wore tight trousers or short skirts, which was happening less and less as feminist symbol earrings, baggy dungarees, and unshaved legs slowly became my fashion of choice. I read more and more about the liberation of women, and he seemed to agree in principle, but seemed hardwired for jealousy and possessiveness.

I couldn't quite face that while he was trying to understand, he hadn't really changed that much at all.

I continued as chair of the university's Anti-Apartheid Group and learned that Zimbabwe was calling for university graduates to come and teach. It had been two years since Rhodesia had become Zimbabwe, when my fellow activists and I ran to each other's dorms and celebrated in a dance of excitement. Now Zimbabwe needed concrete help, and I was more than ready to volunteer. I called Martin to tell him that I was going for an interview at Zimbabwe House in London. I called my father to tell him about it, too, and he thought it was a great idea. He had never liked Martin, and he said, half-jokingly, "Maybe you'll find a nice Zimbabwean revolutionary to marry." I wanted to be offended because he was not respecting my relationship with Martin, but I also fantasized about a new life in Zimbabwe, part of me hoping Martin would say he wasn't coming, and I would be free of him. But when Martin told me he wanted to come too, I wondered if Zimbabwe might be our chance to start over and all would be well after all. But there was a catch.

Martin needed one more year to complete his teacher training—a year's practical experience—and I reluctantly agreed to wait; that way I would not be alone in a strange new land, a situation that excited and terrified me in equal parts.

So the summer after we graduated, instead of packing my suitcase and adventurously flying to Zimbabwe to teach education-starved children how to read and write, I moved with Martin into a cramped flat above a launderette in a grey mining town called Golborne in Lancashire. My father was proudly from Lancashire, and I hoped I might feel a sense of belonging. But I was in shock. I couldn't tell where one town stopped and another began because where I came from there were fields and hills and cows between one town and another. Here they merged into each other in an endless chain of buildings, streetlights painting everything an eerie yellow all the way from Manchester to Liverpool. There was a reason my parents left Accrington as soon as they could, I thought.

Martin and I didn't have a car, so there was no escape to the nearby Yorkshire Moors, Lancashire countryside, or Derbyshire Dales, where my father took my mother on his motorbike during their courtship.

I couldn't see the moon or stars because of the sickly streetlights. The adventures of France were a distant memory. There was just Martin and me and the rain, and I couldn't have been further from Zimbabwe if I tried.

# Chapter Four
## "NO MORE WAR" BRONSKI BEAT

BUT I WAS not so far from Greenham Common.

I was washing dishes in our kitchen when I heard them on the radio. Women singing, chanting, and yelling as the police dragged their deliberately limp bodies from the gates of the military base. I put down my sponge, wiped my hands, sat at the kitchen table, and turned up the volume. Greenham women were in the headlines pretty much every day those days. They lived in makeshift camps outside the United States military base at Greenham Common in Newbury, close to my childhood village, and regularly broke into the base or lay down together in the road in huge, singing, laughing piles to stop military vehicles from entering or exiting the base.

It was the height of the Cold War, and the United States had 102 bases in the United Kingdom—a country the size of the state of New York. Imagine if the British government set up 102 bases in New York to reciprocate. The Royal Airforce Base at Greenham Common was loaned to the Americans during the Second World War but was not returned to the local community at the war's end. It sat on hundreds of acres of what was once—and still should have been—common land, dating back to Roman times, a place for the local townspeople to walk their dogs and water and graze their animals, disturbing only the occasional wild deer, rabbit, or pheasant. Now, it was closed off by wire fences, scarred with concrete bunkers and tarmac roads, and protected by fresh-faced young British soldiers, while further inside the camp steely-jawed American soldiers were poised to launch cruise missiles, first strike nuclear weapons, at the Soviet Union at any moment.

I had been to Greenham twice already on demonstrations, once with my mother in December of the year before. She was a member of the local Women for Peace and Freedom group, and I was part of a women's peace group in Bath. I'd arrived on a bus filled with women in multi-coloured clothes carrying hand-made banners, and my mother and I had met at one of the gates to the camp. I carried a constant feeling of dread deep inside me about nuclear war, avidly followed the doom-laden news, and often woke in the night covered in sweat from nuclear nightmares. I felt a surge of belonging and hope holding hands in a chain of 30,000 women as we formed a circle around the whole base, while others attached homemade patchwork banners to the fence—"Women Say No to the Bomb," "Take the Toys from the Boys."

Since then, I had followed the antics of the Greenham women avidly in the news. They weren't able to stop the missiles arriving, but they certainly knew how to bring attention to them. I thought back to the famous photograph that had graced the front pages of our newspapers—and many around the world—the previous New Year's Day, when dozens of women broke through the fence and made it to the silos being prepared to house the cruise missiles, the same silos that Margaret Thatcher's Minister of Defence had declared the most secure in the whole of Europe just days earlier.

The haunting and inspiring image showed dozens of women holding hands and dancing in a joyous circle on top of a silo at midnight to ring in the New Year, jubilant and triumphant. Silhouetted against the bright lights of the base were huge rolls of barbed wire that had been no match for their bolt cutters. It was an image that made my heart race just that little bit faster whenever I thought of it, as if the peace activist seeds it had planted all across the country were also taking root inside me, waiting for their moment to rise into the sun. I thought back to the first signs of the Americans' arrival in our village and suddenly it felt personal. Like Pierre in France, these women were living their ideals. Today, as they faced eviction, they sounded angry. They sounded indignant. They sounded happy. They sounded free.

"We need more women to join us." A passionate Greenham woman's voice filled my lifeless kitchen. "We need to show the authorities that we represent thousands of women who oppose war. They can't get rid of us. We will not be intimidated."

The next morning, I rushed to my new job at Wigan Women's Aid, an organization that ran a battered women's shelter and hotline, and asked my co-workers Meg and Briana, if they fancied visiting Greenham Common with me. They both said yes. Meg was a teenager from an

unhappy home filled with yelling and incriminations, and she was up
for any adventure that would get her out of the house. Briana was the
first real lesbian I had met, as far as I knew, and she liked the sound of
visiting a community where women like her were welcome. Martin did
not object—not because he had truly changed: he still questioned my
every move, criticized my clothes, disapproved of the music I liked, and
I still hadn't dared to make friends again with the male friends I'd lost
because of him. Martin didn't object because he couldn't imagine what
could possibly go wrong if I were with a bunch of women.

A few days later, we packed our bags, got a lift from a friend to the
nearest motorway entrance, put out our thumbs, and were immediately
picked up by an enormous lorry. We climbed into the massive cab,
laughing at the tiny cars beneath us as we raced the two hundred miles
south along the motorway. Like most people in the United Kingdom
at the time, the driver knew all about Greenham Common, and he was
happy to do his bit to support us. We rolled joints and smoked them,
leaving a small pile behind for him to enjoy after his shift.

The driver dropped us off in the centre of Newbury, a small market
town surrounded by a complicated necklace of roundabouts. We turned
to wave as he drove away, honking his horn as he disappeared around a
corner, en route for France. Part of me wanted to go with him. It was late
afternoon, and a cool drizzle brushed across our faces as we completed
the last mile or so of our journey on foot, through housing estates
dotted with red phone boxes, across smaller and smaller roundabouts,
until we reached Greenham Common, on Newbury's outskirts. I was
just fifteen miles from my family home in St. Mary Bourne with its
thatched cottages, watercress beds, three pubs, and three churches, but I
could have been on another planet. The vast grey military base with its
wire fencing topped with rolls of razor wire stretched before me, with
muddy pathways along its perimeter where thousands of women's feet
had walked in protest. I could just make out the silhouettes of soldiers
holding guns and standing at attention inside the base, feet away from
a group of colourful women on the outside of the fence, bundled up
in layers of clothing, sitting on filthy armchairs and wooden crates,
huddled around an open fire.

As we got closer to the large metal gate at the edge of the forest, the
picture became clearer. A handful of uniformed policemen were standing

in front of the gate chatting with some British soldiers who were behind the gate. Outside the gate, dozens of confident looking Greenham women with playful faces and wearing big boots and heavy jackets were milling about. Some were sitting around the fire and singing, while a Goth, looking like a witch from a fairy tale with her jet-black hair and clothes, was stirring a massive pot of bubbling stew that was balanced precariously on a metal grill sitting over the fire. I could easily tell who the visitors were—there were men, for one thing, but also women whose hands were clean, like mine, who were wearing conventional clothes, and whose shoes were not encrusted with mud. They were wearing sensible anoraks as they unpacked gifts of clothing, firewood, food, and bedding from the backs of cars and vans, watching over children in yellow and red wellingtons splashing in the recently formed puddles. Like me, they had come in answer to the women's call for support in the face of imminent eviction. I heard them thanking the women for what they were doing, saying they wished they could do more.

Standing alone in front of this bustling scene, I was at a complete loss. I had borrowed a tent, but I didn't know how to put it up. I hadn't been allowed to join the boy scouts, only play football for them, so, unlike Robert, I'd never gone camping. He'd gone on a camping trip with them, where he got to sleep in a sleeping bag in a tent and play games and sing songs around a campfire under the stars. I had dropped him off with Mum and watched him disappear in a gaggle of green-clad excited boys while I looked enviously over my shoulder as we drove away. Now it was my turn to camp and sit by a fire and eat under the stars and I had no idea where to start. Briana and Meg had disappeared into the woods with their own tent and were confidently setting it up together, leaving me to fend for myself. While my enamel red earrings crafted in the shape of the women's symbol and baggy denim dungarees seemed fitting, my curly perm with tiny highlights felt all wrong; I had the wrong shoes that were not even waterproof; and I didn't know one end of my tent from the other. These women seemed to be capable of anything, and I wondered how I would ever dare speak to any of them. I resisted the temptation to ask a passing man to help me out.

"Welcome to Blue Gate." A woman with long, wild, dirty-blond hair with shaved sides and multiple ear and nose piercings, was striding toward me. Before I knew it, my tent was being erected, a word I soon learned was very funny here, because this was a women's peace camp, with a lot of lesbians, and a local law had just been passed banning "erections on the common"—hence the recent attempts at eviction.

"My name's Elena," she said in a broad Yorkshire accent as she pushed the last tent peg into the ground and stepped back to admire the now upright orange tent that would be my home for the next week. "Come and have some tea at the fire."

I followed her shyly to the fire pit, where we squeezed between two visitors who moved apart to make room for us. A posh-sounding woman with a deep voice and short hair dyed to look like camouflage was speaking to a rapt group of visitors. She was talking about her hair.

"It's a spider's web gone wrong," she said. "I'm waiting for it to grow out. I feel the worst about Biscuit."

She pointed to the kitchen where a large, white, wiry-haired dog was looking for scraps. The dog had bright blue ears.

Suddenly a middle-aged man, his face tight with fury, strode past, very close to us, his dog at his side. Biscuit and his dog exchanged glances and the women laughed.

"That's the Fiddler," Elena said. "He walks his dog through the camp every morning and every night and refuses to change his route, even if there's a tent in his way. He walks right over it."

Elena was smiling and rolling a cigarette in liquorice paper, her filthy fingernails poking out from fingerless gloves, delicately creating a perfectly rounded roll-up.

"Do you want one?" she asked.

I did, but I was afraid of how badly I rolled them, and I hesitated. She put the cigarette in her lap and started rolling another, and I breathed a sigh of relief. Then she lit them both, placed one to her lips and handed one to me. I was reminded of a famous scene from a Bette Davis film, unable to remember which one, as I smiled inside, thinking of how different the two of us looked from the elegant couple in the film standing in the window on a dark evening, as the dashing hero took two cigarettes in hand, lit them, and handed one to the heroine. I looked into Elena's blue eyes as she lit my roll-up. I took a drag, and looked away, afraid she would be able to tell that I thought she was the most beautiful person I had ever seen, with her smiling eyes, aquiline nose, slender frame, and carefree nature.

THE NEXT MORNING, I was in a deep, dreamless sleep when I was jolted awake by someone whooping loudly. I opened my eyes and turned to ask Martin what the noise was all about, saw the side of a tent where Martin's face should be, remembered where I was, wriggled onto my belly in my sleeping bag, and poked my head blearily out of the tent flap. The drizzle had gone, and there was a sparkling wash of dew on the grass before me. My breath formed small clouds in front of my face, and the smoke from the fire drifted lazily over the fence and across the soldiers, blurring them so that they looked like an out of focus photograph. Silhouetted against the base in the pink morning light, three large bin lorries were discharging several bulky men. It was an eviction.

The men raced around the camp, grabbing anything they could get their hands on, throwing tents, sleeping bags, food, and clothes into the back of the lorries, while the policemen looked on. Women raced behind them, pulling on their belongings, while two women, one of them Trish, the witchy Goth who had cooked the night before, were dragging the kitchen supplies cabinet out onto the road on wheels—how ingenious, I thought, as I pulled on my jeans and sweatshirt, jumped out of my tent, and started to take it down, following the lead of the women around me, who were hurriedly dismantling tents and rolling up sleeping bags. My heart was racing, not with fear or anger, but with a kind of joyful excitement. I was being evicted along with the Greenham women. This was why I was here. I was one of them!

When they were done, the fire stamped out, and the camp erased, we gathered at the top of the hill, on the pavement at the side of the road, and stood in an indignant group clutching our remaining belongings, yelling a favourite singing taunt:

"Which side are you on, boys/Which side are you on?/Are you on the side that don't like life?/Are you on the side of racial strife?/Are you on the side that beats your wife?/Which side are you on?" Between each verse, we turned and laughed to each other, breathless, then took a collective deep breath to deliver the final verse in even louder roars: "Are you on the side of suicide?/Are you on the side of homicide?/Are you on the side of genocide?/Which side are you on?"

Eventually the police and bailiffs moved on. And then we went back and set up camp again. Elena was already at my side, smiling. While Trish the Goth and Lucy of the camouflage hair re-started the fire, and women all around us started to rebuild the camp, Elena and I put up my tent to the sound of women singing softly in the background. I heard a rumbling sound and turned to see the kitchen supplies unit trundling along the road, two laughing women having pushed it out from the hedgerow where it had been hidden.

As we worked together, giggling and tripping over the ropes, Elena told me that, until recently, most of the women had lived in handcrafted shelters made of plastic sheeting draped over bent tree branches. They covered the soft green moss on the ground with plastic sheeting to keep out the damp, then lay their sleeping bags on top, while candles balanced on homemade shelves of stone or wood made for cosy, glowing, hobbit-like homes at night. They called these structures benders, because the tree branches only needed to bend a little to give shelter. Elena said she'd had a beautiful bender half way to Green Gate, deep in the woods, which she didn't think was an eviction risk, since it was so far from the road. But the bailiffs had gone further into the woods one day and taken it down, making sure there were no more benders, no more "erections" on the common. I'd seen many photos of them, and I'd seen them up close on my previous visits to the camp, but I had never gone inside one. I imagined how lovely it would be to sleep on the moss in a bender deep in the woods, my new friend, Elena, at my side.

Elena told me the women were always making up names for themselves—like Anna Key, Eva Brick, and Freda People—when they were arrested. It seemed English law allowed you to use any name you liked when you were arrested, and when I was arrested the next day for breaking into the base, nobody asked me for any ID. When dozens of women called themselves Karen Silkwood after the American anti-nuclear activist and broke into the base on the anniversary of her death, that wasn't questioned by the authorities either.

On my second night at Blue Gate, I sat shyly at the campfire next to a woman called Diana who was visiting from Oswestry on the Welsh border, and her quiet friend, Linda. I'd lost track of my co-workers and, in any case, I was staying a week and they were departing earlier. At the fire, we all jostled for warmth as we listened to the Greenham women sharing stories of actions and arrests. Trish the Goth was there, with her strong Northern Irish accent and twinkly smile; and Lucy, too, her large dog, Biscuit, sitting adoringly at her side; while Elena sat across from me. I could have told who the seasoned Greenham women were even without their grubby fingers, smoke-smelling rainbow clothes, and big boots, by their raucous, unselfconscious laughter.

"We found a tunnel that goes right into the base," a woman who gave her name as Zee said, her eyes glowing beneath her shaved head in the light of the fire. She had a slight lisp thanks to the piercing on her tongue. "A disused sewer pipe, or something."

I couldn't imagine anything more claustrophobic, and my admiration for the women went up a thousand notches when she said, "So me and Drummer and Rebecca get in it and start walking. Spring and Elena put the manhole cover back on and it goes pitch black. It's not too low, you can stand if you bend over. We had a torch, and we just kept walking."

There were around eleven of us at the fire pit, the visitors, myself included, leaning forward in the glow of the fire, enraptured by the story. "Were there rats?" a visitor asked, in her squeaky clean jeans, anorak, and sensible walking shoes.

"I didn't see any," Zee said. "Just a couple of spiders, maybe, but no rats."

Trish was squirming in her seat. "Don't say any more about rats. That's why I refused to go."

"How long did it take?" the same visitor asked.

"I dunno, we walked for about fifteen minutes?"

The others nodded.

"Then we see a light ahead and it's a manhole cover, but it's not completely closed. We open it and there we are, bang in the middle of the base. There are no police, no soldiers, nobody. We can't even see the fence we are so far in. So we start walking around to have a look and there is a control tower right in front of us. With nobody in it."

"So Zee goes up to the door and opens it and just walks right in, just like that," Elena said, smiling. "We climb the stairs and look around—there are a few dials and switches, and we wonder if they have a massive telescope to see what is going on at the camp, but we can't figure out what everything is. Rebecca starts writing peace messages over these manuals she finds. Then we get hysterical imagining what would happen if we started pressing and turning every button and knob."

"That's when Zee decides to roll a spliff," Spring said, who had a single plait running between her eyes and down the front of her face and body. As we all laughed with incredulity, I resisted the urge to put her plait behind one of her ears so that I could see her face properly.

"Yeah, that's right," Zee said, grinning. "That made it a hell of a lot more fun. Then we see a phone and I pick it up and it connects me with someone right away. I say, 'Hello, this is Zee Bra here. I am in your control tower. Which button do I press to destroy the cruise missiles?'"

We all laughed at her bravado. A woman at her side, sporting a short, red Mohican and adorable dimples leaned into her and whispered something. I didn't know it then, but in a few months' time Sally would become one of my closest friends, when I would really need a friend. They smiled, stood, and left the circle, and I didn't hear how the story ended.

Diana turned to me, her strong face shining in the orange glow of the dancing flames. "I have some bolt cutters. Want to break in?"

I swallowed hard. I couldn't think of any good reason why not, so I said in a voice that I hoped was not as small as how I was feeling, "OK."

I glanced over to see if Elena might join us, but she was deep in conversation with Trish, and I didn't want to interrupt, so I got up, reluctantly, and Diana's friend Linda followed.

I knew that breaking into the base was a regular nighttime activity for the women. Sometimes they went for a pint to one of the two pubs in Newbury that still served Greenham women, where some played pool with local men in tense games filled with a rare mutual respect. And sometimes they found a patch of fence and cut it down and saw how far they could get into the military base without being arrested. They were like American groundhogs, but instead of looking for food, they were deliberately being a nuisance, and making a political point at the same time. I would rather have been going to the pub to play pool, even though I was not very good at it. But instead, I was about to do my first action, and my heart felt as if it had broken loose and was battering on my chest to find its way out.

We stepped away from the comfort of the fire and made our way to Diana's tent, where she crawled inside to extract three pairs of bolt cutters. She smiled as she handed a pair to me and to Linda, and said, "They are gifts for the camp, but we can try them out first, right?"

She was fearless and I smiled wanly. Part of me was excited at the thought of having an adventure like Zee's, as long as there were no tunnels or rats involved. It felt like the rite of passage to being a true Greenham woman. And of course the famous image of the women dancing on the silos was at the back of my mind. But there were only three of us right now, and there'd been almost fifty of them, and it was only my second day and already I was about to break the law, and I didn't feel the least bit prepared. Diana and Linda were only visitors too, and I wondered at their bravado.

As we made our way along the fence, I glanced back at the women at the fire. Some of them would be up all night, on the lookout for local men who sometimes came to trash the camp, driving their bikes through the kitchen area knocking things over, calling the women names. Once, someone stuck a knife through a woman's tent while she was sleeping, and ever since, all the gates around the base were aglow at night with night watch fires, small groups of women huddled around them drinking tea, smoking, and telling whispered stories into the early hours, while their sisters slept.

I wanted to tell the night watchers what we were doing, so that someone knew, but I was too shy, and I didn't know what the protocol was and didn't want to appear foolish, so I said nothing. It was midnight as we walked around the perimeter fence past Turquoise Gate and toward Green Gate, the darkness of the forest on our right, the floodlights of the base to our left.

"Here," Diana said, pointing confidently, and the three of us set to work with the bolt cutters, snipping away at a section of the fence, which came away easily as we pulled it toward us. We crouched low and climbed through the fence, looked around us at the emptiness, crossed the brightly lit road that ran along the edge of the fence, and set off on the grass and into the base. There were buildings ahead of us on an incline, and we set off toward them, with no real plan in mind but to get in as far as we could. There was no moon, and thin clouds created a veil across the sky, obscuring then revealing the stars. But our way was well lit from the floodlights of the base, as the dark of the forest, the safety of the women's dwellings, and the glow of the fire pits slowly receded behind us.

We hadn't gone very far when we heard a shout, then another, and suddenly several British soldiers in full uniform were running down the hill toward us, yelling. There was no time for us to turn and run as they surrounded us, a pack of young, angry men carrying guns.

"Keep walking," one said, "to the top of that hill."

We obeyed, glancing at each other nervously. When we arrived at the top, the ringleader, a Londoner with straw-coloured hair and small blue eyes, ordered us to lie belly down on the grass.

"In a star shape!" he yelled. "Open your arms. Open your legs."

The soldiers laughed out loud.

We obeyed, arms and legs splayed flat on the ground, our faces pressed into the damp earth. Then they stood around us, their guns pointing down at us. All I could see was their big boots.

"We're not calling the police, you know," the ringleader said. "We've got our own way of dealing with sluts like you."

"No one knows you're here," another said with a sneer. "We're gonna rape you and kill you and throw your dead bodies into the lake."

I turned my head in panic to look at my new friends, and the ringleader yelled, "Don't move!"

I squashed my face back into the grass. Lifting my head ever so slightly, I could see the barrel of his gun and his boots.

"Don't move an inch, just do what they say," a whisper came to us from one of the soldiers, while his mates laughed raucously, discussing what other horrors they planned to inflict on us. He had a Northern Irish accent, like Trish's. "Don't move and you will be alright."

We lay frozen to the ground in silence for a long while, the soldiers' scenarios getting uglier, their laughter louder. The soft-spoken soldier whispered reassurances to us, becoming my anchor, my only hope.

I wondered what would happen if I sat up, began talking, disobeyed. But I didn't test it. Diana was not moving either, nor was Linda, so I assumed they must think we should do as he said, too. I decided to trust this one soldier because he seemed to be looking out for us, and he surely knew more about his friends' intentions than we did. Perhaps he had a sister our age, perhaps he saw her lying there at his feet, and he wanted to help. I held onto him in my mind, imagining him as a friend of my brother's, a decent bloke, someone who wouldn't hurt a fly but who had wound up in the army anyway, because he needed a job, because of the promise of stability, because that was what everyone in his family did. He was our only sliver of hope. Back at the gate, nobody knew we were in here or even knew who we were. They certainly wouldn't think to look for us.

I was shivering uncontrollably, from being so close to the ground, from the crisp night air, from terror, and then I heard the sirens, saw the blue flashing lights of a police car, and hoped with all my heart it was coming to arrest me. I heard tyres crunching over the gravel, doors opening, low male voices talking. Then I heard and saw boots approaching, appearing and disappearing in the flashing strobe lights of the car.

"You can get up now," a voice said, in the Berkshire accent I knew so well.

I got to my feet and glanced at the others, mouthing, *Are you OK? Yes, Yes.* We followed the officers to their police car, our heads down, not daring to look at the soldiers. I sneaked a quick glance, hoping that the one who had become our ally might make himself known, but none of them gave me eye contact. We climbed into the back seat of the police car, its lights creating flashes of blue trees and bushes in the surrounding countryside. I grabbed Diana's hand and she grabbed Linda's and we sat in shocked silence as we were driven to Newbury Police Station, where the police officers on duty put us in separate cells. No one said a word about finding us lying on the ground at the feet of the soldiers, and we were too traumatized and grateful to be rescued to mention it. None of the Greenham women had ever talked about this kind of treatment. They appeared that much braver to me now.

I forgot about my claustrophobia until they locked the door on me to a windowless cell in the middle of the night. I pounded on the door. I yelled. I screamed, "Let me out! Open the door!"

At last a policeman came and opened the door. He looked to be in his fifties, with grey hair and crinkly eyes, the same age as my father.

"OK, you can come out," he said, and called to a policewoman, who was about my age and wearing a prim dark skirt uniform, and who agreed to sit with me in the hallway.

She told me she was from Andover, where I went to sixth form college and met Martin, and we chatted about the town, and how it had changed with all the London overspill housing and roundabouts and shopping centres, and I asked her how long she had been in the police force, and she asked me how long I had lived at the camp. She made me a cup of tea, and I was sitting on the floor, feeling quite comfortable, when the morning shift arrived and she was sent home and I was ordered back into the cell. I asked if I could keep the hatch open so I could see out, but that was not allowed. Apparently I might hang myself. I was exhausted and felt a little ashamed of my screams and what it must have felt like for my new friends to hear me from their separate cells. I fell into a fitful sleep. But despite the horrors, I knew I was where I should be.

# Chapter Five

## "SATURN" STEVIE WONDER

THE DOOR TO my cell opened abruptly, and I jumped off the narrow bed and onto my feet, blinking in the bright light. A male police officer jerked his head to tell me to follow him into a windowless interrogation room, where Diana and Linda were already sitting. I joined them at the metal table in the centre of the room.

"Are you OK?" Diana asked.

"Yes, I'm fine. I'm sorry I made such a fuss. It's just that I'm claustrophobic," I answered.

She gave me a warm hug and I sank into it, feeling that it was all worthwhile.

The police officer sitting opposite us charged us with trespassing and breaking and entering. You could tell he'd done this many times before as he handed us the forms, sighing heavily as he pointed where to sign. He told us to come back for a court hearing in a month—just enough time, I thought, to pack my bags and tell Martin it's over. I gave my name as Stephanie Cady, after the nineteenth-century American feminist Elizabeth Cady Stanton, whom I had recently read about. Diana gave her name as Isaac Hunt. Linda called herself Fran Tastic.

We stepped out into the early morning light, and as we walked the two miles back to the camp through Newbury's sleepy streets, we held hands. When we reached the forest, we walked toward the fire, where two figures were sitting, steam rising from their mugs of hot tea. They were Elena and Sally, who welcomed us as if it were quite normal for women to turn up from Newbury at six in the morning.

"Great, you can take over at the fire," Sally said.

We sat down next to them and sheepishly told them our story, a little ashamed at how unhappy the experience was. Sally told us of a case where soldiers had tied some women up in barbed wire—that had been bad, she said, but it was exceptional. The squaddies didn't normally do this kind of thing, she said, they were just young working-class men doing a job, from backgrounds like those of many of the women at the camp. Elena slid over next to me and took my hand.

"Want to go on a bike ride?" she asked.

I wanted to crawl into my tent and fall asleep, but the idea of spending time with Elena was too exciting to miss so I was ready to say yes to anything.

"Let's go after lunch," she added. "I need a nap after night watch and I bet you need one, too."

Before I could sleep, I needed the toilet, and I made my way to the shit pit, a large hole dug in the ground that served as our latrine. As I squatted over the hole, the cold air brushing against my exposed backside, I heard a rustling behind me. I wondered if it was the black dog that liked to hang out at the camp, and hoped that it was not a local yobbo come to taunt me. Then Spring stepped past me, her long plait dangling down the middle of her face, and squatted right next to me.

"How are things?" she asked.

I mumbled a few words as I wiped myself, mortified, and wondered if, as much as I loved being in this community, I could ever really live here. I quickly threw a trowel of dirt over my contribution, then scuttled back to my tent, zipped myself in, and fell into a heavy sleep.

When I emerged, Elena was standing by the fire, pumping air into the tyres of one of two bikes that were leaning against a tree. The bikes were covered in bright women's peace stickers.

She smiled upon seeing me. "Let's have a cuppa. And then let's go to Orange Gate and invite ourselves for lunch."

I picked up the boiling kettle from the fire and took it to the kitchen area, a collection of crates and wooden tables where pots and pans and plates were jumbled with jars of jam and half-eaten loaves of bread, cooked vegetables and rice in plastic containers, and dried rice and beans in plastic bags. This was more like it, I thought. The kitchen at home was my least favourite place. I didn't like to cook, I didn't like to wash dishes, I didn't like to shop for groceries. Here, pretty much all the food was donated by supporters, and it was arranged in an anarchic display that made me smile. What if I did this at home, I thought, imagining Martin's face. Cooking for others terrified me, and I was delighted that there were women here, like Trish the Goth and her girlfriend, Trina, who enjoyed cooking for us all.

I found a packet of Tetley's squashed under a plastic bag holding orange lentils and an open jar of instant coffee. I placed one teabag into a chipped mug with a woman's peace symbol on its side, and another into a mug with a line drawing of a dove flying above the peace symbol, then poured steaming hot water into the cups as I placed them on the flattest, driest piece of ground I could find. Then I rummaged around for milk—it was a choice between Coffee-Mate and soya milk. On my first night, Elena had shown me how to create a mini-fireworks display in the fire by pouring Coffee-Mate onto it, so I opted for the soya milk, partly because I didn't want to drink all those chemicals, and partly because I was toying with the idea of becoming a vegan, like so many of my favourite women here, and so it seemed I had better get used to soya milk, though I could never get used to the drink made out of barley that some women said passed for coffee. I poured the almost brown "milk" into the mug and it curdled instantly, turning the tea a mottled yellowy brown. It tasted strange and nutty, but it was hot and strong and just what I needed to wake up, and I was grateful.

Elena finished pumping the tyres and joined me at the fire to drink her tea and smoke a roll-up. There was no one else around—a local woman had arrived in a van about half an hour earlier, Elena told me, to take anyone who wanted a shower to her home, and all the women at the fire leapt at the chance and crammed into her van, leaving Elena alone at the fire and Sally still sleeping in her tent after night watch. Sitting sleepily beside Elena in front of the crackling logs, I felt a sense of calm and belonging. The low voices of policemen and squaddies in the distance reminded me of the fading voices of my parents as I dozed in the back seat of the car when we set off early in the morning to take the cross-channel ferry to France for our summer holidays, and I would slowly drift asleep leaning on one of my sisters or my brother, feeling safe and excited. I took one last sip of tea before jumping onto my bike, the old-fashioned sit-up-and-beg kind, while Elena climbed onto her equally rickety, but infinitely more cool, racing bike.

We cycled south along the narrow, empty road, the expanse of wire mesh fence to our right, barbed razor wire attached to its top in tightly curled rolls. On our left there were a few homes, then forest and scrub and open sky, and soon we saw a funnel of smoke merging into the clouds in the distance. A group of women huddled around a campfire came into view on our right, their tents perched on the edge of the road. We waved and they waved back.

"This is Violet Gate," Elena told me. "They are too serious here, because it's a new gate. They want to talk about war and peace and breaking and entering strategies all the time. Let's keep going and have some fun."

A few minutes farther around the nine-mile perimeter fence, we saw another funnel of smoke in the sky, this time on our left, and another cluster of tents came into view, nestled in a small opening in the forest.

As we sailed by, the women at the fire stood and waved and we waved back.

"That was Red Gate," Elena said. "They are very tidy. Maybe we'll stop for tea on the way back."

The terrors of the night and my reservations at the shit pit started to fall from my shoulders as the freewheeling minutes passed. The sky was grey, with streaks of yellow in the distance where the sun was trying to emerge.

At last we saw Orange Gate, a cluster of tents and benders among the trees, far back from the quiet road.

"Let's pretend we're visitors," Elena said.

"OK," I said, thinking that this was hardly a pretence for me.

"Where shall we say we are from?"

"France?" I suggested.

"Brilliant, let's do it," she said.

"Do you speak French?" I asked.

"No," she said, shaking her head as she overtook me, her hair flying in the wind. "But I can do the accent."

We lay our bikes on their sides in the bushes and walked toward the women sitting at the fire, the birds singing in the cool air. It was lunchtime, and a freckled woman with curly ginger hair was serving a steaming lentil stew into cracked plates, which were being handed from woman to woman around the fire.

"You're just in time," she said.

"Zank you," Elena said and we sat down, accepting our bowls of food and metal spoons to eat it with.

"Where are you from?" one of the women asked.

"We are from Parree," I said.

"We are 'ere to visit ze camp," Elena said. "We are at Camp Bleu."

I giggled and wondered why she didn't worry that someone might recognize her later, and then I realized, it wouldn't matter if they did. They would just laugh.

"Too bad Zelda is not here today," the woman with ginger hair said. "She speaks perfect French."

Elena and I smiled at each other.

"Oh, 'ow wundeerful," I said, my mouth full of spicy stew.

Elena snorted and tried to cover her face.

"I am sorree," I said, channelling my French friends as I did so. "My friend sinks my English is verry, 'ow you say, funnee?"

We put our heads down to focus on our food, hoping to finish our meal in a hurry, as we shook with silent laughter.

"I hear some women from Blue Gate were harassed by squaddies last night," one of the women said, and as a wave of ice washed over me, I glanced at Elena and signalled with my eyes that it was time to leave.

It took us forty-five minutes to cycle all the way back past Red, Violet, and Blue and on to Green Gate, where I couldn't see a camp, or any women. All I could see was forest and a funnel of smoke where the fire must be.

"We're not stopping here," Elena said. "They're too middle-class and spiritual, all into Goddess worship and full moon rituals, and they don't like boy children. That makes me mad." She got off her bike anyway, and I followed. "But it's easier to get to Yellow along the fence than the road. So let's creep past without them seeing us."

We wheeled our bikes along the perimeter fence, and when we arrived at Yellow, we were no longer French, because Elena seemed to know everyone. She waved or kissed the women on the lips as she passed. I didn't see any press, but I knew that Yellow Gate was the main gate to the base, with the largest encampment and the greatest number of soldiers and police, where the American women tended to live, and where the media always went. I recognized one or two women from TV coverage, and I felt excited and even more connected to this great band of activist women standing up for what was right. I wanted to be one of them, too. I may not have made it to Zimbabwe yet, but at least I was standing up against the might of the United States' military and its Cold War madness right here in my own backyard.

# Chapter Six
## "SHOULD I STAY OR SHOULD I GO" THE CLASH

BACK IN GOLBORNE, I could think of nothing but my first ever action as a Greenham woman. Martin talked about school and I thought about Blue Gate. He told me about his colleague Mike's latest divorce sorrows, and I inwardly walked myself through our action moment by moment, dwelling on Diana's touch as we held hands in the back of the police car and Elena's embrace when we said goodbye. I considered what and what not to tell Martin and was glad that I had the perfect excuse to go back soon—a court hearing. I would be with Diana; I would see Elena. Martin played me a new Elvis Costello track, and I heard women in my head singing, "You can't kill the spirit, she is like a mountain."

On my second night home, Martin made me spaghetti and we sat together to eat in the kitchen, Joy Division playing in the background.

"I'm proud of you," he said.

I was touched. "Thank you."

"I want to get the bastards who did that to you," he added, his eyes clouding over with anger.

"What do you expect?" I said. "They're soldiers, that is what they are trained to do. Don't worry. I'm fine."

Then the phone rang. I ran to the living room and picked it up. My heart beat that much faster and a smile came to my lips as I heard Diana's voice.

"How are you?" I asked.

"Fine, excited, can't wait to get back," she said.

"Me neither," I said.

We chatted for half an hour, and when I hung up the phone, Martin was scowling.

"Why do you talk to her in that tone of voice?" he asked.

"What tone of voice? I've no idea what you're talking about," I lied. For the first time in our six years together there were actually grounds for his jealousy.

He left the room, sensing, I'm sure, that things were changing, and they were. My job at the small run-down Women's Aid office in Wigan opened my eyes to a whole new world—which was alarmingly familiar. I answered the phone to women desperate to leave abusive husbands. I helped terrified wives hurriedly pack their bags before their husbands got home, and helped furnish a safe house at a secret location for women and children fleeing violent homes. As I listened to story upon story of violence and degradation it started to dawn on me that—apart from the physical violence—my relationship with Martin may not have been so different from those of the women we were rescuing.

ONE MONTH LATER for my court hearing, I took a train from Golborne to Diana's hometown of Oswestry on a clear moonlit night, the only passenger on the entire train, racing through the Shropshire countryside as a pink dusk fell slowly over the earth. Stepping out to greet Diana on the empty platform, I breathed in the country air, grateful that it was truly dark here, with trees casting shadows from the light of the moon. I stayed overnight with Diana in her stone cottage and my heart fluttered whenever she looked at me, undeterred by the presence of her boyfriend. I would never dare tell her how I felt anyway. It was enough to watch the way her lips moved when she spoke and how her eyes sparkled when she laughed.

We picked up Linda the next day and, as Diana drove us the four hours to Greenham Common, we sang snatches of songs we had learned at the camp. "Men call us names to be nasty and rude/Like lesbian, man-hater, witch, and prostitute/What a laugh/Cos the half of it's true."

When we stopped at the Little Chef on the side of the motorway, we weren't sure they'd serve us. All the Little Chefs in the country had banned Greenham women, making it hard to find food or tea when travelling. Since there was no other food choice on the motorway and because we were hungry, we sat down and ordered a meal of chips and baked beans. When the waitress didn't bat an eyelid, I realized I was disappointed. I wanted to be known as a Greenham woman, a peace activist. And I was looking forward to my day in court, to telling the world that war was the real crime and what we did was simply a protest to stop it.

By the time we arrived at Blue Gate, it was dark. We chose a spot in the woods and tried in vain to connect the poles that seemed to have no relationship to each other or the canvas that was supposed to drape over them. In a tent a few feet away, some women were listening to Bob Marley on a cassette player, waving to us through their tent flap now and then as we struggled. I could smell the sickly odour of the pot they were smoking. As Bob Marley sang "Don't worry about a thing," they sang, "Don't worry about your tent. Cos every little tent is gonna be all right!" then dissolved in hysterics, and I was cross. In the end we gave up, and used the tent as a big sleeping bag. Lying next to each other in a row, our heads poked out of the zipped tent opening, and when we woke to our day in court, gentle rain was falling on our faces.

Diana, Linda, and I were still huddled close to each other a few hours later, only on a bench in the waiting area in the court building. And this time the Greenham women had come out to help in full force, a tribe of fifty or so in multi-coloured clothes, all of us smelling of wood smoke. I looked in vain for Elena, but she was not there, and my heart sank a little. Penny from Bradford had come, with her multiple pigtails, freckles, and smiles, and so had Lucy, with her braying laugh, and Spring, with her one long plait trailing its way down between her eyes and breasts, all the way to her belly button. I recognized a few women from my bike tour of the camp, but I could not place which gate I'd seen them at and hoped nobody realized I was not French after all. I also recognized a couple of women I had seen on TV, but had never laid eyes on most of the women, and I filled with pride.

I was excited to be holding Diana's hand, as a group began singing and another group gathered around Elena (she was here!) who was doing a pretty good imitation of the BBC journalist who recently got furious when a Greenham woman insisted on cartwheeling behind her every time she tried to do her report.

"Can't you see you are stopping yourselves getting coverage by doing this?" the journalist had yelled, adding, "You're being such a tit."

Today Drummer was the cartwheeler, while Elena used a rolled-up magazine as a microphone and shouted, "Can't you see I am trying to get you all on television, you tits? Why can't you just all behave? Why are you all so unladylike?"

These were the last words I heard before a court official stepped into the hall and a hush fell over us. In the silence the three of us stood and waited for our names to be called to enter the dock. Instead, the official walked over and showed us our names, "Is this you?"

Diana didn't even get to hear him say, "Isaac Hunt."

"All charges dropped," he said. "You're free to go."

"Why?" My breath caught in my throat. "We want our day in court."

He shrugged and walked away.

The night of the incident, we had told the police about the soldiers' treatment of us, but they had made little of it, and now it didn't occur to us that they might have been dropping the case so the soldiers' behaviour wouldn't come to light. Lucy said that it was most likely part of a larger strategy on the part of the authorities to stop arresting Greenham women to help curb publicity. And then a cheer came up among the women, and Elena, aka the BBC journalist, ran toward us with her magazine microphone and asked for our reactions at this emotional time. We jumped up and down and clapped and hugged each other. Drummer did a cartwheel, and I thought, I am home. I am a Greenham woman.

# Chapter Seven
## "ME MYSELF I" JOAN ARMATRADING

A WEEK AFTER our court case, I was sitting on our cheap futon-sofa giggling and whispering with Diana on the phone, her Welsh accent sending delicious tremors through my body, as we lamented losing our chance to speak out against the United States stationing nuclear weapons in our own country, poised to start a nuclear war.

"Why do you always have to talk to her for so long?" I heard as I hung up. I hadn't noticed that Martin had entered the room. "And why do you always use that tone of voice?"

I glanced around the small living room, with its shelves brimming with books and records, the wonky standing lamps, the armchair we found in a skip. My eyes settled on the poster pinned into the wall, a famous nineteenth-century depiction of a riverside picnic in France, a housewarming present from Martin's older brother. I'd put it up because we didn't have anything else to put up, but it wasn't my style. It faced, on the opposite wall, the green and red anti-apartheid poster from my university days, featuring a map of Africa with chains around the southern part of the continent, blood dripping from the chains. I looked at the woman walking across the grass at the picnic, wearing a bustle and carrying a parasol, and wondered if she ever escaped the man in a black top hat holding proprietarily onto her arm.

"I don't know what you mean," I said, looking directly into his eyes, knowing absolutely what he meant.

"That quiet tone of voice. So soft. Almost a whisper. Like, like . . ." He couldn't bring himself to say *Like a lover.*

"That's how we talk to each other at Greenham. Because we're women."

We spent the next week in our routines. He drove to school and back in the car we'd recently bought. I took the moped and rode along the grey roads to the Women's Aid office in Wigan to listen to more stories of abuse, neglect, and violence. Late in the week, on an overcast, chilly afternoon, my colleague Lizzie and I accompanied Grace, a tiny middle-aged woman with thick glasses and a shaking, quiet voice, to the suburban bungalow she shared with her abuser on the outskirts of town. Grace did not have any children, so she had no son or daughter to run to, and she did not want to face the shame she felt by asking her younger sister to take her in, so she was coming to our shelter for safety and was here to collect a few items of clothing and toiletries to take with her.

There was no car in the driveway when we arrived, which we took as a good sign. Her husband must have been out—probably at work, Grace said, but he might come home within the hour, so she had to act fast. The lawn was perfectly mown, with neat flowerbeds at its edges, empty of colour now. I imagined the inside of the house being just as impeccable, with a shining kitchen, gleaming furniture, and not a speck of dust anywhere. But I wouldn't get to see for myself, unless the two police officers, who were parked just a few doors down from the house in case they were needed, told us we could go in with her. They wouldn't even allow us to accompany her to the door.

I wondered how many neighbours in this quiet cul-de-sac would be curtain twitching, wondering what was going on, how many had known for years, and to how many her departure, and the reasons for it, would come as a complete surprise. Or perhaps nobody had ever noticed the quiet mouse who hid at the end of their road, terrified, beaten, and alone.

I WAS SITTING with Lizzie in her car, parked on the opposite side of the road to the police. She was small and sharp, smoking one cigarette after another, throwing the butts out onto the pristine street as the car filled with smoke. This was the first time I had done anything like this, but Lizzie had been working with battered women for many years and she was as worried as I was. We knew that Grace's husband had beaten her unconscious. He had burned cigarettes into her skin. He had called her terrible names and stopped her from having her own friends, her own job, her own life. He was twice her size and he might come home at any moment. I had a sudden panic that he was already home and that his car was at the garage for repairs.

I looked at my watch. An hour had passed.

"Ask them to go and check on her," Lizzie said. "They don't know you. They're fed up of me haranguing them all the time. They might be nicer to you."

I nodded, got out of the car, and walked toward the police car, grateful that Lizzie was here to tell me what to do.

I knocked on the window, and the driver, a sandy haired man in his thirties with a pink complexion, slowly wound down the window. He flicked a cigarette butt into the street, then glanced at me before looking away, as if I were a horror to behold.

"An hour is too long for what she is here to do," I said. "Something must have happened. Will you go and check on her? Can I?"

"He's not even home, so what could possibly go wrong?" the police officer said, leaning back, tapping his fingers on the steering wheel.

*He isn't taking this seriously at all*, I thought, and my mind leapt back to a few months earlier when Martin and I had been walking home to a friend's house in Bath late one night when we heard sounds coming from a nearby flat of a woman screaming, dull thuds, a man's voice yelling, then more screaming, more thuds. We thought of knocking on the door but were nervous about it, so I ran to a phone box and called the police instead, the first time I had ever dialled 999. By the time the police car arrived, quietly, no sirens, the noises had stopped, and the police officer said, "Well, it must be alright then, mustn't it?"

"Can you just check?" I asked. "She might be horribly injured."

"Sorry, love, we can't knock on someone's door without good cause," he said.

And that was that.

Now another police officer was shrugging his shoulders while just a few feet away a small, scared woman may have been facing down the man who had beaten her for decades.

"We can't be absolutely sure he's not there," I said. "Can we?"

"Well in that case, maybe they're making up." He smirked, winking at his colleague, a young policewoman whose thick black hair was tied into a strict ponytail under her police cap. She didn't return his smile.

"He has assaulted her many, many times," I pleaded, looking hopefully from one to the other, my voice trembling with rage and worry. I became more and more aware of how posh my Southern accent must sound, and wondered if this was why he was being so unfriendly and whether Lizzie should have spoken to him after all. "When battered women leave their homes, that is often the time their husbands do the worst."

"Well, as far as I know, we don't have any record of violence at this address," he said.

"Of course not," I replied. "Most women don't report it when their husbands beat them. Because *you* don't take it seriously."

His face clouded over.

"Well, if you ask me, we're wasting our time," he said. "But we're here, aren't we?"

I looked over to the policewoman at his side and forced a smile, searching for a glimmer of solidarity, which she did not offer.

Then the door opened and tiny Grace stood there, a suitcase in one hand, a Sainsbury's carrier bag in the other. Lizzie jumped out of the car, her arms open wide, ready to embrace her. My heart leapt and sank at the same time. Grace was alive. But she looked so alone as she walked away from the only home she had known for thirty years, the home she had spent a lifetime building, only to leave it with a carrier bag and a suitcase, and little chance of ever seeing it again.

I wondered when Grace's husband started hitting her. Was it soon after they met? After they got married? Had she tried to talk him out of it? Had she tried to leave him before? Martin only hit me once, at his parents' home. We were making a bed in his younger brother's room at the top of the stairs and had just tucked in the bottom sheet when I said something critical about his mother. I felt a sudden hot sting as he slapped me across the face, hissing, "Don't ever talk about my mother like that again." I considered that I had hit him that time in France, which made us equal, maybe—even if he was stronger, and a man. But I didn't abuse him verbally or question him constantly in a need to control him.

One morning I took a call from a young woman living on a council housing estate who had been married just one year. She told me she hadn't left home for five days.

"Why not?" I asked.

"He won't let me," she said. "He says he'll know if I've gone anywhere without him. He thinks I am looking at other men, or other men are looking at me. I can only leave the house to go shopping, and then he has to go with me. He doesn't give me any money."

"Has he hit you?" I asked.

"No," she answered. "But he calls me a bitch all the time. He says the clothes I choose are to attract men. He won't let me have any friends. I used to have so many. But I don't have any friends anymore."

She started to weep. When she regained her voice she said, simply, "I feel like a prisoner."

"You are a prisoner. I know how you feel," I said as I wondered at my qualifications for helping her.

In my own way I had been terrified, like Grace, and it came as a sudden awakening to discover that I was not alone in my suffering, that I didn't have to keep quiet about what Martin had been doing, and it was not love. Only I was going to walk out thirty years earlier than Grace did—because I had found Greenham Common.

I asked Briana and Meg to go for a drink after work, and over three pints of bitter, in a dimly lit pub on Meg's council estate, I declared, "I am going to live at Greenham," and a surge of energy rushed through me. I was going to save the world from war, women from violence, and myself from Martin.

They both jumped up and hugged me and we ordered a second round to celebrate.

"It's about time you left that bastard," Meg said, wiping the white foam from her top lip after taking a swig of beer. I was surprised at her vehemence. She had only met Martin once, and I didn't remember telling her anything about him.

She saw the surprise on my face.

"I can tell," she said, nodding.

I hadn't been alone after all.


THE NEXT NIGHT, Martin and I had just had a dinner of pasta and vegetables, a nod to my newfound vegetarianism. I put down my fork and said bluntly, "I'm going to Greenham again next week. And I'm not coming back."

He looked confused.

"You're leaving?"

"I'm leaving."

"For good?"

"For good," I said, feeling powerful. Slapping his face in France was nothing compared to this.

His face crumpled and he put his head in his hands. When he looked up, he had tears streaming down his face. I had never seen him cry before. He looked small and lost, and it dawned on me that he, too, was still finding his way, and I felt a softening of my heart. I had been dragging him behind me as I pursued my dream of going to Zimbabwe, when he would have been just as happy taking a job down south where he could eat dinner with his parents once a week, go to the pub with his mates in the evening, and play cricket on Sunday afternoons with his brothers.

"You're going to leave me here? Where I don't know anyone?" he said. "I only came here for you."

"You could go and live with Mike," I said.

Mike was his colleague in the PE Department whose wife had recently left him. I pictured the two of them patronizing jazz clubs and drinking together, maybe even joining a football club, finding new girlfriends. Mike had a large, lonely house with several bedrooms and an extensive wine cellar in a tree-lined suburb of Manchester. He had room.

"You've really thought this through, haven't you?" he said, accusingly.

"It's a very strong feeling I have. I have to play my part. This is our chance to show the world that we don't want American weapons on our soil. Who am I if I don't join? Why would I spend my time here in this godforsaken little town where nobody will ever like me because I don't wear makeup or heels or shave my legs? What is the point of that?"

"What about Zimbabwe? I only came here because you want us to go to Zimbabwe. Don't you care about that anymore?"

But there was no energy in his voice; he knew there was no way he could win. He'd seen my determination at work before—campaigning against apartheid, getting accepted to teach in Zimbabwe, standing up to my parents. And in the last two years, I had slowly but surely directed it at him. His mother had once told him to watch out for me, I was trouble. It turned out she was right. I almost felt sorry for him.

He didn't ask the unspoken question hovering in the air. *Are you a lesbian?* I didn't know what I would answer if he did.

When I was younger, the only person I really cared about was Bridget, and when she moved away from Whitchurch when we were fourteen, I was heartbroken. I would not have called what I felt for Bridget "attraction." I did not consider myself a lesbian, and had only heard the term used as an insult. But I liked being with Bridget more than with anyone else. It was her I thought of when I fell asleep and when I woke up, and when we stayed over at each other's houses we sometimes tickled each other's backs in an ecstasy of sensation before we fell asleep. But it would never have dawned on me that I could actually fall in love with her, that I could desire her like I was supposed to desire boys. The first time I knew this was possible was at Greenham, and even that came as a surprise. The media never talked about the lesbians, the strong, sexy women who walked upright and fixed things and played and held hands and kissed each other on the lips. They focused on mothers and grandmothers and wives sacrificing their family time to save the world and create a better future for their children and grandchildren. Of course, many of the women *were* mothers and grandmothers and wives. But they were also sisters and daughters and friends—and lovers. They were women who wore whatever they liked, reminding me of the village tomboy, Theo, whom I had admired from afar as she strode past my house at the edge of the village in her boots, jeans, and green military parka, her hair cropped short, not giving a single concession to the pressures around us girls to be as feminine and weak as possible. She was strong and independent and had been my hero, as these women were now. But just as I hadn't dared speak to Theo, and despite my crushes on Elena and Diana, I couldn't truly imagine myself as the lover of one of them.

Martin was sobbing. I watched, my heart cold. I got up, went to the bathroom, and brought back a wad of toilet paper for him to blow his nose on. I sat down opposite him at the kitchen table and watched, thinking of all the times he had seen me in tears, and all the times he had refused to offer comfort. When he was done, I reached over the table and took one of his hands. He squeezed it tight, like a drowning man holding on for one last moment before he lost me altogether. I slowly pulled my hand away and got up to make some tea.

As we drank it, we talked quietly about the logistics of my move. I would go in a week's time. I would take the train to Newbury and

walk from there. Martin offered to drop me at the railway station in
Manchester and agreed to keep hold of my records, clothes, and books
until I knew what to do with them. All I needed was the minimum
clothing that would fit into a backpack. I didn't even need a sleeping bag
or a tent, because visitors brought bedding all the time, and someone
would find space for me in their tent. I could even sleep on the ground
in a Gore-Tex bag, if it came to it. I couldn't wait to start packing.

We stayed up into the early hours drinking French tisanes and
smoking roll-ups. I talked about my plans for Greenham, we talked about
how to bring peace to the world. Like my father, Martin believed in the
power of education to create change, and told me he was introducing
girls' football the following term. I told him I was proud of him. It
felt as if nothing had happened, when in fact the inevitable had finally
happened, and with it, the tensions and expectations had dissipated,
quickly, and finally. We were simply two young people who had become
involved too young and who had suddenly washed up together safely on
a quiet unfamiliar shore after years on a turbulent sea. When we at last
went to bed and made love one last time, it felt like love making for the
very first time.

The next morning, I woke up earlier than Martin. A ray of sunlight
was washing over his sleeping face and the rings of sadness under his
puffy eyes. I felt a tug of sorrow and an even stronger tug to get away.

I slid out of bed, made my way to the kitchen, and turned on the
radio. It was playing Joan Armatrading's "Me Myself I." I turned it up,
smiling as I mouthed the lyrics and prepared coffee. And I smiled at
the radio, too, a blue and white 1960s classic that had accompanied
me from my home in St. Mary Bourne to university in Bath to my year
abroad in France and to here. I thanked it, silently. If it wasn't for you,
I said, I wouldn't have heard the women being evicted from Greenham
that day, and I wouldn't be here, now, in this sunny morning kitchen, on
the cusp of adventure and freedom.

I poured my coffee and sat at the kitchen table and smiled.

# Chapter Eight
## "ALISON" ELVIS COSTELLO

A WEEK LATER, in my dungarees, boots, thrift store winter coat, and a backpack on my back, I stood at the top of Newbury hill, struck by the brightness of the stars pricked into the dark sky and the silvery light of the full moon rising above the camp. The air was crisp and I could smell the wood smoke inviting me to its warmth. I stayed there for a good long moment, breathing deeply, smiling at the distant sounds of my new family talking and laughing at the fire pit. As I approached, the first person I saw was Elena, who welcomed me with a warm hug.

"Come for a visit?"

"No," I said, thrilled that Elena was the first to greet me. "I am here to stay."

Taking my hands in hers, she stood back and looked me up and down. "Really? You've come to stay?"

"Yes. I left Martin." I giggled with excitement.

"Hey!" she shouted to the women at the fire pit. "Guess what? Beautiful Steph is here to stay."

"Great!"

"Wow!"

"Brilliant!"

One by one the women around the fire got up and gave me a welcome hug—Penny with her short, tiny pigtails; Lucy with her dog, Biscuit; Spring with her single plait running down the front of her body; feisty Little Chris; the Goth Trish and her girlfriend, Trina; Sally and Zee; and two women I had never met before.

I couldn't stop smiling. I'd left my life behind and Elena had called me beautiful. I was home. But there was still one thing missing. I hadn't kissed a girl.

THEN I MET Alison, in April, as the buds were slowly uncurling on the trees, the snowdrops were wistfully waving on the roadsides, and the bluebells were creating carpets for fairies in the woods. Alison had curly blond hair and a sweet laugh and she lived at Indigo Gate—the hardcore gate with very little grass and no trees, set right next to the perimeter road. There were only two full-time women at this gate, and Alison was a weekender from Portsmouth, where she studied design.

One day, after a fifteen-minute walk from Blue Gate along the perimeter fence, I arrived at Indigo and joined the three women sitting at the fire. I was feeling quite confident because I had a whole new Greenham look, a transformation I started in Bath the week before, where my friend Hannah, from my anti-apartheid activism days, put me up every two weeks so I could sign on the dole to receive unemployment benefits while I devoted my life to full-time activism.

Hannah's hairdresser friend had been happy to tackle my curly perm and make it into something more exciting. I hadn't gone for a Mohican straight away, but rather a short, bright orange, spiky cut with pink highlights on the almost-shaved sides. Hannah's boyfriend, Joe, had given me a pair of his Doc Martens, which, surprisingly, were a perfect fit. Looking down and seeing them on my feet, I was reminded of the football boots I never had as a child and always craved. For most people, Doc Martens are a symbol related primarily to men, including skinheads and punks. But they will forever remind me of the rainbow women of Greenham Common striding through the woods, lying down in front of military vehicles, singing peace songs, letting their bodies go limp to be dragged by the police into police vans, or sitting huddled in circles around campfires. Hannah had also given me a couple of pairs of cotton overalls—one grey and one emerald green—that tucked nicely into my boots and made me feel as tough as I would ever feel. Along with my short skirts and vest tops for the summer, baggy sweaters, and a few pairs of knickers and socks (no bras required), I had all I needed to be a true Greenham woman.

At the fire at the newly formed Indigo Gate, it was early evening and still light, another wonderful harbinger of spring. When Alison turned to me, I noticed her blue eyes, curly hair, freckled cheeks, and earnest, fresh energy. She told me that she had been visiting the camp every weekend for several months, but somehow the dirt hadn't wedged under her nails or the smoke in her hair. She was clean and wholesome and adorable.

We ate a vegan stew of lentils, potatoes, onion, and carrots out of chipped plates as we sat with the other women by the fire, but our eyes and conversation were just for each other. After dinner, we walked in the moonlit woods, holding hands, jumping in excitement at strange animal rustlings in the bushes. Finally, we found ourselves in her tiny two-person tent on the small strip of green wedged between the tarmac and perimeter fence of the military base, just me and her, woman to woman. She turned to me and offered me her soft sweet lips. I could not believe it was happening, so soon, and with someone so beautiful. I melted into her.

We saw each other for a few more weeks, mostly at my tent, which was just as small as hers, but in the woods, so we woke up to birds singing in the trees, not the voices of policemen and soldiers at the gate. I even visited Portsmouth with her for a few days where she awkwardly introduced me to her university friends, who didn't quite know what to do with this new development in their friend's life—I was her first girlfriend, too—the woman with the bright orange hair and big boots she had suddenly shacked up with.

Then Alison number two came along.

I WAS SITTING alone at Blue Gate drinking tea and gazing into the fire one sunny afternoon, when a tough-looking woman with a stiff red Mohican, Doc Marten boots, a black army surplus jacket, black jeans, a red armband, and a mischievous laugh, set herself down next to me, put out her hand to shake mine, and said, "Hi, I'm Al. Who are you?"

I already knew who she was. Rumours had been circulating around the camp for days that Al, a bass player in a two-girl anarcho-punk band called On the Rag, was coming to stay for a few days—and she fitted the description perfectly. Friends at Blue Gate had swooned a little just at the mention of her name, so of course, I was curious. I learned that On the Rag played at all the anarcho-punk venues around the country, supporting such legends as The Poison Girls and The Nightingales, espousing causes like the Miners' Strike and Workers Against Racism, and sending their primarily female audiences into fits of pogo-ing as the two of them raced maniacally around the stage, spitting savage feminist lyrics and freedom songs into each other's faces. They had two records out. My heart pounded as I told Al my name. She took my hand in hers, and instead of shaking it, she put it to her lips and looked gallantly up into my eyes.

"Wonderful to meet you, beautiful Steph," she said, in her gravelly voice, tinged with a slight Midlands accent.

I was hooked.

"Do you want to go for a walk?" she asked.

"Yes, of course, why not?" I stuttered.

"You can show me around." She jumped up, took my hand in hers, and pulled me to my feet. She was so strong I almost fell into her. She laughed as she steadied me, though I was tempted to keep falling so she could catch me.

"I was at Yellow Gate when I lived here," she said.

*That figures,* I thought. *That is where the cool women go.*

"I never made it over to Blue. So I don't know the neighbourhood at all."

She didn't let go of my hand as we walked through the bluebells in the spring woods bursting with new life, and told me about her band, her life in Birmingham, her time at Greenham getting arrested and singing at the campfire. She told me how she met the other half of her band, Zephyr, at a WONT (Women Opposed to Nuclear Threat) meeting in the Midlands. They came to Greenham together, Al all in black, Zephyr with her dyed black and white hair teased into a lion's mane. At the fire, the women sang one of their famous peace songs, and Al and Zephyr began to harmonize, their voices blending above the chorus. They became lovers, wrote songs together in the woods, and plotted to form a band when they got home to their native Birmingham.

"We both loved the Poison Girls and one day we hitched to see them play in Nottingham," Al said. "A minivan pulled up and we got inside and it was Ranking Roger from the Beat."

"Oh my God," I cried. "I love the Beat."

"'Stand Down Margaret, Stand Down Please. Stand Down Margaret,'" Al sang in a deep strong voice, and I soon joined in, and then she was pogo-ing and so was I. We sang the whole song together, from start to finish, collapsing in a laughing heap on the damp grass when we were done.

Al turned to me, brushing some stray hairs back from my face. "Then at the concert we went backstage and we met Vi Subversa, the lead singer of the Poison Girls, and she said, 'How many songs have you got?' We said 'Three,' and she said, 'You're opening for me tonight.'"

"That's so amazing," I said, also amazed that I was lying on the grass next to her and that her face was so close to mine. I tried not to smile too much, afraid it would make my feelings too obvious.

"Zephyr and I are not together anymore," Al continued, looking crestfallen, and moved away from me to lie on her back, her hands behind her head. I rolled over onto my back, too, and watched white clouds puff across a blue sky filled with promise. "At least, not as lovers. We are still partners in music. She's my best friend. And I am still in love with her. But she's not in love with me. She's decided she's more into men."

"Crazy," I said, because that was the closest I could come to expressing what I really wanted to say. *Is Zephyr nuts? She wants a man when she can have you?* I felt disappointed that Al was in love with Zephyr.

Al jumped up, turned to offer me her hand, and pulled me to my feet. We stopped for a split second and looked into each other's eyes, then she smiled and turned, and offered me her hand. As we walked back toward Blue Gate hand-in-hand, I noticed how Al walked like a bloke, and even looked like a bloke, with the androgynous appearance I was starting to find so compelling in women, the excitement of knowing what was really under her unisex black T-shirt and tight black jeans. She stopped, reached into her pocket, and pulled out a pair of headphones. She placed them on my ears so that I could listen to her singing "Strange Fruit" on her Walkman, the first time I ever heard this sad and moving song about lynchings in the deep south of the United States. Then she played her favourite On the Rag song, "Other Girls Like Me," where she and Zephyr pelted out lyrics about freedom and women's rights, Zephyr's saxophone dancing with Al's pounding, rhythmic bass: *Don't wanna wear your heels/Don't wanna cook your meals/Don't wanna sit on the sidelines/Just want to run, run, run like the boys/Just stop playing with your*

*war toys/Other girls like me/I'm looking for other girls, other girls like me/I'm*
*all right now cos other girls, other girls like me . . .*

When the song was done, we continued walking. I told Al that I
had just arrived at the camp, that I had studied French and Russian at
Bath University, that I cared about apartheid, that I'd had a possessive
boyfriend for six years, and that now I was a lesbian. I told her that my
family lived a few miles away and that we were not talking, really, and
that this part of the world was home to me. I told her that my parents
were disappointed with me for choosing to live at the camp, despite
their support for Greenham, that they were afraid I was a bad influence
on my younger sister, Sarah, who admired me so much she wanted to
change her name to mine. I wondered as I told Al this whether Sarah
still did.

By the time we made it back to camp, Al's arm was around my
waist, and mine rested on her strong shoulders. When her eyes caught
mine as we talked, I was overcome with the desire to throw her to the
ground and make crazy love. Instead, I flirted. I found it hard to believe
that she was actually interested in me. But she was, and I was alarmed
and delighted at the effect she was having on me. We laughed, we told
stories, we shared indignation at the horrors of war, the stupidity of
nuclear weapons, the all-encompassing damage done by the patriarchy,
the cruelty inflicted on animals, and how much better things would be if
women were in power, ignoring, for a moment, that Margaret Thatcher
was our leader. I learned that Al had the same Scorpio birthday as the
first Alison, and I realized, as we crawled into my tent in the middle
of the afternoon, that I was about to drop sweet Alison for tough and
complicated Al.

We squeezed into the tent, then turned to take off our Doc Martens.
You can't really rip off someone's Doc Martens in the heat of passion.
You can always keep them on . . . but we didn't, not this time, and
instead we struggled with the laces for what felt like an eternity, laughing
hysterically and conspiratorially, because we knew what was about to
happen and we could barely stand the tension. Finally, they were off,
and we closed the tent zip behind us. I turned to face her. She brought
her face close to mine and stared into my eyes, then at my lips, then
back into my eyes. She placed a finger on my lips and gently traced their
contours, humming quietly and deeply to herself. Then she abruptly

took my face in her hands and kissed me with more passion than I had ever been kissed before. We undressed each other slowly and playfully, and something woke up in me that I was determined to keep awake. "Are you sure I'm only your second female lover?" she purred as we lay in each other's arms two hours later, the tent flap open, our eyes gazing up at the swaying branches with their fresh green leaves and the blue sky above. I felt insanely proud—and I immediately wanted more and pulled her back into the tent, zipping up the flap. Where Alison was gentle, Al was strong. Where Alison was sweet, Al was feisty. She liked to play games and roles and I played along, our imaginations tangling with the leaves above the tent, or the gauze curtains that hung around the bed in her small flat in the Moseley neighbourhood of Birmingham, where she told me, often, that I was beautiful. Martin had never said this to me, and I liked it. I even began to think it might be true. She liked my eyes, my lips, my smile, my body. She liked every part of me, and every part of me liked her back in gratitude. She made sure I enjoyed myself in bed, which to her was a playground, not a battleground, where words were sweet, sexy, and witty, not cruel, unkind, and hurtful.

But Al was busy. While she was mine as often as I could make it to Birmingham, for three nights a week she entertained her other female lover from Newcastle-upon-Tyne, and for two nights, her boyfriend, Rick, an anarcho-punk fan of On the Rag, and a former lover of Zephyr's. Al managed to keep her three lovers neatly apart for the most part, and it helped that I was busy, too, at the peace camp, too busy to notice, really, that I was far more in love with her than she was with me, and that when she told me that I should never rely on her, I should have taken notice.

I ONLY VISITED Al occasionally because I was occupied at the camp. For one thing, there was Cruise Watch. You never knew when the gates would fling open and the dreaded cruise missiles would propel out onto our country roads in huge convoys as they took part in full-on military exercises. So we looked out for tell-tale signs. We'd notice a gradual increase in police officers and soldiers on duty and a general air of edginess inside the base. Then the minute the convoy burst out of the gates, we jumped into our VW vans and onto our motorcycles and chased it through the narrow country lanes, hollering and whooping, making sure their secret launch locations were not so secret.

ONE SUMMER DAY, a few months into my stay, and not long after I'd met Al, they did it differently. It was early evening and Trish and Trina, with their identical jet-black hair and black humour, were cooking a familiar bubbling stew on the fire. The rest of us were sitting on the ground in a large circle deep in the woods, playing a strange game with some newly arrived day visitors who had come loaded with cans of vegetables, bottles of juice, packets of rice and lentils, and, the all-time favourites, Cadbury's milk chocolate and maltesers. One of the visitors, an imposing-looking woman with strict metal-rimmed glasses and a tight bun, told us she was a Brown Owl with a Brownies troupe in Leicestershire and we laughed and whooped in recognition as memories of Brownie badges, Brownie uniforms, and the Brownie pledge came flooding back. I'd only been a Brownie for one day. I'd pulled out the new brown dress from its cellophane packaging, slipped it on, and discovered to my dismay it was as short as my gym skirt. Then I'd picked up the ugly yellow cravat, wondering what it was before it dawned on me I was supposed to tie it around my neck. Then I'd walked down the village street to the Salvation Army hall, where a handful of girls from the primary school were standing in an unfriendly huddle. They glanced at me, but didn't invite me to join them, so I stood alone, kicking my foot back and forth, looking around at the unwelcoming walls, breathing in the musty air. An earnest woman with buck teeth and calling herself Brown Owl taught us a song about how we were here to lend a hand, and asked us to recite a pledge of allegiance—to the queen, country, and God. I shuddered, wondering if my dad knew what they made us do in here. After Brown Owl told us what to expect in coming weeks—sewing, cooking, drawing, performing good deeds to earn a badge, and then, adding insult to injury, sewing the badges onto our dress sleeves—I'd stomped home in a fury.

"I'm not going back to the Brownies," I'd announced to my parents. And I never did.

"I'm Brown Owl of Blue Gate," Lucy cried, sitting next to me at the fire, and she went on to list a set of badges the rest of us had to earn—

best fire-starter, most creative camp insurgent, most prolific practitioner of non-monogamy. I hadn't made it past my first day in the Brownies, but I decided to be Brown Owl's pet and began accusing others of being monogamous, refusing to do night watch, eating milk chocolate when they were vegan.

The women I accused protested, laughing, and I shook my head. "I saw you!"

"How about Biggest Creep badge?" Sally said, who was sitting next to me, smiling her dimpled smile. "You'd be a good one for that." She slapped me on the knee.

"Well, I could tell everyone about last week," I said, giggling, thinking of how Sally, this great animal rights activist and vegan, had gobbled down a milk chocolate bar, swearing me to secrecy.

"Don't you dare," she said, her eyes flashing.

"What did you do, Sal?" Penny asked, her part-time lover, another animal rights activist, with a short crop of multi-coloured pigtails and a gentle Yorkshire accent. "Did you sleep with Steph?"

"Oh, she'd get Brownie points for that." I laughed.

As I glanced at Sally I blushed. Al was making me cocky and I realized I was flirting.

Sally and I were still laughing when we heard a holler from the gate. "Cruise Watch, Cruise Watch!"

We all jumped up and raced through the woods, leaping over tent pegs and skirting around tree roots at top speed, visitors and Greenham women alike. When we arrived at the gate, dozens of police officers were already running up the hill from town, a sea of dark blue descending upon the camp like a blot of ink, spreading to form a huge barricade protecting the entrance to the base and blocking us from the road. Their fast action left all of us stranded in the forest, unable to get into our vehicles and follow the convoy.

I watched helplessly from behind the line of police officers standing shoulder to shoulder, facing us. We couldn't even get to the phone box on the housing estate half way down the hill to call our Campaign for Nuclear Disarmament friends in Newbury. When they got the tip-off, they would set into motion a sophisticated telephone tree of Cruise Watchers in neighbouring villages, each person picking up the phone to make a new call as soon as they hung up. These ordinary and extraordinary men and women stopped in the middle of baking bread or gardening or fixing cars or watching TV and leapt into action. They jumped into their vehicles and fanned out around the Berkshire and Hampshire countryside to track the nuclear monsters as they crashed along our narrow country lanes. Once, my mother saw one lurching ominously across the bridge in front of Dove Cottage—with its cooing doves living on its thatched roof in St. Mary Bourne's village square, more used to Morris Dancers in bells than nuclear missiles on convoys— winding like a dragon along the Bourne Valley before returning to its lair, as if Sauron the Lord of Mordor had reached the Shire, and all was lost.

The British soldiers standing to attention inside the base were wearing what looked like World War II gas masks. They looked vulnerable as they watched two police officers open the gates for the monsters to appear—a convoy of massive military vehicles rumbling out at top speed, with American soldiers poised on the steps in glaring white head to toe protective gear, machine guns at the ready, as they took off between the sweet-smelling hedgerows toward a secret hidden spot where they would rehearse the moves they'd use to launch the deadly weapon.

For some of us, including me, this was our first view of the Americans, and it was not a pretty one. Around me women were wailing with frustration; others burst into protest songs, and this slowly caught fire until we were all singing at full volume, holding hands, or each other. I turned to see Penny crying silently at the sight of so much hate in the midst of so much verdant life, Sally holding her in her arms.

We knew this was most likely a practice. But we also knew that one day it might not be. A chill formed in my heart as the reality sank in that these weapons of mass destruction were roaming around our countryside and may one day be launched when a President of another country thousands of miles away deemed it necessary, and there was nothing we could do to stop it.

Later that evening, when it was all over, an electric stillness descended upon the gate. We assumed the convoy had returned through a different gate, because the police had dispersed and no convoy had come back through Blue Gate. No one had the energy to sing songs anymore to take the edge off our collective jumpiness. I was sipping tea from a cracked mug and walked to the entrance of the gate to chat with a familiar police officer who was rubbing his hands to keep them warm. The police didn't have fires like we did. He and I had made friends a few weeks earlier when I had learned he was from Whitby in Yorkshire, where my long-lost friend, Bridget, and her family had moved to years ago, leaving me bereft at Testbourne. The last time he had been on leave he'd found out for me that Bridget had moved to Canada, with no forwarding address. What would Bridget make of my adventures? Would she join me if she knew?

It was dark, and the peace camp was invisible from where we stood in the eerie pool of yellow light at the entrance to the base. We were brightly illuminated for all to see, as if on a film set.

"Don't you realize that nobody offered you any protection?" I said. "The Americans get the white super suits, the British soldiers get outdated gas masks. But you? You didn't get a thing. So you'd be dead now. Doesn't that bother you?"

He shrugged. He didn't know what to say. He was just doing his job.

# Chapter Nine
## "WE ARE FAMILY" SISTER SLEDGE

"YOUR FATHER IS here to see you."

It was just a few weeks after the night of the cruise convoy excursion when Lucy came to find me at the fire, her hair shaved short, no sign of the camouflage pattern any more. It was late afternoon and overcast, a chill was beginning to form in the air, and I was telling a group of rapt visitors about the night of the convoy. One of the funniest people I knew, Lucy was not smiling now.

I looked past her and saw my grey-haired father standing in the distance. He was still handsome, still looked like Gregory Peck, but he was paler and thinner than usual. As I stood up, Sally squeezed my hand, and I heard her picking up the convoy story where I left off as I walked toward him.

I hadn't seen my father since I took a group of Greenham women for a shower at our family home in St. Mary Bourne a month earlier. Liz, a tall, calm weekend visitor with short, red, spiky hair, had offered to drive four of us to my home. I felt as if I had just arrived from another planet with some new alien friends as we drove through the thatched roofed villages of the Bourne Valley, with everyone saying how pretty it was, past the road leading to Cluny's house in Stoke, past Gangbridge Lane and the horses in the Macnamaras' field, until we reached our modern bungalow nestled behind the village primary school.

My mother was a proud Greenham supporter and had attended many demonstrations herself. But she didn't like my new friends at all.

"Why are they so rude?" she whispered loudly to me in the kitchen as she cracked eggs into a frying pan. "Marching into my house as if they own it, not even taking off their boots."

I was chopping white, freshly peeled potatoes into perfectly ridged chips with the metal chip maker and dumping them into the big pan that always stood at the ready on the stove. The fat was usually white and congealed, with the metal chip strainer stranded in it like a ship stuck in ice, but now it was hot sizzling liquid, ready to turn the chips a perfect crispy golden brown.

"They're not rude," I said. "They're not used to being inside. We forgot about taking off our boots."

"And why do you all have to look so untidy?" She glared at my overalls and baggy sweater.

I stroked the woollen baggy sweater covering the turquoise overalls that Hannah had given me and I loved so much. "We live at a peace camp," I said, watching the clear of the fried eggs turn white and take shape in the crackling fat. "Elena and Zee don't eat eggs. Can I open a can of beans?"

My mother sighed and nodded. "I still don't understand why you don't become a lawyer." She crashed mugs onto the table. "We send you to university to get a degree, and you waste your time sitting outside a military base when you could be standing up for the Greenham women in court."

When I was fifteen, I briefly considered a career in law. My mother found a lawyer who lived in Hurstbourne Priors, a village just south of ours along the Bourne Valley. One Sunday morning she drove me to meet him in the living room of his low-ceilinged thatched roof cottage with a crackling open fire and leather upholstered furniture.

As I perched on the edge of his armchair sipping tea and eating digestive biscuits that I didn't dare dunk, I decided I didn't like the posh lawyer at all. He kept stealing glances and smirking at my mother's white, Russian fur hat that made her look like a dandelion about to spread its seeds. She didn't remove it because she hadn't washed her hair, she told me in the car later, and because when she wore it she felt like Julie Christie in *Dr. Zhivago*.

I didn't like the way he looked at my mother, and so then and there I decided I would never be a lawyer.

But I didn't tell my mother this as together we put plates of fried eggs, baked beans, and chips onto the Formica kitchen table for a bunch of Greenham women.

"I thought you supported us," I said.

"Of course I do, I'm a Greenham woman myself," she snapped. "I come and go, like most women. But you, why do you have to take things to the extreme all the time?"

"If you didn't have women living there full-time, you wouldn't have a camp at all," I said as, one by one, my Greenham friends filed into the kitchen, clean and scrubbed from their showers, followed by Sarah and my father.

My mother and I glared at each other, but said no more.

War was very personal to my mother. Evacuated at the age of seven to Tideswell in Derbyshire just days before the relentless bombing of our major cities began, she and her younger sister Barbara sat silently on a noisy steam train surrounded by equally petrified children until they reached the dark platform where the children were lined up and chosen by adults one by one. Her mother insisted the girls remain together, and so she and Barbara were the last to be chosen—by Advent Huntstone, a towering local stonemason who scooped the two girls up in a warm embrace and walked them in the darkness to his stone cottage at the edge of the village. We often sat spellbound by our mothers' war stories— how her father took a slow train with blacked-out windows from Crewe to Liverpool to collect Christmas presents for the children from the grandparents, walking alone down empty streets on the Liverpool docks, burning buildings on either side; how an incendiary bomb landed on the bed in his parents' home on that same visit and how he ran down the stairs to drop it down the toilet; how her mother and the two youngest huddled in bomb shelters when the air raid warnings wailed; and how she and Barbara soon joined them back in Liverpool, her mother unable to bear the separation. How she saw a German plane crash and watched the pilot float down like a seed from the sky in his parachute to land in a tree not far from her backyard. She was a good storyteller, but she wasn't in a storytelling mood now.

"How's Robert?" I asked as we sat down and began eating. I missed him and his heart as big as his smile. He was working with developmentally disabled adults in a group home, and I knew my parents didn't approve. My younger sister, Sarah, shot me a look as if to say, *Don't go there.* But I couldn't help myself. "I think the work he is doing is amazing," I added, addressing the unspoken comment hovering in the air: Why is he working in a group home when he could be at university?

Only Kate seemed to be doing the right thing. She had acquired a degree, a husband, and a teaching job, all in the right order. Yet for some reason, it was me that Sarah idolized.

Now, Sarah and I smiled at each other across the kitchen table as I wondered what it was like for her to be the only one left at home.

"So, how are things at the camp?" My father smiled paternally at the motley group of young women gathered around his table, their hair wet from their showers, shovelling food into their mouths in the most unladylike way. Without even looking at her, I could feel my mother shudder with every swallow.

"Fine, thank you," Liz said. "Though I'm just a visitor, from Oswestry, you know, on the border with Wales."

"Yes, a beautiful part of the world," my father said. "My side of the family is originally from Wales. Davies, you know."

"I didn't know that was your last name," Liz, said, turning to me.

"I don't know your last name, either. Or anyone else's, come to think of it." I smiled at my Greenham friends, who smiled back.

Our last names were really the names of our fathers, anyway, and when we got arrested, we never gave our real names.

"That's because we call ourselves whatever we feel like," Zee explained. "Freda People, Anna Key, Eva Brick . . ."

My father chuckled.

"We bring supplies down every month," Liz went on. "We have a very active women's peace group."

"Why does it always have to be women?" Mother said. "Men care about war, too, you know."

I had annoyed my mother, and now she was looking for an argument. "That makes no sense," I wanted to snap at her. "You're a member of a women's peace group yourself." But I didn't want my friends to witness one of our arguments, so instead, I looked over to my father at the head of the table for help. He caught my eye, but I couldn't catch his thoughts.

"Oh yes, they do, that's very true," Liz said. "My boyfriend collects food for us from his health food cooperative to bring down. And lots of men bring supplies to the camp."

Thank goodness Liz was there and could mention a boyfriend. Then Sally slurped her tea, an absolute crime at our table, and Sarah and I glanced at each other, stifling a giggle.

I glanced at Elena, who was shaking the tomato ketchup bottle so that she could get enough out to dollop over her chips. My mother looked on in helpless fury. You were supposed to put vinegar on the chips and tomato ketchup on the side.

"Women don't start the wars," Zee said, looking directly into my father's eyes.

"Margaret Thatcher did." My father looked right back.

After dinner, or as my family called it, tea, my friends went back to Greenham, and I stayed on for one more night, Liz promising to come and pick me up the following evening. After my father had left for work the next morning, my mother took me aside, all a-flutter.

"It's horrible. I found pornography under the bed," she said. "Your father said he confiscated it from the boys at school. But he also said he and the deputy head had a bit of fun reading through it themselves. How disgusting is that. And why did it have to make its way here?"

I could tell she was hurt and confused and needed an ally, and who better than her newly lesbian, man-hating Greenham woman daughter? But when my father came home from school on his motorbike that same afternoon, she said nothing. She kissed him as he walked through the door, took his helmet from him, and ushered him into the living room where she had a cup of tea waiting for him, and where I sat, scowling.

AND NOW HE was here, in my territory at the peace camp.

I walked toward him awkwardly, and it almost seemed as if shaking hands was most appropriate. We managed a brief, English hug.

"How are you?" he asked.

"Fine. How are you?"

"That's one of the reasons I'm here. Can we go for a chat?"

He told me that Sarah was in the car, and I glanced over to see her silhouetted in the front passenger seat of his dark blue Humber Imperial, parked on the other side of the road. I wanted to run to her and hug her and ask about her tribe of friends at Testbourne and the neighbour's horse she rode every week. Instead, I looked behind me at the parked car as we headed into the woods, feeling a mixture of love and resentment for my father. Even before I had moved to Greenham, my parents had tried to stop me having "too much influence" over my younger sister.

As I became more and more rebellious, my parents worried that Sarah would follow in my footsteps. A few weeks earlier, I had called her from the red phone box on the housing estate closest to the camp. We were chatting away when suddenly it was my father's voice on the end of the line, not hers. "Sarah has homework to do, don't you Sarah?"

I could hear her protesting in the background, but I couldn't hear the words.

"We haven't finished," I said.

"Yes you have." He put down the phone, in an uncharacteristic display of anger.

But now he wanted to talk.

As we walked in silence along the perimeter fence and deeper into the woods, I thought back to our last serious talk, when I had decided not to attend my university graduation ceremony because I thought the keynote speaker was a capitalist pig, and I didn't want to wear the cap and gown that I thought were elitist symbols. My mother yelled and cried, and later my father took me aside, chain-smoking in the living room as I stared sulkily at the floor.

"I understand why you don't want to do it," he said.

I looked up.

"But will you do it for your mother's sake? You know she never went to university, her father would only send her brother, but none of the three sisters. It means the world to her to see her girls graduate."

He looked sad and so I gave in. I did it for him. And now I wondered how many concessions I had made to spare him upset ever since I was eleven years old and my mother walked into the living room and told Kate and me that our father was a member of Exit. "A group for people who want to kill themselves" was how she described it. I felt lightheaded and glanced at Kate, who had turned white as a sheet. "It's because he's depressed," Mum told us. "He doesn't think about what it means for the rest of us."

Neither Kate nor I had known what to say, so we said nothing. I stole glances at the television, playing my favourite show, *The Liver Birds*, as Mum continued to sit in silence, which was almost as unnerving as one of her outbursts. I glanced at Kate, then at the TV, then stood up and turned it off, before heading for the door. Kate looked daggers at me, and I felt guilty leaving her alone with our mother, but I didn't know what else to do. I went up to my bedroom and lay on my bed to look through the skylight at the grey mass of clouds, thinking that joining Exit must be something depressed people do, like joining a stamp-collecting club. I called my dog, Che, up onto the bed, and buried my face in his soft, blond fur, then turned to let him lick the tears from my eyes before they had time to track down my cheeks. Images flashed through my mind: my father with a knife in the bath, a bottle of empty pills at the side of his bed, a noose attached to a rafter.

From that moment on, I worried constantly that something I might do or say would tip him over the edge and we would lose him forever. I talked to him about politics whenever I could and tried to forgive him for not letting girls play football in PE at school and for encouraging me to be girlier than I wanted to be. Whenever our parents went out for the evening to the pub or a dinner or a party, I'd lie awake, scarcely breathing, willing my parents to come home, waiting for the soothing sound of the car wheels crunching on the gravel driveway, the arc of the headlights sweeping across the darkness like a searchlight.

Sometimes I found my mother standing and quietly simmering, her hands gripping her hair, her body shaking with rage, saying not a word over some frustration we were not aware of—I wondered if it was something one of us had done or said, though the evidence may have been just next door, lying on the living room floor listening to Sibelius or Rachmaninoff or Beethoven: my pained father barely able to move because of his bad back, the dimming effect of his tranquilizers, his depression.

Now, as we walked along Greenham's perimeter fence toward Green Gate, my father told me, "I've not been feeling well." It was still light, but it wouldn't be long before night fell. "I am having headaches and losing my concentration."

He glanced at the British soldier standing on duty inside the fence, and when the soldier greeted him, my father nodded, but said nothing.

"It's probably stress," I said, noticing his pained expression, not sure that I was the right person to be coming to for advice. After all, I lived outside a military base, broke the law, and was going out with a female anarcho-punk singer. I could hear Zee in my head saying that his visit to me was about male energy curtailing female freedom, the patriarchy coming to wrench me back into its clutches.

I asked if my mother knew.

"Yes, she knows. But she doesn't know how worried I am."

I was at a loss as to what to say. If she didn't know how serious he thought it was, why did I?

"How about Kate?"

"Kate just started her new job, I don't want to worry her."

It dawned on me that I was a safe place for him to deposit this information. I lived outside of the normal life of the family, and I never spoke to my Mum, and rarely to Kate, and he knew I wouldn't burden my younger siblings with the news. I glanced over at him as we walked. His almost grey skin was dry and the back of his neck wrinkled in small folds above his shirt collar. He looked old.

"What does the doctor say?" I ventured at last.

"He is sending me for some tests," he said. "I can't read a whole page of writing any more. I used to speed read—well you know that. That is why I only read poetry, because if I read a novel I just read it too fast."

I thought about the dark blue hardback book he gave me full of graphic, sad anti-war poetry—from Siegfried Sassoon's moving World War I poems to angry American poets protesting the Vietnam War—which I devoured alone, in my attic bedroom, memorizing entire verses. It was at Martin's, now, with all of my books.

The late day sun came out briefly one last time, sickly yellow and weak, illuminating the distant silhouette of a lone soldier carrying a rifle on the hill far behind the fence. I wondered if it was the same hill where I had been forced to lie face down on the ground, if this soldier was among those who held us at gunpoint. The words to Wilfred Owen's "Anthem for Doomed Youth" popped uninvited into my head, along with an image of a young Wilfred on the battlefield trying to bring his comrade back to life.

> Move him into the sun—
> Gently its touch awoke him once,
> At home, whispering of fields unsown.
> Always it woke him, even in France,
> Until this morning and this snow.
> If anything might rouse him now
> The kind old sun will know.

I wondered how the soldier on the hill had become my enemy when Wilfred was my friend. Because the soldiers in World War I were drafted, I told myself, because they were kids—like my dad's father, who suffered a terrible head injury, who knew nothing of politics, who suffered shell shock, who had no choice about going to war. But were these squaddies really that different just because they chose the army as a career? These working-class lads with few options in life, doing the bidding of the upper and political classes? I wanted to ask my dad what he thought of this, to have one of those long political conversations we used to have, about civil rights, colonialism, the miners' strike, the struggles of the working classes. But when I looked over at him, his eyes were tired and he looked sad and confused, and he was telling me he was ill. I had no words.

As we walked in silence, the sun went behind the low clouds one last time before the looming shadows appeared, letting us know it had finally sunk over the horizon.

My father said, quietly, "It's not just your mother, you know. I want you to leave the peace camp, too."

"Really?" I stopped abruptly to face him, feeling a hot flush of betrayal. "I thought you supported us?"

I thought of the time he scrawled "Yanks Go Home" on the mirror of a pub bathroom in felt pen after he saw a group of American soldiers drinking at the bar.

"Of course I support Greenham," he said. "But is it really best that you live here?"

His hazel eyes looking directly into mine were full of care and worry. My eyes were clouded with confusion and disappointment. "You want me to go back to Martin?" I spat out. "You don't even like him."

"Of course not," he said. "But you can do so much more good as a lawyer representing the women, or as a journalist reporting on them."

"But they're just part of the system, too," I said. "We're here to oppose a whole system, to highlight what's wrong with a whole system." I didn't use the word patriarchy. "If people aren't prepared to take risks, then society doesn't get anywhere, does it?" *Aren't you the one who taught me that?* I wanted to add, but I didn't.

What he didn't say was that he was afraid for my life, that he didn't want his twenty-two-year-old daughter to get hurt by men in uniforms carrying guns, that he couldn't protect me as a father when I lay down in front of military vehicles and let the police drag me away by the armpits as I fell limp into their arms. As long as I was here, he couldn't do his job as a father, and he was at a loss.

What I didn't say was that Martin had been far more dangerous than the men in uniforms at Greenham, that here I had friends who understood and cared about me, that I had learned that love and sex could be fun, not terrifying, and that I was experiencing a freedom I had never imagined possible.

I didn't hear what he didn't say and he didn't hear what I didn't say. All I felt was betrayal because my socialist parents had taught me to fight injustice and stand up for my beliefs, and now that I was taking part in the country's biggest, most effective anti-war campaign, they were disappointed in me. When my mother expressed disappointment, I expected it, because everything—from the clothes I wore, to the boyfriends I chose, and even the way I walked—seemed to disappoint her. As long as my dad was still with me, however quietly, however implicitly, I felt all right. But now he was abandoning me too.

I thought back to the time I confronted him about why I had never been given a female author to read all through my so-called progressive education. It was the last year of university, when the first rays of a feminist awakening were creeping into my consciousness. Just a year ago. A lifetime ago.

"Why do they teach us Sartre and Camus but not Simone de Beauvoir?" I'd asked as we finished our rice pudding at the kitchen table.

My parents exchanged weary glances.

"Because they are the masters of modern French literature?" my father offered.

"We haven't studied one single female author," I said. "Not all through school at Testbourne. Not all through university at Bath. What's that about?"

"Because men are better writers?" my father said, winking at my mother, who smiled back.

I put down my spoon, pushed my chair back, and stormed out of the room. I couldn't bear to be teased about something so important. I was determined to educate my father about women's lack of access to things that men had; to the evils of pornography; to sexism in the media; to the degradation of women in advertising. I still cared about apartheid, I still cared about the rights of the working classes, I still marched for peace. But I was discovering more hidden injustices, ones that directly affected me, his daughter, and I wanted him to care about them, too. But he didn't.

And now that I was on the frontlines of the country's largest civil disobedience movement, he wasn't there for me again.

A sudden urge to cry welled up in my throat. I didn't want him to notice, so I turned away and coughed, remembering the recurring dream I used to have as a child of being alone on a street and seeing my father walking ahead of me. He turns a corner, not seeing me as I try to call out but can't, because I have no voice.

"I thought you would be proud of me," I said quietly.

He said nothing.

We turned and walked in silence back to the gate, and I wanted him to go so that I could be alone in the woods and cry a little before telling my friends at the fire about it. I knew they would be indignantly and vocally on my side. But there was one more thing I had to do before he left.

"Can I see Sarah now?" I asked, swallowing my sadness, feeling it harden in my throat and tighten my shoulders as Blue Gate came into view.

"Of course you can see Sarah," he said. "But before you do, I have something else to ask you, Steph."

He stopped and looked at me sadly. His voice was quiet, gentle, almost a whisper.

"What?"

"I think it's best you not come home for a while," he said, and I thought I saw his eyes well up, but it was dark, so perhaps I didn't. "It upsets your mother. And when your mother gets upset, it makes things harder for me."

A flash of fury lit up my entire being, then left as quickly as it came, leaving a hollow, sad feeling in its place. My tall father looked small, weak, afraid. I was at a loss.

"That's fine," I said, glancing over his shoulder at the light of the fire glowing in the distance, wishing I could run there and take refuge with my new family. "It's hard for me, too."

It was dark now as we walked back to the car, the yellow lights of the base lighting our way. My dad was walking stiffly, slowly, with difficulty. But he always had a bad back, I told myself, he was probably suffering from stress. I reminded myself of his depression, the tons of pills in the top drawer of the chest of drawers in his bedroom, his sleeping late on weekend mornings while my mother waited in pent-up frustration for her weekends to begin.

When we got back to the camp, Sarah was sitting at the campfire.

"Look, Sarah's joined Greenham," I said, unable to help myself, knowing how much this would annoy him.

"I saw this poor little thing sitting all alone in the car crying," Lucy said, who was sitting next to her. "So I told her to come here and have a cup of tea."

Lucy glared at my father, who stood awkwardly a few feet away from the group of women around the fire as Sarah and I hugged each other. Sarah was not such a little thing, being taller than Lucy and almost as tall as me. But she looked young and vulnerable and her eyes were red.

"Nice haircut," Sarah said.

"Don't say that too loud," I whispered. "He'll think you'll want a bleached Mohican next."

We climbed into the Humber, me in the front, Sarah in the back, and my father drove us to the nearest of the two pubs in Newbury where Greenham women were still welcome. The car was dark and spacious, and I sank back into the leather seat with a feeling of familiarity and calm as it purred evenly along the winding roads and pulled up gently in the car park. In the pub we found a corner table in the dimly lit lounge bar where Lionel Richie's "Hello" was playing on the jukebox. This was one of Sally's secret favourites, and I looked round to see if she was there, but there were no Greenham women in here tonight, just the regular locals—couples whispering in corners, family groups laughing around tables, a few lone red-faced drinkers talking to the barmaid at the bar. I was the odd one out tonight. My father ordered two pints of bitter, one for me and one for himself, and half a cider for Sarah, who was sixteen, so could now drink in pubs. Sarah and I held hands as I told her excitedly about life at the camp, omitting the bits about Alison and Al. She told me about school and her friends, and about Bella, the horse she rode every weekend. When Madness's "Baggie Trousers" came on the jukebox we danced the jerky ska dance in our seats and laughed.

"Must you hold hands all the time?" my father said.

We dropped each other's hands. It was true, in our family there was very little touching. Since I had been at Greenham I had learned to hold hands with women, hug strangers, and stroke the prickly softness of freshly shaved heads at the fire. It was only natural now to want to touch my sister to show my love for her, but it was breaking a family code and my father didn't like it.

I took her hand back in mine.

# Chapter Ten
## "(I'M NOT A) REAL WOMAN" POISON GIRLS

AT THE CAMP, things were clear and straightforward: war was wrong, women liked peace, nature was beautiful, animals needed protecting, if you believed in something, you did it with your whole heart, and if that meant uprooting your life, career, studies, and relationships, so be it, and we would all celebrate your liberation with you.

When I hitched a ride to Brixton in South London to attend my first real punk concert, where I would finally see Al perform onstage with On the Rag, everything appeared dark and secretive and a bit scary. The concert was held in a basement filled with unwashed-looking men and women drinking beer out of bottles; they wore Doc Martens, spiky haircuts, and tight-fitting pants adorned with large safety pins, and with their piercings and tattoos some could pass for the most extreme Greenham women—except they were not friendly.

I was not used to being around men anymore and had come to see them as the enemy: the perpetrators of war and violence against women and the creators of an oppressive patriarchy that relied on the subjugation of women. It was not just political. I experienced this patriarchy quite personally—the soldiers who held me at gunpoint and threatened to rape me; the men on the street who leered and made sexual comments, something that didn't stop when I got my Mohican, big boots, and baggy clothes; Martin. I suppose it didn't help that Martin was coming in a few days with my things, which Al had agreed to keep at her place.

I hadn't seen Al for two weeks, and I was excited when I spotted her Mohican in the crowd. She had her back to me and I skipped toward her, only to be stopped dead in my tracks by the sight of a black-haired Goth with her arms around Al's waist, kissing her passionately on the lips. I felt sick to my stomach. It must have been her girlfriend from Newcastle. It was easy to forget that Al had two other love lives, even though one of her other lovers had often just left a few hours before I arrived at her flat in Moseley on one of my regular visits. She would tell me what a great time she had had and how happy she was to see me, and I pretended to be the centre of her attention as she showered me with songs, homemade meals, and kisses. But what was happening at the concert felt like a betrayal. It was my turn to be with her, and I had come a long way. I didn't have anyone else to stay with, and I wondered what I would do.

I stepped back toward the door, and a tall woman with a mane of white and black hair took me by the arm, kissed me on both cheeks, and said, "You must be Steph."

"You must be Zephyr." I recognized her from photographs. I was taken for a moment by the piercing blue of her eyes, but then could not keep my eyes from Al and the Goth in her arms.

"Look, this is really uncomfortable," Zephyr said. "I am sorry, I am not sure what she's up to. But I just want to say I am really happy to meet you, and"—she took both my hands in hers, stepped back, and looked me up and down—"Al's a fool if she doesn't try and hang on to you."

"Thanks," I mumbled, blushing, then felt a pair of strong arms encircle my waist, a kiss at the base of my neck. I jumped and turned to see Al behind me, the Goth slinking back into the crowd.

"Steph. Sorry," she said. "I didn't know Danny was coming. But it's the Poison Girls. Hard to keep away. You've *got* to come and meet Vi, she is *dying* to meet you." She knew I had become a big fan of Vi Subversa. I caught a look in Zephyr's eye that I couldn't quite read, but it might have been disapproval, even exasperation.

"It's lovely to meet you, Steph," she said as she winked at me. "I hope you enjoy the concert."

I nodded as Al took my hand and whisked me out to the dance floor where the Clash's "London Calling" was playing, and we pogo-ed around together energetically until she left me alone to prepare for her set. I loved the Clash and thought of some of the women at camp who would only listen to women's music. Men may have been the enemy, but I wasn't going to give up listening to Stevie Wonder, the Jam, or Madness.

As Al and Zephyr strutted around the dimly lit stage—Al's deep husky voice harmonizing with Zephyr's higher, sweeter, still feisty tone—I was proud to be Al's girlfriend, and hoped one day to be Zephyr's friend, but

I couldn't keep myself from stealing glances at the Goth as she smiled at Al the same way I was smiling at Al. By the time the Poison Girls played, I just wanted to be back at Blue Gate, sitting at the fire and listening to camp stories under the stars.

Al and I hitched back to Birmingham the next morning, and during our next few days together I was preoccupied with Martin's visit. But Al didn't want to talk about it. She wanted to make love and play like puppies. The day before his visit, she made me chase her for miles through Moseley Park and the residential streets around it, and stopped every now and then to belt out Nina Simone songs at street lamps before racing off again. By the end, I was pretty tired of the whole thing but did not say so. I didn't say much about what I felt. I wanted to ask her to leave her boyfriend and girlfriend and be mine alone, but that seemed old-fashioned, and when I even hinted at it, she reminded me that the person she was really in love with, anyway, was Zephyr.

"Just accept me as I am, Steph," she said. "And be my drums," then tapped out rhythms on my bare stomach, laughing, putting her head back and singing loudly, until I started laughing, too.

I gave my musical lover no indication that I played classical guitar, that I could sight read and had performed at school concerts; though what I enjoyed most was playing quietly alone to myself. Nor did I tell her how Martin had stopped me from playing because he was jealous of everything I did that didn't involve him, or that among the things he would deliver the next day was my guitar.

Al had gone to write songs with Zephyr, and I'd been sitting rigid on the sofa, suffering the pain of unrequited monogamy, when Martin arrived, unshaven, his hair tousled, his eyes tired and heavy with bags under them. He had lost weight, and I noticed how his usually muscular frame was almost skinny under his jeans and sweatshirt as he carried my bags in one by one. There wasn't much: my clothes, shoes, records, guitar, my two childhood teddy bears, Maximus and Polaris, a lime green suitcase filled with letters from friends and family and a few photograph albums. I had let Martin keep all the kitchen things because I couldn't imagine having a kitchen ever again.

I made us both a cup of tea in Al's sparse kitchen. The soya milk curdled a little and I apologized. She was a vegan, and I was now, too, so there was no cow's milk. We sat across from each other, and he said, "Looks good," indicating my hair, which was blond and spiky.

He told me he had moved in with his friend Mike in Manchester and that he loved the city with its vibrancy, music, clubs, and pubs. I felt at the same time familiar and awkward with him. He looked around the small living room, his eyes resting on a large photograph of Al on stage with Zephyr.

"Which one is she?" he asked.

"The one with the red Mohican," I said, proudly.

"Funny you'd end up in the punk scene," he said. "It took you a while to even like punk music."

*It's the woman I like,* I wanted to say, but I didn't say it. And anyway, he was right. He had played the Sex Pistols and the Clash and the Stiff Little Fingers for hours on end before I actually came to appreciate them.

Our tea had gone cold and I wanted him to leave. But I could tell he was hoping to meet the person who had replaced him. Or maybe he knew this was our last cup of tea together and didn't want it to end. I didn't want Al to meet him because I didn't know how she would treat him, knowing, as she did, how he had treated me. He had been hurt enough and I didn't want him to be hurt by her as well. I was starting to feel sorry for him. I looked at the clock.

"It'll be getting dark soon," I said.

"When does she get home?" he asked.

"Late," I lied. "She'll be home really late."

"So are you happy with her?"

"Yes."

I didn't want to answer his questions. I had had a lifetime of answering to him, and now I wanted to exercise my freedom by telling him absolutely nothing. He was desperate for some kind of connection, but after six years I had nothing left for him at all. I could not bear the tension in the room and in my body, and I willed him to leave. When he finally drove away into the night, I cried. I never saw him again.

Minutes later, Al burst through the door with a case of beer, grabbed me around the waist, and pulled me toward her for a long, deep kiss. She pulled away just as abruptly and jumped into the kitchen, where she opened two bottles of beer, then sat next to me on the sofa, her legs planted squarely apart, and placed the beers down on the table in front of us.

"We had a wonderful session. Zeph is so amazing." She looked wistfully into the distance then back at me. "Your eyes are red. What did he do?"

"Nothing. He didn't do anything. I just feel a bit sad, that's all."

"I know what you need." She jumped up and rifled through her record collection. "Aha. The Poison Girls!"

She pulled out the record, took it out of its sleeve, put it on the record player, and placed the needle down on the track she wanted. There was a brief crackling sound before the music filled the room, and she leapt around, singing along to the raucous rapid-fire lyrics, gyrating in front of me:

> I'm not a real woman, I don't nod my head
> Or patiently wait for your favours in bed
> I don't wear lace panties, at waist away prices
> Or bondage and scanties at masochist dances
> I'm not a real woman, I don't waggle my hips
> Or flapple my eye lids or shackle my lips
> And I'm not a lemon, so please don't squeeze my pips

I swallowed down my sadness and managed to laugh. She was right. I wasn't a real woman. I jumped up and joined her. We danced a punky dance together, jumping and twisting, and yelling the words to the chorus at each other as our heads almost clashed:

> I'm generous I'm mean
> I'm a law unto myself
> I just laugh at everything you say
> Don't be surprised
> If I don't look into your eyes
> My eyes are on a million miles away

When the song finished we collapsed breathless on the sofa, laughing. Al kissed me on the lips, then turned to lie on top of me, weighing me down deliciously. Suddenly I felt as if Martin was a distant nightmare, Al was all mine, and everything was right with the world.

# Chapter Eleven
## "HAPPY HOUSE" SIOUXSIE AND THE BANSHEES

THE ONLY OTHER place where everything was right with the world was Greenham, where I sat night after night with my friends around the fire pit, surrounded by trees, under the dark starry sky. But this was an illusion. Sometimes we had to leave camp to do actions elsewhere or support sisters who had broken into military bases in other parts of the country—which was the case when I travelled with Zee on a National Express bus to Wakefield. Little Chris, who seemed to get arrested and jailed more than anyone else at camp, had recently broken into a military base in Yorkshire with Little Steph (I was Big Steph because I was tall) and they were facing a trial at Wakefield Magistrates Court. A group of us planned to set up camp in front of the court building to show our support.

Zee and I were picked up at the bus station by Little Chris, who lived nearby with her girlfriend and didn't feel safe being out as lesbians, so they spent as much time as they could at Greenham. I didn't like how bleak it was where Little Chris had chosen to set up her tent and where the rest of the women from Greenham were supposed to meet us later that day. It was a desolate abandoned lot, far from houses, lights, or civilization. We lit a small bonfire with twigs and dead branches we had collected beneath the scrubby trees dotted around the edge of the deserted lot, which was probably illegal, but since when had that stopped us from doing anything? The sky was grey and heavy as Chris and her girlfriend spent the afternoon in their tent poring over notes for the trial and Zee and I drank cups of tea by the fire, wondering why no one else had shown up. Then a man from a local peace group pulled up in an old car sporting several anti-nuclear stickers, with an offering of an Indian takeaway, and told us that the trial venue had been changed to Leeds and that our Greenham friends had gone straight there instead of joining us here.

I wanted to join them right away, but Chris's girlfriend protested that Chris was tired and had a big day tomorrow, and anyway, it was already starting to get dark. And so we agreed to head over first thing in the morning. I was pouring Zee another cup of tea when something whizzed past my head and landed bang in the middle of the fire pit. It was a brick.

Zee jumped up, and another brick whizzed past, almost grazing her head and landing just beyond the fire. We both ducked and peered into the darkness, but could see nothing. Then there was another thud—a brick had landed a few feet away from Chris's tent. "Dykes! Perverts! Die!" We couldn't see the men and couldn't tell how many of them there were, but they were close.

Chris and her girlfriend crawled out from their tent and lay next to us on the ground, belly-down, behind a collapsed brick wall we hoped would protect us, as brick after brick landed around us. I felt sick to my stomach and clambered to a squatting position, not entirely hidden, now, but determined to be on my feet, unlike when the soldiers forced me to lie flat on the ground inside Greenham. I looked desperately around as the bricks and epithets landed around us.

"Bitches!"

Thud.

"Whores!"

Thud.

"Lesbians!"

"Jesus Christ!" was all I could muster.

"Let me get the buggers," Chris said, struggling to stand as her girlfriend grabbed her arm to prevent her. I wondered if we should all jump into Chris's car, but that would make us easy targets. I turned to Zee, whose eyes were closed firmly and who appeared to have gone into a trance.

"I can get them to go away," she said quietly, opening her eyes briefly, then returned to her trance. We all knew that Zee was a bit "cosmic," as we liked to say.

I sat back on my heels, trembling, as five minutes passed and there were no more voices. Had they crept up quietly, were they going to grab us right here at the fire? Another five minutes passed. No more bricks. No more voices.

Zee opened her eyes. "There."

That night, as Zee slept soundly beside me, my mind raced over the events of the night, jumped to the soldiers at Greenham threatening to rape us, then to the men riding through our camp on bikes trashing our belongings or driving past hurling bottles and insults out of their car windows. It wasn't because they supported nuclear weapons that they hated us. It was because we threatened their sense of their place in the world, just like I had threatened Martin's whenever I stepped out of the narrow confines of what he thought a girlfriend should be.

The feminism I read about in magazines when I was at university— the sexual revolution of women in the 1960s wearing mini-skirts and popping the pill, of 1970s braless hippie feminists in their flowing, flowered skirts—was nothing compared to the androgynous tribal freedom of Greenham. Whether we were lesbian, straight, or bisexual, we shocked wherever we went because we did nothing to conform, please, or titillate. England had never seen anything like us. We didn't shave our legs, our armpits, or our pubic hair. We didn't pluck our eyebrows or wear nail varnish. We wore men's clothes if we liked, and we often went topless at the camp, or at least some of us did. We were altogether natural, except, of course, for our multi-coloured hair, which we wore as though we were our own tribe of Amazonian women. The freedom we felt in our own company was matched in intensity only by that of the looks, taunts, and rage directed at us whenever we stepped out into the "real" world.

When we arrived in Leeds the next morning, everyone was already settled in tents pitched close to each other on the small manicured lawn in front of the Town Hall building adjacent to the courts. Seeing the women milling among the tents, my heart churned as if I were about to be reunited with a new lover. There must have been at least fifty of us here. Sally and Lucy rushed over to ask where we'd been. I told them about our terrifying ordeal in Wakefield, and with each murmur of sympathy and gasp of indignation the horrors of the previous night slowly dissipated.

The court case lasted three days, and I was proud of Little Steph and Little Chris as they stood before the judge in the windowless courtroom to proclaim their right to commit a crime to prevent the greater crime of war. Greenham women were crammed into the viewing galleries, and when two detectives gave evidence against them, we booed every time the detectives said anything, continuing to boo and applaud and sing throughout the proceedings, like a Greek chorus. On the last day, as the verdict was read, a cheer went around the room—suspended sentences! We whooped and hugged each other before our excited tribe packed up and, like colourful nomads, we made our way back down the country to Greenham Common, my home, fanning out to our separate gates, kissing and waving each other goodbye.

THE FOLLOWING MORNING dawned bright and sunny, and I was wondering what to do with the luxurious day stretching before me when the base gates sprang open and the cruise missile convoy came pounding out of the base, surprising us all. Unlike before, there was no sudden police presence, just a loud rumbling, and before we knew it, the convoy was on its way, white-suited American soldiers brandishing terrifying guns, leaving us unprepared to follow, stunned and indignant on the side of the road.

"Let's go to London and lie down in front of the Houses of Parliament," Lucy cried.

It seemed like the most rational response, and so we raced in our cars the sixty miles to London, some of us driving first to the other gates to get our sisters to join us.

When we arrived at the Houses of Parliament, I leapt out of the car and joined the seventy or so Greenham women gathering as nonchalantly as they could on the pavements and at traffic lights, trying to merge in with the bustling urban scene. It was a warm spring day, and many people were in shirtsleeves or summer dresses. Looking around at my Greenham tribe, I was reminded of the suffragettes, doing their best to blend in as they gathered on the streets to set off bombs in mailboxes or chain themselves to the fences at this very same Parliament as they fought for the right to vote. Of course, like them, it was not easy for us to blend in with the tourists, office workers, and passers-by. We had set a time for the action, and had told our press contacts this, but the police presence was getting larger by the minute.

"Are they on to us?" Sally said. She was holding my hand and looking nervously at the police officers appearing on street corners.

"Well, we did all yell, 'Let's go to the Houses of Parliament and stop the traffic!'" I said. For sure the policemen at Greenham would have called the Metropolitan Police and told them to expect us.

So before the press arrived, before our London supporters arrived, before we were really ready, we raced into the street as one and lay down on the hard tarmac yelling, "Take the toys from the boys!" "Send cruise missiles home now!" "Women say no to war!" We linked arms as we lay in the middle of the road and I felt happy looking up at the blue sky, thinking back to my early morning walk in St. Mary Bourne when Bridget dared me to lie in the middle of the road. I wished she were here to share this moment, as I heard tooting horns and drivers yelling in the distance and the women around me taking up our signature song, "You can't kill the spirit/She is like a mountain/Old and strong/She goes on and on and on."

I joined in the singing full pelt and felt a tug on my left as Sally was grabbed by a police officer. Like dark blue birds of prey, swooping en masse from vans parked on hidden streets, the police descended on us. We held onto each other's hands more tightly, then I felt the hard fingers of a police officer grab me under my shoulder blades. He pulled hard, dislodging Sally's hand from mine. I did my best to remain limp in the policeman's arms, my boots dragging heavily on the road. My heart pounding and feeling exhilarated—my first London action!—I twisted my head around to see if any press had arrived, but there were no photographers or TV cameras to be seen. I could see the legs and boots of the police mingled with the Doc Martens and jeans of my fellow Greenham women as they, too, were dragged one by one to the waiting vans, and we sang in rounds to the tune of "Frères Jacques," "We are Women, We are Women/We are Strong, We are Strong/We Say No, We Say No/To the Bomb, To the Bomb."

"Why can't you just get up and walk?" the policeman hissed into my ear in a thick London accent, his breath smelling of sweet milky coffee and cigarettes. I wondered if I would have bruises as his sharp fingers dug into my armpits, and I continued to sing as loudly as I could, looking round at my friends. A second policeman grabbed hold of my feet, and I was lifted into the air and dumped into the back of the police van, where I smiled at two Greenham women I had never met before.

Inside the police station, we lay on the ground and refused to sit or stand, forcing the police officers to lean over us to ask questions as they filled in their paperwork.

By the late afternoon we had been discharged, and we drove back to camp in our own convoy of cars, jubilant, even though we didn't get any press, which was really the point of the whole exercise. Still, I thoroughly enjoyed disrupting the traffic and annoying the police and doing a normal action where normal things happened.

BACK AT THE camp, Lucy's upper-class friend, Samantha, who had joined us on the protest, sat at the fire with us. She had first come to the camp to pick up Biscuit when Lucy was in prison and had decided to stay. We all adored her, with her wistful eyes, curly hair, and the kind of accent that made you do her bidding whether you wanted to or not, despite your class politics. It was visceral, instinctive almost.

"I'm just fed up of all these Autumns and Leafs and Skys and Trees," she said in her terribly posh accent, referring to our habit of changing our names to reflect our love for the natural world. "I'm from London and I'm proud of it. I'm going to call myself Pavement from now on."

Lucy whooped in delight and put on a faux serious voice. "I've given this a lot of thought, sisters. And I have decided I, too, need to change my name to reflect my roots. From now on, please call me Lamppost."

Lucy swore to be working class, despite her frightfully upper-class accent. Her grandmother had been a servant to a grand London family and married a man who had been a servant from the age of twelve. Then when Lucy's mother married a Jewish violinist, she and her new husband were cast off by both their families in disgust at what was then seen as a mixed marriage. Lucy acquired her accent at Oxford University as a survival mechanism to stop the real upper-class people from sneering at her, but found, on returning to London, that if the accent didn't come with the privileged networks it has long been associated with, it wasn't worth so much. But it still helped, sometimes, such is our class-ridden society, and anyway, now it had stuck.

Class mattered at the camp, too, especially to me, because this was the first time I had spent so much time with people of such different backgrounds. My father swore he was working class, too, despite living a comfortable life in a quiet village in Hampshire, and despite his profession. We used to tease him about this sometimes, because the worst thing you could accuse him of, apart from being a Thatcherite, was being middle class. I considered myself firmly middle class, because of my accent, my education, because of where I lived. But most of the women at Blue Gate really were working class: Elena from Sheffield, Trish from Northern Ireland, her girlfriend, Trina, from Liverpool, Little Chris, Little Jane, and a couple from London who came every weekend and whom I was a bit in awe of. I thought they didn't like me because of my posh accent, but they were laughing at Samantha and Lucy, who were much posher than me, so I wondered if they just didn't like me.

The following morning, there was a newcomer sitting alone at the fire pit, and she was completely covered by a blanket, making a high keening sound as she rocked back and forth. Trish whispered to me that the newcomer had just arrived in a car with a couple of women from Green Gate who had gone to talk to Lucy because she was a social worker and they wanted her advice. Apparently the woman often ran through the woods naked, cried out unexpectedly at the fire pit, and required help remembering to eat, drink, and go to the shit pit. Green Gate was afraid that if the authorities saw her she'd end up in a mental hospital.

The woman lived at Green Gate because it was the most hidden gate, and I was glad she didn't live at Blue Gate because I didn't know how to handle the moaning. Then Lucy and the two women emerged from the woods and I relaxed. Weeks later, I learned that she had been taken to live in a teepee community in Wales.

They were leading her back to the car just as Dee, a quiet and shy young woman we called Plant-a-Tree Dee, arrived, leaning forward slightly from the weight of her backpack. We called her this because she loved the trees so much. Dee seldom spoke and when she did she had a soft upper-class lilt and a softer stutter. Her shoulder-length brown hair covered her face most of the time, because she liked to look at the ground, avoiding eye contact. She sat next to me at the fire and I smiled.

"Welcome back," I said.

She smiled nervously, glanced up at me quickly, and said nothing.

Nothing remarkable happened that morning. But it's a morning I will never forget because this would be the last time I ever saw Dee.

A few months later, on one of her hitchhiking trips home, she would be brutally murdered by a travelling salesman for refusing his sexual advances. It was a horror that suddenly and directly brought us all face to face with the brutality of men that we talked about so often, the violence they were capable of, the hatred toward women so many of them seemed to carry deep inside. The women of Blue Gate planted a tree in her honour—and the murderer got life in prison.

I never knew if women disrupted the murderer's court case, met with her devastated family, wept and held each other as the news hit home. I never knew if they wrote letters of outrage to the papers, created a petition, or held angry demonstrations. I never knew any of this because by the time this happened my father had died and I was living and weeping in a small, damp stone cottage at the side of a stream in Wiltshire. I thought of Dee every so often when I looked at the many trees around me on my solitary walks through the countryside. Sometimes I touched their rough bark, imagining her spirit living "on and on and on" in the sacred trees back at Greenham Common. But mostly I was engulfed with grief for my father and only thought of Greenham because I had to. In another few months, I would have a court case in Reading Crown Court, and the precedent for my crime of breaking and entering a nuclear research establishment was nine months in jail.

# Chapter Twelve
## "TWO TRIBES" FRANKIE GOES TO HOLLYWOOD

WE DIDN'T MEAN to break into a nuclear research establishment. We meant to break into Abingdon Royal Air Force base and spray paint some planes with peace slogans.

It seems a bit odd that it all began with the idea of inviting ten million women to Greenham for ten days. There had been such a groundswell of support from across the country, and around the world, that some of us were getting ambitious. Rumour had it that Linda McCartney and Yoko Ono had sent food hampers to Yellow Gate. Our antics were reported on the news almost every day and regularly made the headlines. Our numbers swelled on weekends into the hundreds as cars and buses descended upon the gates, disgorging women of all sizes and ages, some with children in tow, who brought gifts of food and sleeping bags and toiletries, often staying overnight as weekenders, joining in actions, or doing night watch at the fire to give the full-time women a chance at a good night's sleep.

I had been at the camp for four short, exciting months, long enough to feel that I belonged, that my voice mattered. I didn't like the idea of ten million women and nor did anyone else at Blue Gate. So one warm summer's day I walked with Penny, Zee, Sally, Elena, Lucy, and her dog, Biscuit, the thirty minutes to Green Gate to discuss the ten million women action. The women at Green Gate were a mixture of articulate, hardcore feminists and spiritual women in purple and orange and green who organized noisy Goddess circles and full moon rituals, so I didn't go there very often. Although at Blue Gate we agreed with them on most things, we prided ourselves on being a bit more down to earth. But at that moment, it was Yellow Gate that concerned us.

"You know Yellow Gate will do all the talking," Sally said.

I took Sally's hand and we swung our arms like children in the playground. Yellow was the main gate of the camp, the one that the press and the scarily confident American women gravitated toward.

"We're counting on you, Lucy," I said, because we all knew Lucy wasn't afraid to speak her mind.

When we arrived, the astonishing sight of more than a hundred women sitting on the ground, leaning against trees or each other, greeted us. Quite a few were topless, something I found quite distracting. A naked toddler was running back and forth screaming in delight across the circle between her two mums, to the delight of many, and irritation of some. The meeting had already begun, so we sat at the edge of the circle, on the grass, the tree branches swaying overhead, distant clouds scudding across the bright blue sky, the occasional sound of wood pigeons accompanying the discussion.

A skinny American woman with a shaved head stood there saying quite forcefully that ten million women were enough to bring down the cruise missile program, get the Americans out of our country, and end the Cold War. I was distracted by the tattooed snake running the length of her back and curving around her left hip to lose its face beneath her belly button and down the front of her cut-off jeans, so I only vaguely heard what she said. A frisson of agreement ran around the group. Then Lucy stood up, topless too—the only Blue Gate woman I knew who didn't feel weird taking her top off in public, having lived in a lesbian hippie squatting community for six years before arriving at Greenham.

"What about the trees and the common? Have you any idea what an influx of twenty million feet would have on the common land we purport to love and respect so much? And why ten million? What kind of patriarchal number is that?"

The Blue Gate contingent laughed in approval. Then Rebecca from Yellow Gate stood up. She was perceived by the media to be one of our leaders, because she was pretty and earnest and articulate, and so they often sought her out for comments. But we had no leaders, and this fact had thrown the police off more than once. They just couldn't fathom how we organized without a hierarchy. Rebecca, however, was one of the most determined.

She brushed her long brown hair out of her eyes and said earnestly, "Lucy, I have thought about this long and hard and I absolutely agree with you. But we've held rituals to ask the trees how they feel about it. We've *talked* to the trees. They say they are willing to sacrifice themselves."

I was too shy to stand up and say what I thought about the absurdity of the trees speaking to us—let alone to imagine that the trees would care more about accommodating a huge demonstration of women than about their ability to drink in the sun and water and provide refuge to the birds and squirrels and spiders—and us. It seemed terribly ungrateful at best—murderous at worst. The discussion continued, heated at times, and in the end, Rebecca's contingent won out, and ten million women it was.

I like to think it was the welfare of our beloved trees that made me agree to the action that evening. I was sitting at the fire with Zee and four visitors—Maggie, a Scot living in London; Karen, a soft-spoken Midlander; and Jane and Susan from Dorset.

Zee's eyes were aglow with excitement as she said, "We need to divert energy away from Greenham, we need to show there are many military bases around here, not just this one. We have fallen into the patriarchal trap of centralization. We need to do our bit to take attention away from here for a change. We've become egotistical. We need to branch out like the Greenham women who are supporting the miners' strike. And what about the working-class women who can't come here because they have kids and jobs and abusive husbands? What are we doing for them?"

I wasn't sure what this last point had to do with what was to come, as I nodded in agreement with this seasoned queen of actions—who had been arrested and sent to jail many times and who had a certain cachet because she had been part of the group who made it into the control towers.

Then she said, "Let's go to Abingdon and spray paint the planes." And I agreed to that too.

Jane had a car and drove like a madwoman for an hour along the dark unlit roads, the full moon just visible on the horizon as it began its ascent into the inky sky, but we could not find Abingdon. We were on our way back to Blue Gate, when Zee saw a sign for Aldermaston. "That's something military. Let's go there instead."

We were all sure that Aldermaston was an important military site, but none of us could remember why.

"I think it's British, isn't it?" I said.

"Maybe, it doesn't matter, they are all the same," Zee said. "Men waging war."

And so it was that I ended up lying flat on my stomach on the damp grass scoping out the military facility through the same kind of mesh metal fencing we had at Greenham—no match for our bolt cutters. The scent on the warm Berkshire air and the dark silhouettes of the trees reaching up to the stars reminded me of night walks in St. Mary Bourne. But this was not St. Mary Bourne, it was a military establishment, and after my last experience of being threatened with rape, I wanted to run right back to join Susan, who had preferred to be our getaway driver than join us on the action. But I didn't have the courage to admit I didn't have the courage. I could see a guard illuminated in lights in the distance, far inside, but no police or security personnel anywhere along the perimeter fence. There was nothing to stop us, really, and my heart fell as I realized we had no choice but to start cutting.

Zee cut into the fence easily with her bolt cutters and we crawled through. When it was my turn, I snagged my black tuxedo jacket and ripped the top of my trousers, then I crawled on my stomach behind the others under a rope and through an area of long, damp grass, until I made it to a paved, well-lit road where my friends were crouched in a huddle. Zee cut another hole in yet another fence. We crawled through and as we stood in an unnatural, eerie pool of light I looked around for soldiers, but none appeared.

"What now?" I whispered as we made our way to the cluster of buildings ahead. It was a warm summer evening, but I couldn't stop shivering. I glanced behind me, and the fence we had just come through was invisible in the darkness.

"There's nobody around," Zee said. "Let's just take a look."

Zee and I walked ahead, looking around at the low buildings. She stopped at a sign standing in front of one of them and grabbed my arm as she read aloud. "Accident in 1967. Do not go within fifteen feet of this building with a naked flame."

"Why do you think?"

"Got a match? We could light it and see what happens."

"No, you don't." I wasn't sure if she meant it or not.

By now the others had caught up and were reading the sign too.

"If we had a camera we could show it to Greenpeace," Zee said. "Maybe they'd know what it's all about."

"Let's pose anyway," someone said, and we did, and I even found it in me to laugh at us all hamming it up for the imaginary camera.

We continued to stroll around, almost casually, and I started to relax as if I were window shopping on Newbury high street.

"Look at this," Karen called, from a few feet ahead. To her right was a building with flashing lights coming from its darkened windows. To her left was an open storage area where we could see white protection suits hanging on hangers next to a van. We walked over to take a closer look, and saw that the van had a Geiger counter, a box, and a clipboard with delivery sheets on its dashboard.

"Spooky," Maggie said.

"Let's try on the suits," Zee said.

Before we could debate the wisdom of this suggestion, I saw a flash of light above me and crouched down to the ground. Everyone followed suit as a flashlight streaked across the ground before us in a sweeping arc that disappeared slowly into the distance as the small figure carrying it walked away from us.

As we continued looking around, I pointed to the piles of full, black bin bags strewn in front of the buildings and asked, "Why so many?"

Then Zee asked, "And why do they have radiation stickers on them?"

A rabbit hopped through the shorn grass in front of us. I looked around at the non-descript buildings and the radiation stickers, and suddenly there seemed to be no air to breathe even though we were outside.

"I'm cold," I said. "Let's go back."

I led the way this time, more than ready to race to the safety of our campfire at Greenham. I ran toward the grassy area we first crawled through, which was carefully sectioned off with rope, like a crime scene. I had only half-noticed this on the way in, but now I could see it was deliberately cordoned off, and for a reason. Planted firmly on the grass facing us was a sign with a radiation sticker on it, warning:

RESTRICTED AREA: DO NOT ENTER.

"What do you think that means?" I asked Zee, in a whisper, as we scurried through the hole in the fence.

"It can only mean one thing," Zee said. "We've been radiated."

Back in the car, we all began to panic.

"Why restricted?"

"It's a nuclear place . . ."

"There must be radiation."

"We crawled right through it."

"I'm getting a headache."

"I'm getting a rash."

"We should call Greenpeace and ask for a Geiger counter."

We sat in silence as Susan drove us to Yellow Gate. I was shaking and Zee took my hand in hers, which was shaking even more than mine. I got out of the car and made my way to the fire pit at Yellow, and a jumble of words fell from my mouth as I told them what had just happened. I asked for a number for Greenpeace, which, luckily, was pinned to a crate along with other emergency numbers, easy to find by the light of the full moon—the Quakers, Cruise Watch, the barrister, Izzie, and the solicitor, Janet, in London, who offered free legal support. I wrote down Janet and Izzie's numbers too.

"Please tell Blue Gate what happened to us," I told the night watchers at the fire, and a couple of them nodded. They didn't seem that impressed or concerned about what was going on, and I felt disappointed. I put it down to the fact they were at Yellow Gate and had become a little jaded.

We drove to the council estate close to Blue Gate, just ten minutes away, and I made the call to Greenpeace in London, my trembling hands barely able to dial the numbers in the red phone box, with its distinct damp smell and the familiar clanking as the coins fell one by one into the machine.

"We don't have one," the Greenpeace activist said, sleepily.

*How can Greenpeace not have a Geiger counter?* I thought.

"We do actions, not testing," he said. "The only way for you to get tested for sure is to get Aldermaston to test you. You're going to have to hand yourselves in if you really want to know what happened. Or you can wait until morning and we can connect you to the laboratory that tests us, but they are going to have to believe your story before they take you in. And if you don't hand yourselves in . . ."

"Aldermaston can say we never went in," I finished.

"Exactly," he said.

We talked more before I put down the phone and walked dejectedly onto the dimly lit street and climbed into the car where the others were waiting for me.

I told them everything, plus, "Aldermaston is Britain's premier nuclear research establishment. Atomic Weapons Research Establishment Aldermaston. It's where they make Trident, the British warhead. It has uranium, plutonium, the works. He says if we don't hand ourselves in, chances are the authorities will deny we broke in. They won't want it out that it's that easy to walk around Aldermaston for as long as we did. So handing ourselves in is the only way to get the testing or treatment we might need."

"It's a trap, he's got me," Zee whispered quietly, but I didn't understand.

"I think we should do it," Karen said, and we all nodded, all except Zee, who was rocking back and forth, holding herself in her arms.

"He's got me, he's got me," she said, looking up. "Either way he's got me."

"So that's a yes?" I asked.

She nodded.

I got back out of the car and opened the heavy red door to the telephone box, unable to quite grasp what I was about to do.

"We just broke into Aldermaston," I told the officer on duty at Newbury Police Station. "I'm with a bunch of Greenham women and we think we've been radiated. Will you arrest us so we can get tested?" There was a silence at the end of the phone.

"We'll need to verify your story," he said at last. "But in the meantime, make your way to . . . Red Gate . . ." I managed a smile as I heard him use our terminology. "Yes, to Red Gate. There'll be someone there to meet you."


IT WAS THREE in the morning when we arrived at the designated spot. Three police officers, two male and one female, were waiting for us next to a white police van. They refused to touch us.

"Thank you, ladies, please get into the vehicle," one of the male officers said, standing a safe distance from us. "The scientists from Aldermaston will be here as soon as possible."

"Can we have a drink?" I asked, suddenly parched.

"We can't offer you anything to eat or drink until you have been declared free of radiation," he replied, then added, "You might ingest the radiation."

I glanced at Zee and whatever colour may have been in her face drained out.

"Can I go for a pee?" I asked.

I set off into the bushes, the young policewoman following me at a safe distance behind. I could run off, I thought, and the policewoman wouldn't catch me because she was under instructions not to touch me, which made our predicament all the more real.

When I got back to the police van parked in front of the gate, Zee was still muttering, "He's got me, he's got me."

Karen, Maggie, and Jane were talking about the signs and symptoms of radiation poisoning. "Isn't it headaches? Memory loss?"

"Your hair falls out and you get cancer."

"How long does it all take?"

Meanwhile, I was fixated on the rip at the top of my trousers and how I had been lying down in the grass and so the grass must have touched my skin.

Next to me, I felt Zee shaking, her eyes bright with terror.

"He's got me now," she said.

"What are you talking about?" I asked.

Then it dawned on me. She was talking about the sixteenth-century monk who was chasing her across the centuries. He had been stalking her ever since she took up camping outside military establishments to protest nuclear war. It started at Porton Down, near Salisbury, a Ministry of Defence research establishment. She and her then-lover, Sally, lived for almost a year in a caravan on a busy road facing the main entrance to Porton Down to protest the use of animals in military experiments.

It started one morning when Zee looked up from her breakfast and saw a tall monk in full brown robes, his face hidden by the shadow of his hood, standing in the caravan doorway brandishing a rope. She immediately knew who he was—a witch hunter searching for the soul of a witch burned on Salisbury Plain—and that witch was she.

When Sally returned later that morning from grocery shopping in Salisbury, she found Zee passed out on the floor, and when Zee eventually came round, it took several hours before she could tell Sally what she had seen. Since arriving at Blue Gate, Zee had run into the ghostly monk in the woods more than once, screaming before passing out from fear. Penny and Lucy once spent a night at the fire summoning the monk in the hopes of getting rid of him and thought they had been successful. Apparently they hadn't.

I couldn't help feeling a little indignant. *Why is he taking us all down with you?* I wanted to say.

But I had not yet learned to say what I thought, so instead I took her shaking hand in mine and remained quiet as we waited for the scientists from Aldermaston to come with their Geiger counters. Looking out of the police van window as dawn transformed the trees from shadow and the bright stars faded, I thought of my childhood bedroom, fifteen miles away, where my sister Sarah now slept. As a teenager, I often gazed at the stars or clouds through the skylight as I entertained activist fantasies—of being Che Guevara's girlfriend in the Sierra Maestra or a friendly white ally risking her life to save black activists in apartheid South Africa. It had never occurred to me that I would put myself in danger for a cause I believed in so close to home.

# Chapter Thirteen
## "I LOVE A MAN IN A UNIFORM" GANG OF FOUR

THE SCIENTISTS FINALLY arrived, in the pink dawn light, a po-faced man with a sour-faced woman carrying a metal box. They did not look us in the eye or smile. When the police officer sitting in the driver's seat ordered us out of the van and into a line, the male scientist opened the metal box and took out a Geiger counter, then proceeded to run it over each one of us head to toe. We watched, spellbound, wondering what it meant that the Geiger counter sped up to a rapid-fire crackling noise, like the static on a telephone amplified, a couple of times on each of us.

The scientist still hadn't spoken a word when he nodded to an officer to take us away.

The officer said, "No radiation, then," as he grabbed me roughly by the arm, then frog-marched me through the gates and into the base behind Zee, who was on the arm of another police officer.

We were officially declared radiation free, then loaded into the van again, where we all agreed in whispers we would not admit to having cut the fence in order to enter the base.

We were surprised when we were not brought to Newbury Police Station, but farther into the base, where we were unloaded in front of a low nondescript building, then led single file into a dingy reception area with scuffed wooden tables and hard metal chairs, where two plainclothes detectives were waiting for us, the older one sitting tipped back on one of the chairs, his feet crossed on the table in front of him. The younger, heavier detective was standing and smiling, almost genially. There was something familiar about them, and when Zee turned and whispered, "Wakefield," I realized why. They were the very same detectives who had worked on Little Chris and Little Steph's case.

I hadn't slept all night and was feeling parched and punchy when the younger detective asked us our names. I was too exhausted to be imaginative enough to think of a meaningful false name, so I just changed my last name to Bell, for the American writer bell hooks.

They asked us to sit down, then took us, separately, into a dark, musty office with no windows, where they played good cop, bad cop. Perhaps because I was so exhausted and perhaps because of my relief at not being radiated after all, I giggled maniacally at just about everything they said.

"Who put you up to this? Who's your ringleader? Do you know how serious it is to enter a nuclear research establishment? We could be talking long sentences here." This from the older detective, who identified himself as Detective Osland and who seemed to come straight out of a BBC crime series, with his dishevelled suit, grey hair in need of a haircut, never smiling face.

*We got disgruntled with the ten million women idea, so we set off for Abingdon, got lost, and decided to break into Aldermaston when we saw a signpost to it, even though we didn't know what it was, and then we walked around inside until we got bored*, did not sound like the kind of seriously planned action we had apparently committed. But it's what I said, minus the ten million women part, and he snorted.

"Why don't you just tell us how you knew where to best enter the base?" the younger man said, who was introduced as Detective Williams, and who sat on the desk leaning forward in a friendly, hey, I could be your brother manner. "Why not just tell us the real story, and we'll all be able to go home a lot earlier."

"I know you," I said. "Weren't you the detectives on the case in Wakefield, the one that got moved to Leeds?"

"Yes, I recognize you, too," Detective Osland said.

"Really?" I was surprised, adding, "Why did you change the court case from Wakefield to Leeds?"

"Security reasons," Detective Osland said. "Now, tell us your real name."

"This is my real name."

"I don't think so. Do you know how serious it is to use a false name? What if there is a murderer in Glasgow by the name of Stephanie Bell? You could get yourself in serious trouble."

"I doubt there is a murderer in Glasgow called Stephanie Bell. And if there is, how likely is it I would fit her description? Anyway, most murderers are men." Detective Osland was annoying me and I was surprised at how outspoken I was being.

"That may be true," Detective Williams said. "But nonetheless, by using someone else's name you put yourself at all kinds of risks." He smiled.

I shrugged. "You know we got attacked at Wakefield? We never told the police, but we got attacked by a bunch of men." And I told them the story.

"You should have reported it," Detective Williams said.

"Women never report things like that," I retorted. "We don't trust how you will treat us. You know around half of reported violent crimes are woman battering and most women never report it anyway, so imagine how many women are being raped and beaten every day." I learned all this from my job at Women's Aid.

"We can't catch the rapists and batterers if victims don't report it," Detective Osland said.

"Well, women get put on trial when they go to the police," I said. "They are asked why were you wearing this, why were you doing that. They end up being violated twice. That's why they don't report."

"We're as keen as anyone to catch rapists and batterers," Detective Williams said, leaning forward earnestly, and it seemed as if he meant it. "I have a wife and two daughters. Do you think I want those men on the streets?"

I wanted to say that most crimes happen within families, and I stopped myself. We seemed to have departed from why we were there, and I wondered if they were going along with this conversation as a police tactic to get me to let my guard down.

"We should have women judges, women officers, and women doing the interviews when women have been raped," I said, hoping to annoy them.

To my surprise, they both agreed.

"The problem is we don't have enough of them," Detective Osland said.

"Not yet, at least," Detective Williams added.

I couldn't tell if they were being sincere or manipulative. I went silent.

"Wouldn't you rather be back at the camp with all your friends?" Detective Williams said. "I know I would rather be home right now,

I can tell you. The sooner you tell us the truth, the sooner we can all get out of here. So, did you cut the fence, or was it one of the others?"

"We didn't cut the fence," I said each time they asked. And they asked this often.

"But you entered the base, didn't you?"

"Yes we entered. There was a hole there already. So we just went in. And then there was no security. Imagine. A nuclear research establishment with nobody to protect it."

"It is perfectly well protected, as you well know." Detective Osland scowled. "How did you know where best to break in? How long had you been planning this crime?"

I giggled. "We didn't plan a thing. But it is shocking that five untrained women could get so easily inside a high security nuclear establishment and that we were the ones who had to get ourselves arrested. Don't you think?"

We'd agreed to stick to the same story women often used for our actions at Greenham—that we had entered the base to show the world that lethal weapons were being held in our communities and that the authorities were too incompetent to keep them safe, thereby putting us all at risk.

Back in the reception room, all of us except Karen, who was being interviewed, compared stories and found that our interviews had gone along pretty much the same lines. We were released back to the van and in a few moments asked to return to the building, where Karen informed us, "They just told me that Aldermaston is denying we entered."

If we didn't admit to cutting the fence, the police would let us go because Aldermaston did not want to press charges. That way it would not come out that their security had been so lax. And if we didn't get charged, and if Aldermaston denied we were there, we wouldn't be offered any further testing. We'd heard the Geiger counter clicking and were convinced we needed further testing and for that we had to admit we cut the fence. So we admitted to it and were taken to Newbury Police Station and charged with criminal damage.

Apparently our crime was much greater than if we had broken into Greenham, though it was not clear to us why. Instead of the usual magistrate's court, we'd be facing a judge and jury in Reading Crown

Court, and for that we needed to get seriously prepared with a plausible defence.

"You're looking at nine months or more," Detective Osland said, smiling for the first time.

IT WAS GREY and misty when we arrived at Blue Gate. Women were emerging, blurry-eyed, from their tents in the woods, making steaming cups of coffee and tea in the kitchen area, and sitting around the fire, talking in low, sleepy voices. We made our way to the fire, relieved to be home and among our sisters. Elena took my shaking hand in hers, while Sally sat down on my other side. I stroked her shaved head, and she meowed and purred like a cat, pushing her head into my hand for more, making me smile.

When we'd finished telling our story, Lucy said emphatically, "You must talk to Zol," and because I always did what Lucy said, Zee and I walked over to Yellow Gate after breakfast and found Zol, a formidable and capable looking Australian woman in her forties who always wore a large outback hat. She told us that she had been radiated on an action in her home country in the late 1970s and gave us phone numbers for scientists who worked for SANE—Scientists Against Nuclear Energy—and Trevor Brown, a local Liberal Councilman who had lost his job at Aldermaston after trying to get safety measures put in place. Then she gave us each a big bear hug, and I thought that Yellow Gate women weren't so scary after all.

Later that afternoon, Zee and I got a ride to Bath with two men who had just delivered firewood to the camp. We went straight to Hannah's, my friend from my university anti-apartheid days. I spent the afternoon on the phone to several scientists and learned that: we should have been told to shower immediately after the action (we still hadn't); if the Geiger Counter sped up at any point that was proof of radiation exposure (it did); if we breathed in radiation, there were no available tests to measure the impact; we should try and get a sample of the grass we crawled through; radiation exposure was particularly bad for children and women of child-bearing age because our cells change so rapidly; we should put our clothes in bags and take them immediately to the National Radiological Protection Board (NRPB) in Harwell, a government laboratory in Oxfordshire responsible for testing anyone suspected of radiation exposure; radiation can go right through you and cause no ill effect; worst case scenario, we could be looking at leukaemia, anaemia, or lung cancer in twenty years' time.

Forty-two seemed a long way away, and I felt vaguely relieved.

Then I called the NRPB, and a friendly sounding woman told us to come for a full body scan the next day.

When Zee and I arrived, after hitching from Bath, Maggie, Karen, and Jane were already standing in front of the large corporate looking NRPB building. We hugged and cracked some radiation jokes—"Zee's lost all her hair!"—before entering the reception area. I was stoned and hadn't eaten and felt light headed as a smiling blonde woman in a pressed suit, crisp shirt, pink lipstick, varnished nails, and carefully coiffed hair led us into a conference room, offered us tea and biscuits, explained the testing procedure, then left us alone.

After about half an hour, Zee said, "Oh forget this," and pulled out her tobacco pouch and rolled a joint, and we passed it around the room. We flicked the ash into a tissue that Zee had dampened a little with water from the water cooler in the corner of the room and cupped to form an ash tray. She opened the window, hoping the sweet smell would disperse. When the blonde woman came back, we were devouring the biscuits and gulping down glasses of water. And I had a question for her.

"What were the black plastic bags we saw inside Aldermaston? They had radiation stickers on them."

"There was a strike," she said. "So the rubbish wasn't being picked up. They would have contained materials with low level radiation in them, like gloves."

Before I could continue my detective work, we were interrupted by a knock at the door.

"Who first?" a man in a white coat said.

I put up my hand.

"Two at a time," he said, and Zee stood up to follow me.

He led us to a shower room where he instructed us to shower and then change into some pale pink pyjamas that were hanging on a hook on the bathroom wall. We giggled nervously as we pulled on the thin cotton pyjamas, then entered the laboratory barefoot, to see a group of men and women in white coats scattered around the room in front of machines and devices you only saw in sci-fi movies. My body was shaking, but it wasn't cold.

The scientist led me into a cubicle and entered my name (Stephanie Bell), address (Greenham Common), and age (22) into a computer and asked me to sign a form giving him permission to conduct the tests. I signed without reading it. Then he led me into a small dark room. There was a flat table in the middle, like a doctor's examination table, and he asked me to lie down. I complied. A huge metal machine loomed over my head. He swung two side arms over my body and clicked them into place. My first thought was, how will I escape if I need to? The metal bars went across my hips and my chest, so I could wiggle myself down to the bottom of the machine, perhaps, but I wondered how my shoulders would get through. For a moment I felt like Emma Peel in *The Avengers* and imagined creating a dramatic escape, with Zee acting like John Steed in the wings, ready to trip up the scientists with an umbrella as they chased me around the lab.

"This will take about half an hour," he said. "The machine will pass slowly over your entire body, scanning it. So, just relax. If you need anything, remember we are just next door."

And with that he left.

I didn't want to scream to be let out like I had at Newbury Police Station. I also didn't want to be left alone in a dark room strapped to a machine with small flashing lights making strange clicking sounds as it slowly made its way over my body. I was utterly stoned so had no idea whether I had been lying there for thirty seconds, five minutes, or three hours already, and a panic formed in my chest that they might forget about me and I would be stuck there for days. My mouth was dry, and I was desperate for a drink of water. So I did the only thing I could think of. I talked to myself.

"OK, so you will be seeing Al tomorrow. She'll make you a nice dinner, you'll drink beer, and make love and walk in the park and then you are going to see her concert, which will be great, and Ming will be there, and she'll make you laugh, and maybe while Al is rehearsing you and Ming will go for a curry, or visit Zephyr, and you can just hang out with all your new Birmingham friends (here I lapsed into a Birmingham accent) . . . and we'll dance . . . and then . . . and then . . ."

When the door clicked open and the scientist released me from the table, a flood of relief washed over me. He led me back to the glass cubicle in the centre of the large open office space, where Zee was waiting, seated between two white-coated scientists.

"Lucky they have that microphone in there in case you need something," she whispered, with a wink, while the scientists fussed over a computer monitor that was presumably connected to the machine I had been lying on.

"You mean . . . ?" I began, and I struggled to remember what had just been broadcast into the laboratory.

"You probably taught them a thing or two," she added, winking again, as they led her small frame with her bald head, wild tattoos, and pink pyjamas into the dark room.

When we were all done, the scientist gave us our test results then and there—printouts with incomprehensible numbers on them, a chart, and some scientific text.

"You have as much radiation in your bodies as we'd expect from testing that took place in the Pacific in the 1950s, which sent radiation over here, affecting our atmosphere," he said, matter-of-factly. "So there is nothing to be worried about."

Then he handed us back our clothes, all except my lovely tuxedo jacket, which I didn't notice until it was too late and we were back at the camp. Jane drove us back to Blue Gate where someone immediately handed us a copy of *The Sun* newspaper, a tabloid that featured a topless woman on Page Three every day, not the kind of paper you'd expect to see at the camp. Inside there was a short article entitled, "Greenham Gang in Atom Scare," describing our night's antics. We laughed. But none of us really thought this was funny.

# Chapter Fourteen

## "WHERE HAVE ALL THE FLOWERS GONE" JOAN BAEZ

WHEN AL TOLD me not to rely on her if I was ever in trouble, it never occurred to me I ever would be. I didn't believe her anyway, and I believed her even less when I visited her shortly after the radiation testing, and she was all flowers and wine and kisses and proposed a holiday in France—my favourite place in the world—which I enthusiastically agreed to.

But our trip was postponed abruptly when my sister Kate called.

"Steph, I've got some bad news about Dad," she said immediately, never one to beat around the bush.

"His headaches . . ." I said, my voice barely louder than a whisper.

"Yes, his headaches, and blurred vision, and swinging moods," she said. "Are you alone? Are you with Al? Or friends?"

Even though I felt Kate disapproved of me, I also knew she always looked out for her younger siblings. She didn't want me to be alone, she wanted to be sure I had support.

"Yes, I'm with Al," I said.

"Ok, good." She let out a big sigh. "I just spoke with Dad. He told me he went for a test at Southampton hospital a couple of weeks ago, and he just got the results."

I leaned my head against the wall and craned my neck to look out of the window, but all I could see were sickly yellow streetlights, no stars or moon to offer guidance or comfort for what might come.

"He's got a brain tumour, Steph, and it's quite advanced. He needs an operation next week. July 26."

I scribbled down the date, as if I would ever forget it, and when we hung up I sat stunned on the sofa.

I called my mother. I didn't ask if I should come home right away even though I desperately wanted to see my dad, because he had asked me not to come home and I didn't know if he still felt that way. I wondered if he only said it because of the brain tumour, if it had affected his mood, his decision-making. She asked me to go home the day of the operation and to stay for a few hours with Sarah while everyone else was at the hospital. Sarah was too young, my mother said, to accompany them, and she didn't want her to be home alone in case there was bad news. In case he died, she meant.

I didn't want to believe my father could die, and I didn't want to go home. But I did want to be there for Sarah. I spoke to my father, briefly, and he tried to be upbeat. He said all would be well and he told me I should still go to France. So I stayed a couple more days with Al, who continued to make plans for our trip as if nothing had happened—"We can postpone it for a week, that's no problem, I don't have any shows for a month"—and then I hitched to Greenham in a state of numb anticipation. The morning of his operation, I stood alone at Blue Gate while I waited for my lift from a woman at Green Gate. I was bewildered because I loved my father, but shouldn't I hate him? In ways small and large, he and my mother had imposed upon me expectations of being sexy, accommodating, demure, passive—all the qualities that had made my life a misery with Martin, that led me to give up football—and what kind of parents gave their daughters suspender belts and stockings when they reached the age of sixteen? At the camp some women blamed men for everything, so I had been learning to blame my father for everything because he was a man and men were responsible for all that was evil in the world. Now he was possibly about to die, and I already missed his deep voice, his wry humour, and his gentle guidance.

"Is he dead yet?" Little Jane, the rough, curly-haired seventeen-year-old who had run away from home, called to me. She was sitting at the fire pit with a group of women, and when she turned back to them and said something about one less man to worry about, they laughed.

A number of women at Greenham were radical feminists who saw men as the enemy, the cause of war, as being irretrievably and utterly bad. My recent experience of men had not been so great, and I had found comfort and support from this ideology. But it didn't explain the friends I had before Martin came along—Richard and Raymond and Mark—or Kate's husband, John, or my friends in France, or my wonderful brother, or Dr. Martin Luther King, Jr., or Nelson Mandela, or Gandhi—or even the men who brought us firewood each week.

Exceptions to the rule, I had thought. But demonizing an entire sex still didn't sit right; it couldn't be that simple. And now my dad was seriously ill, and the ideology was no comfort at all.

My father had done his fair share of marching against war—a photograph of him and me on a peace march with a Pax Christi sign right behind us had appeared in a Catholic newspaper, making my atheist father look as if he were, in fact, a Catholic, something that made him laugh out loud, a rare occurrence. I felt betrayed and invisible, standing there at Blue Gate, my sisters laughing at my pain. Yet a small part of me wondered if I was wrong to care that my dad was dying. I felt dizzy and light, as if I were about to float up above the treetops. How I wished I could.

Thank Goddess for Zol, the strong Australian who'd given me the numbers for scientists the day after we were radiated. Striding through Blue Gate that very moment, wearing her outback hat and a wide grin, she noticed me and came over. When she took my hands, I told her what was happening at home and what Jane had just said, and she looked me intently in the eyes, then said, "This is your father, not the patriarchy. He's your flesh and blood. You love him. Go and be with him."

As she stroked my hair from my face, the dizziness passed, and I slowly came back to earth, hugging her as I cried into her smoky jacket.

Indicating the women at the fire, she said, "They are young and Jane is scared and they don't know what they're saying."


MY LIFT DROPPED me off at home, and it was sunny and lovely in St. Mary Bourne, but I felt unwelcome. Only Sarah was home, of course, but I worried that she had been co-opted into my mother's disapproval of me. It didn't help that I had smoked pot that morning and that the main effect for me, beyond giggling, was paranoia. Sarah did not say anything to make me think she loved me less, but she was quiet, and even though I realized she was only sixteen, her father may have been about to die on the operating table, and she was terrified, I didn't know what to say to her. He was my father, too, and I wanted to escape. So I went into the small back garden overlooking the school playing fields, sat on the grass, and tried to roll a joint in the paper packaging from a tampon, because I had forgotten my cigarette papers.

Sarah stayed inside the house, and we waited out separately the three hours before the phone rang. She took the call, then walked out to give me the news.

"He made it," she said.

I gave Sarah an awkward and stoned hug and noticed her eyes were red. But I said nothing.

I was elated that my father was alive, but as I sat in the front garden waiting for my lift back to the camp, I hoped desperately that it would arrive before my family did. I was certain they didn't want to find me there, and I didn't want to see them either. My feelings were a riot inside me, and I didn't want them to see how scared, how relieved, how sad I really was. Sarah came out to join me.

"Why don't you wait to see them?" she asked.

I shook my head.

"We'll be moving to Devon, now," she added, looking lost.

Just before my father got really sick, my parents had made plans to move to the coastal town of Stoke Fleming in Devon, two hundred miles away. My father had retired early because of his health and didn't want to be around to see a new head take over his school, and so he had put an offer on a 1930s semi-detached on a small estate as far away as possible, by the sea, his favourite place to be. I wondered if they would still disrupt my sister's life, and their own. Sarah was about to start sixth form and would be leaving many friends. I knew she was sad about this, but she was the youngest, so nobody asked her what she thought.

I WENT TO Birmingham the next day, where Al and I packed a small burner to cook on, a tent, two sleeping bags, and a change of clothes. We had plans to hitchhike to the Dordogne, where I wanted to visit my old haunts, but I hadn't contacted any of the lovely French men who had given me my first taste of liberation because I didn't know how to tell them I was a lesbian.

Our first stop was Vi Subversa's in London. Normally this would be thrilling to me, but I felt numb. I only half-listened to Al and Vi's talk of their upcoming tour and Al's new twelve-inch single. Al didn't tell Vi about my father or my recent adventure in Aldermaston, and nor did I.

I was consumed by images of radiation poisoning—rashes, headaches, the gradual physical decline into emaciation, then death. I wondered how emaciated my father had become after his operation, what it must have been like to be anesthetized not knowing if you would wake up again, how weird it was that I had got radiated while he got radiation treatment. I planned to visit him the next day before we left for France, and I wondered if my family would be there and what my mother would say to me. My body shook uncontrollably. Al thought I was cold, and when she held me close in bed, I felt comforted.

AT SOUTHAMPTON HOSPITAL, Al waited outside on the grass next to the parking lot. I had never been in a cancer ward before. Walking through the white swing doors to my father's hospital room, I didn't know if my mother, sisters, and brother would be there, and I didn't know if I was still supposed to stay away. I was terrified that I might see them, but when I didn't, my heart fell. I'd already been told I made my mother upset, and I was convinced that my older sister, Kate, was angry with me too, feeling I'd taken my bolshie attitude to the nth degree, with my Mohican, female lover, veganism, and activist life at the peace camp. Always, to my mind, the clever, talented, pretty, funny, stylish girl, Kate taught history at a secondary school in Cambridgeshire where she lived with her husband John, a handsome, kind, dependable man with jet-black hair and piercing blue eyes whom she met at university. She was doing everything a daughter should, and now planned to start a family—while I was convinced she thought I was being difficult and awkward, as always. My younger brother, Robert, ever the peacemaker, was the only person I felt would be happy to see me, but he was not there, either.

THE MAN NEXT to my father was lying flat on his back with tubes in his arm and a mask over his face, in a coma. My father sat upright in the bed next to the window, pale and small in the thin cotton hospital gown that exposed some grey hairs on his chest.

"I love you," he said when he saw me.

This was the first time he had said this to me. We didn't say things like that in our family.

"I love you, too," I said back.

He reached out weakly for my hand and I sat on the edge of his bed. We stayed together like that for a while.

This was my father. The handsome, deep-voiced man who looked like Gregory Peck and who took me on the back of his motorbike through the meandering Hampshire countryside as a child and a teenager, patting my leg as he turned to yell through the heavy helmet, "You make a good pillion rider!" Who railed against Margaret Thatcher and introduced me to Malcolm X and Angela Davis and Che Guevara and the Beatles and Bob Dylan and Joan Baez and whom we all loved to tease about his love for Frank Sinatra.

"How can a socialist love someone who's in the mafia and who's friends with Nixon?" we'd say.

"Just listen to his voice," he replied.

My father, who more often than not, could be found lying on the sofa or on the floor in our mismatched living room in pain from his bad back, listening to Sibelius or Beethoven or Mozart, plunged in the deepest of depressions, far, far out of reach. Now, as I held onto his dry, bony hand in the hospital, I knew for sure he must be sad, afraid, and in pain.

My father, who engendered terror in the children at Testbourne School where he was the headmaster, when he uncharacteristically yelled, "You boy!" to some unsuspecting chap who was breaking a school rule, perhaps one related to integrity, the quality my father chose for the school motto. A headmaster who put the workers first, praising his caretakers and cleaners and cooks as much as his teachers, a man of the people, democratizing classes so that kids of all abilities sat next to each other, in an experiment he was proud to bring to the hallowed halls of conservative Hampshire.

I'd been offered the chance to go to the grammar school in Andover, where my sister Kate went, in case I didn't want to have my father as my headmaster. But I quite liked the idea, and like my father, I believed in the principle of comprehensive education and was opposed to the grammar school system that weeded out kids with the 11 plus exam, starting early on the discrimination that my father believed led to poorer kids being funnelled into technical schools, or secondary moderns, and the more privileged to university. He had a cartoon to that effect on his office wall, of girls and boys climbing up ladders on the side of a mountain attempting to reach the summit of a university education. The ladders for state school students were attached precariously, with students forced to start their climb at the bottom of the mountain, while private and public school kids stepped out onto their secure ladders from very close to the top. The bodies of those who didn't make it flew in the air as they fell to the ground.

My father, who brought home from school stray children whose families had abandoned or hurt them—the stocky, angry Bruce who became a second brother to us, playing guitar with me, and cricket with me and Robert, and the wistful Angel who spoke Spanish and liked to giggle as much as I did. A father I loved to join in front of the telly as he watched the Test matches in a darkened room on the sunniest of summer days, listening to the comforting click, click of leather on willow, the quiet voices of the commentators, the oohs and the aahs of the cricket-loving crowd. My father, whose idea of a good night out was to walk to the local village pub to have a pint with the working-class locals. My glorious, socialist father, who was proud of the "80 Years a Scrounger" badge I wore the day the village celebrated the Queen Mother's eightieth birthday, and who secretly smiled when I slapped a friend of Mr. Macnamara's daughter for trying to stop me from crossing their field, even though there was a footpath there, even though I did this every day. My father, who told me that it's okay to hit someone, but only if they hit you first; who didn't want to pay Mr. Macnamara for the chickens my dog ate on one of his wanderings, offering to donate money to a charity of Mr. Macnamara's choice instead. My father, who, accompanied by my mother in her colourful kaftans or silver halter necks, was obliged to attend the poshest of posh cocktail parties since he was headmaster. My father, who winked at me when he found me in the corridor at school standing outside a classroom because I had been sent out of Religious Education, a topic he did not personally approve of, for giggling. My father who, although by law had to deliver religious assemblies at school, always found a way to bring in social issues—war, homelessness, kindness, justice—and who gave me a book of moving anti-war poetry, seeing in me the light that was in him to make the world a fairer place. My father, who quietly supported me when I decided not to attend my university graduation ceremony because I did not approve of the capitalist keynote speaker, but who implored me to go anyway, just to make my mother happy and his life easier.

It was on the tennis courts in Accrington that he met my mother, with her jet-black Irish hair, Elizabeth Taylor eyes, and magnificent humour, dropping her a few weeks later when he learned she was only sixteen, the same age as his students, only to gallantly reappear two years later on his motorbike to ask her out.

They married and bought a two up two down on a cobblestone street in Accrington, a home filled with laughter and play. He taught English at the local secondary school where the girls swooned at his deep voice and love of Yeats. He wrote love poetry to my mother, who made him laugh with her exuberance, ability to mimic any accent, and her willingness to sit pillion on the back of his Sunbeam motorbike and ride for hours around the Lancashire moors, and once to Paris, where she wore a wide tight-belted skirt with full petticoats on the back of the bike as they rode past the Eiffel Tower, the Garden des Tuilieries, and the River Seine, and who didn't complain once when it poured with rain the whole long journey home.

The two of them had six years of bliss, they told us, before we came along. Kate came first, with her huge green eyes and bright intellect, delighting my dad with her ability to say *onomatopoeia* at the age of sixteen months. I came three years later, making him laugh even as my mother was exasperated at my antics—pouring sand all over the living room floor, needing company at all times, my love for stray, mangy dogs. My father opened the car doors graciously for Kate's imaginary friends and then for mine, Buddha Sugga, Dougala, and Dougala's Mummy. But by the time Robert came just eighteen months after me, a dark cloud had descended over their new home on the busy Stone Road in Stafford in the Midlands, and it never fully left.

My mother told us more than once how my father once fell asleep when he was supposed to be looking after baby Robert in the back garden, most likely affected by the medications he took every morning and every night. Robert climbed out of his pushchair and crawled purposefully through the open gate and as far as the edge of the busy road in front of our home, looking, with his big brown eyes, like a lost bush baby escaped from a zoo. A lorry driver came to a screeching halt at the sight, leapt out of the cab, and scooped up Robert, then carried him to my father, who was just waking up from his nap, oblivious to it all. And so we learned that while our father may well love us, he was too depressed, too sensitive, and too intellectual to be trusted with ordinary things, such as babysitting or making sure his children didn't get run over. When he joined the euthanasia group, Exit, it seemed both inevitable and incomprehensible.

Our attempts to reach him over the years were met, more often than not, with a wan smile and a wave of the hand that said, *Go away. I'm resting,* or, *I can't do that, I have a bad back.* The top drawer in his bedroom filled with more and more pills—for depression, back pain, migraine.

AS I SAT in silence holding his hand in the hospital, the flood of memories threatened to lift me off my seat and carry me on and on and on and out of the window and crash into the car park and beyond. All thoughts of Greenham, Al, and radiation were swept away as I thought of the sunny Saturday, when I was still fifteen, that he took me on his BMW to my county hockey match in Winchester. I was thrilled that he was about to see me play for Hampshire for the first time and felt enormously proud of him as I dismounted from the large green motorbike, hoping that my teammates and the opposition would see us emerging from beneath our impressive helmets. But he didn't stay. Instead, he drove off to a nearby park to play bowls, a boring old man's game, something I didn't even know he liked. It was one of my greatest matches, one where I stopped every ball that came my way, dribbled effortlessly past opposition players, and passed the ball selflessly across the midfield for our forwards to score. When he came back to pick me up, I felt pride, disappointment, and a sense of injustice.

"You won. Why the sulky face?" he asked.

"I always have a sulky face," I reminded him. This was one of the main accusations levelled at me at home.

This was the same man, my father, sitting upright in a hospital bed in a pale blue gown of cheap, thin cotton, the man who didn't hug, or kiss, or effuse, the man separated from us all by the fog of depression, constant pain, a lifetime of prescription drugs, and my mother's possessive nature. But as I sat there holding his hand, any conflict, fog, or separation melted away for a few precious minutes, and I was his rebel daughter again, the one I knew, secretly, he was proud of. And while I didn't tell him about the radiation and the testing and the fear, and how much I needed him at this confusing, terrifying, and exciting time, it was enough for me that he was here holding my hand.

"I'm hitching to France with Al," I said. "She's waiting outside. We're going to catch a boat from New Haven to Dieppe and see how it goes from there. We're going to the Dordogne."

"Where will you stay?" he asked.

"In a tent. We have a tent. There are plenty of campsites."

What I didn't ask was: *Can I go back home now? Or do you still want me to stay away?*

Instead I said, "What shall I bring you back?"

"Nothing," he said. "Just stay safe and have fun."

He didn't say anything about the fact I was hitchhiking or ask me why I was doing something so risky. Perhaps he didn't have the energy to worry. Perhaps he needed all his energy to recuperate from the operation. Perhaps he had given up on me.

"I'll call from France," I said. "We'll be back in two weeks."

On the road in front of the hospital, I joined Al and turned to see my father standing at the window. I wondered if he could see Al from there and what he was thinking. I waved, and as the two of us took off, I wondered if I'd ever see him again.

# Chapter Fifteen

## "GIRLS JUST WANT TO HAVE FUN" CYNDI LAUPER

I AM CONVINCED that my trip to France while my father lay in the hospital presented me with a series of encounters to help me open my heart to men, while not forgetting the danger they can impose, either.

The first two men were Italian and wore dark glasses. We met them on the cross-channel ferry to France, and they graciously drove us in their comfortable Italian car all the way to Paris, European electro-disco music blaring. After a while the music was too high energy for us, and Al asked if we could put on a tape of hers, and I was surprised when Ella Fitzgerald came on. One of the Italians said, "Ella, we love Ella," and I was reminded of my father, how he'd dance with my mother to Ella when his bad back allowed, Ella's velvety voice and Cole Porter's playful lyrics transporting them back to their first dates in the dancehalls of Lancashire in the 1950s. They waltzed and smooched around the living room, oblivious to any of us, making us kids scrunch our noses. "Mum! Dad! Don't be so disgusting," one of us would say, and my dad smiled and said, "Just you wait until it happens to you." Now it had happened to me, and with a woman who listened to my dad's favourite oldies. I couldn't wait to tell him.

Ella was singing "I love Paris in the Springtime" when we arrived in Paris and we all laughed at the serendipity of this. We waited together in the parked car at the side of the busy street until the final note had played. As the smiling driver handed the tape back to Al, he invited us out partying. I had grown to like the Italians, but we hadn't come out to them because we had been worried they might throw us out of the car or drive us into a lay-by and murder us. Al and I felt extra vulnerable because we hadn't hitched together before, and neither of us had done so in a foreign country. So the Italians had been free to chat me up, and I had quite enjoyed it, surprising myself, and angering Al, who had been getting increasingly jealous, grabbing my hand where they couldn't see, looking out of the window sulkily. So if we went out with them now, either I'd continue to let them flirt with me, or we'd have to tell them, so we declined.

We said goodbye and wandered off into the busy, sunny streets to find a cheap hotel near the Gare du Nord. Al had her arm around me, confident now in the safety of the French, stylish crowds, and the likelihood that, while people might stare at her, they would more than likely mistake her for a boy. She enjoyed the subterfuge, and so did I, as she crooned "I love Paris in the summertime" into my ear in her deep, throaty voice, sending thrills through my body.

The next morning. we ate crusty French bread and jam for breakfast on the outdoor patio of a sweet-smelling patisserie and then wandered hand-in-hand around the Eiffel Tower and Jardin des Tuileries, where we drank wine out of a bottle and smoked roll-ups. With Al all in white and me all in black, we must have looked striking because a greying middle-aged man carrying a camera with a big black lens asked if he could photograph us. He reminded me of my father, who loved his camera, taking photographs of the village's thatched cottages and rolling hills, and some of my mother wearing wigs and lingerie, too. I didn't like posing for him, as I once did when I went to a fancy dress party as a St. Trinian's schoolgirl in my short gym skirt, lifting it to show the top of my stockings as I leaned on my hockey stick. But today I was happy to be photographed with my orange, spiky hair, tough looking boots, cut-off black T-shirt, and smouldering roll-up as I laughed and kissed my strong, muscular, boy-like girlfriend with the reddest, spikiest Mohican in all of Paris. The French photographer sent us the photographs a few weeks later and thanked me and my boyfriend for letting him take our photos. I wrote back from the safety of England to let him know we were both girls, thank you very much.

The next day, we got a lift from a small, wiry man in a battered white van, who immediately veered off the highway leading out of Paris and stopped on a quiet exit road. Al sat by the door, and I in the middle so that I, who spoke French, could talk more easily with him.

"I have a gun in the back, but as long as we all behave, nobody will need to use it," he said.

I wondered briefly if he was telling us he had a gun because he thought Al was a man and he was afraid of us. But we were the ones who had good reason to be afraid. He was the one in the driver's seat, he was the one who knew his way around, and he was the one with the gun. Al was as strong as most men, and we were relying on this— as well as the fact most people thought she was a man anyway—to protect us from any aggression men might direct at two young women travelling alone. But her muscles were no match for a bullet. Al didn't understand what he was saying, but she could see that something was terribly wrong.

"Why are we stopped here?" she asked.

"He insists on going to his house to pick something up," I said, and I was shaking. "He says he has a gun in the back and that we shouldn't worry because he has the bullets up front and as long as we all behave, we will be OK."

"Is he nuts?" Al yelled, and the driver looked startled.

"You'd better take us back to the highway. My friend is very angry," I said, careful to be gender neutral.

He turned the van onto a rutted back street with rubbish strewn across it. It was a warehouse district, with very few people around. I wondered whether it was safer to stay in the van or to jump out onto the street. I talked to him, trying to be friendly and chatty, to make a connection. Did he have sisters? A wife? Children? He told me he lived in a Parisian suburb with his sister and her family, so I asked questions about her and her children, which he answered, smiling. I wondered if this was a good sign. He pulled up behind a rundown warehouse, jumped out of the van, and told us to wait there.

"Shall we get out here?" I asked.

"Is it safe?" Al asked.

"We could make a run for it. But what if the neighbourhood is full of hostile men? We don't know where we are."

"We could try and call a taxi."

"Except we don't have a number or much money to pay for it."

We were still debating what to do when he returned, alone, holding a large duffel bag, which he flung into the back of the van.

"See?" he said, smiling and opening his empty hands. "No gun. You can tell your boyfriend that."

"Thank you," I said, relieved that he used the masculine noun, smiling a smile I didn't feel.

I continued to chat with him and persuaded him to take us back to the line of hopeful hitchers at the entrance to the main highway leaving Paris. As we jumped down from the cab, I turned and yelled up at him, "You're disgusting, how could you do that? What were you thinking, threatening us with a gun?"

I felt the same surge of power, the same feeling of liberation, I had experienced when I had told Martin I was leaving him for the last time. I slammed the door, and added, "Just fuck off and leave us alone."

Al took me in her arms. "My hero," she whispered into my ear. "You were amazing."

Al said I didn't need to do anything but look pretty and be her drums. But I was feeling almost giddy from my success and wondered what she would have done without my ability to talk down a mad gunman in French.

We took our place among the thirty or so hitching hopefuls lined up at the slip road to the highway, the only women travelling alone, though it was not obvious that we were indeed both women. Every so often a car slowed down, its driver eyed up the hitchers one by one, and chose who to pick up. It wasn't long before a small battered Renault pulled up, a bearded man wearing a beret in the driver's seat.

"Where are you going?" he asked.

"Perigueux," I said, naming the largest town close to where we were headed.

He looked us up and down.

"Why not give a lift to the precious English punk girls," he said, his smile revealing teeth blackened from tobacco.

He had a wife next to him, so Al and I squashed into the back seat next to a boy and a girl who stared up at us with large curious eyes. I took Al's hand in mine. I was not going to be closeted for the next few hours, and I could already tell that this man was not going to care. He turned out to be a sculptor, eccentric and talkative, bursting into song every now and then, chain-smoking Gitanes, and leading a nonstop conversation the whole way about art, politics, and literature. We helped him fill the car with thick smoke, enjoying the bitter taste of the unfiltered French cigarettes, the tiny bits of tobacco that catch on the tongue. He was curious about who we were and thrilled to find that Al was a singer in an anarcho-punk band, that I was a Greenham woman, and that we were a lesbian couple. We told him about our adventure with the van driver, and he shook his head as his wife, Sylvie, gasped in sympathy.

"You are lucky we found you," she said. "I wish we could drive you all the way. So dangerous, two girls hitching together . . ."

Sylvie was sweet and said very little, and the children sang songs and drew, looking at their strange fellow travellers every now and then with sidelong glances. I never knew what to say to children so I just smiled and answered the sculptor's questions about the camp and Al's music, and listened to his tirades against the Parisian art world and his left-wing political views which, I remembered as I listened to him, were refreshingly mainstream in France. His lively personality was nothing like my father's, but he reminded me of him nonetheless with his indignation at injustice, his hatred of the ruling class, his camaraderie with the working man, his wry humour, and his love of beauty.

I started to feel quite central to our story. Al may have been the singer who could summon a punk rock audience, but I was the one who could talk down gunmen, get us rides, explain who we were, and laugh at jokes in French. I told Claude that I used to teach in the Dordogne, and that I wanted to show Al how beautiful it was. I didn't mention what occupied my mind the most: that I may have been radiated, and my dad, who was lying in a brightly lit hospital room on the southern coast of England, was recovering from an operation, and we didn't know if he might be suffering from a worse state, possibly fatal.

Claude dropped us off at our exit, and almost immediately a young man in another battered Renault pulled up, introduced himself as Michel, then drove us to his parents' home half an hour away where he gave us coffee and a few hours' sleep in his parents' bed (they were away on holiday), cooked us a lunch of ratatouille and warm baguette, then drove us the full two hundred miles to Riberac because, he said, he had nothing else to do that day, so why not? Al and I dozed most of the way, and I thought fondly of the days I had spent at the lake we were headed for with my friends from my university year abroad. They were around the same age as the man who was helping us out right now, and I thought how well they would have got on with each other. As Michel shared with me his scepticism for military service and his left-wing views, I thought how I had almost escaped Martin thanks to the freedom I tasted with my French friends, almost. I wished they could see me now as I arrived at the lake in the late afternoon. We hugged and thanked Michel for helping us, waved him goodbye, then set up camp in the woods, far from other campers, and settled in for a few days to play house in our tiny tent, to swim, and run, laughing, through the woods. We bought cans of vegetables at the campsite shop, and Al cooked our meals on the small burner we had brought along. I told her about how the twelve-year-old students in my favourite class, from my year as an "assistante anglaise" at a school just a few miles from here, loved the photograph I brought in one day of my dad on his BMW, and then I told her about my rides around St. Mary Bourne with my father, and worried that I was talking about him too much.

When Cyndi Lauper's "Girls Just Want to Have Fun" drifted over the lake from the campsite jukebox every evening, this was our cue to go inside the tent and have fun ourselves.


A WEEK LATER, we were in the medieval walled town of Sarlat, with its turrets, worn flagstones, and bustling farmer's market. I was in a phone box talking to my sister Kate, desperately adding coins while Al drank tea in an outdoor café with our new friend, Jean-Christophe, a jewellery maker.

"We must think positive," Kate said. "But the news is this. The brain tumour was a secondary tumour. He has another one in his kidney and it's inoperable. All they can do is make him comfortable."

I tried to let the words sink in, but it all seemed so far away, so unreal. My dad was the person who first brought me to this part of France as a child, he was the one who arranged the school exchanges that led me to request Riberac as the place where I would spend my university year abroad. How was it possible that he wouldn't be able to come back here one day?

Kate was telling me that the family had already started to pack up the house, ready to move to Devon. I asked if we could undo the decision to move, and she said, "No, it's too late. We're moving tomorrow. And anyway, we have to think positive."

I wondered if thinking positive could really cure someone from cancer. I also knew my father wanted to live by the sea and thought how selfish it would be to suggest taking that opportunity away from him now. Kate told me he may have a few months left, so I didn't need to rush home—but I was so far away, and I wanted to be as close as I could. I felt disconnected from my family, and from myself, estranged in a distant French town with an unhinged, singing girlfriend, wondering how to think positive.

I left the phone box and sat at the table on the café patio with Al and Jean-Christophe.

"I have to go home," I said to Al. "My dad has got worse and I need to be closer to my family."

"Don't think about it," she said. "Think about life, about love, about France."

"How can I not think about it?" I asked. "This is my father."

I was taken aback by what came next.

"I told you never to rely on me," she purred into my ear. "Except for certain things, of course."

She smiled wickedly, rubbing the inside of my thigh. I took her hand in mine to remove it from my leg. It was true, she'd told me this more than once, but who wasn't there for someone they love when their father may be dying? So I chose not to believe her. I chose not to see what was there right in front of me and saw, instead, someone who would learn to care, when the time came.

Jean-Christophe was looking puzzled, so I explained to him, in French, what was going on with my father. He raised his eyebrows when I told him that Al didn't want to go back.

"Of course you must go home," he said. "You must stay with me in my cottage tonight, and I will drop you at the entrance to the motorway to Paris tomorrow." He took my hand in his.

"Thank you," I said.

Al was watching us, not understanding our conversation, feeling left out. She leaned forward, stroked my head, my face, and my lips, and looked intensely into my eyes. "Let's go home and go to bed. That'll change your tune."

Then she started to sing to me, loudly, one of Zephyr's songs, called "Sweet Sister," about being there for someone—the words "Just hold on, I will be there before the morning comes" ringing hollowly in my head.

When we eventually went to bed in Jean-Christophe's stone cottage in the middle of a beautiful nowhere five miles from town, I thought of Martin and wondered if he would have been so insensitive to news of my father's illness. I doubted it. It was true that Al was not controlling or jealous, that she gave me a freedom in bed, and a freedom to be who I was at Greenham and in the anarcho-punk underworld she inhabited. But I thought that dating women would be the answer to bad relationships, that women would be kinder, more loving, more supportive. I was beginning to find out I had been horribly, naively wrong.

In the morning, I got out of our iron-frame bed long before Al woke up, showered, dressed, and packed our clothes, looking out of the bedroom window now and then to watch the bees and butterflies flitting from flower to flower in Jean-Christophe's herb garden in the early morning light.

Al woke up, saw what I was doing, and groaned.

"We're leaving today," I said, and she capitulated, sulkily.

I didn't say much at breakfast on the stone patio, while Jean-Christophe hummed to himself as he came in and out of the kitchen with steaming bowls of black coffee, soft fresh white bread with a perfectly crispy crust, and homemade jam. I looked enviously at the local butter and cheese and frothy milk he brought out for himself, but Al remained strictly vegan, so I did too.

After breakfast, he dropped us off at the entrance to the motorway headed to Paris. It was a national holiday and there were very few cars on the road, but we managed to slowly make our way up the country. We were lucky when an older gentleman in a swanky car picked us up a hundred and fifty miles south of Paris. He had short silvery hair and hazel eyes, like my dad's, and a BMW, too, though his was a car, not a motorbike. He drove us all the way to his charming apartment in the sixteenth arrondissement, where he cooked us a vegan meal, and the comparison I'd been making to my father came to a dead halt. *How French*, I thought, *how amazing. Even the men his age can cook.* After dinner, he drove us around the city to show us the sights, the windows wound down to let in the sultry air. At a restaurant on the banks of the River Seine, we chatted over a bottle of red wine. I wanted to tell him about my father and my radiation, but instead I talked about Greenham, Al talked about music, while I translated, and he talked about Paris.

We spent the night in Monsieur Lebon's home, wondering if he was being kind, or if he had ulterior motives. It all felt too wonderful to be true. The next morning, he was waiting for us in the kitchen, a warm baguette, jam, and coffee on the table.

"So what's the hurry to get home?" he asked in English. "Want to stay another day or two?"

Al turned to me and grabbed my hand. "Let's do it."

So I had to tell him. My voice came out as a whisper as I said in French, "I have to get back to my father. He is very sick. He has cancer."

Monsieur Lebon's expression changed to one of concern. "If I could, I would drive you to Dieppe to catch the boat. But at least I can take you to the motorway entrance. Enjoy your breakfast, and then let's get going."

He threw a warm smile in my direction and a puzzled look at Al. We ate hurriedly, picked up our bags, jumped in his car, and at the motorway entrance, Monsieur Lebon took my face in his hands and said, "Beautiful."

At any other time I might have yelled, "Don't objectify me!"

But, instead, I wanted to tell him I may have been radiated and I needed my father now more than ever, but he was dying. I wanted to ask his advice—how did I reconcile my new life with my old, how could I get my family to like me, how could I do the right thing without giving up my ideals and my newfound independence? I looked up into his kind eyes, my own on the verge of tears, and said, simply, "Merci."

# Chapter Sixteen
## "EVERY TIME WE SAY GOODBYE" ELLA FITZGERALD

"HOW IS AL—is it?" My dad was asking about my girlfriend, who hadn't asked once how my father was and who was probably making love to one of her other lovers right then.

He was pale and thin and short of breath, but tried to be cheerful as we talked in the living room of the new family home, an ugly modern house on a small cul-de-sac in the Devon village of Stoke Fleming. Robert was with us and we could hear Mum and Kate making dinner in the kitchen, the comforting murmur of Radio 4 playing in the background, while Sarah was upstairs in her room, writing to one of the many friends she had left behind in Hampshire.

"Al's fine," I said. "She has a big concert supporting The Nightingales in Birmingham in a couple of weeks, so she's busy rehearsing." I wanted my father to be proud of me for having such a talented lover. I wanted him to like her and could not face the fact that I had walked headlong with my heart open into another dreadful relationship. I wanted my dad to think I was loved. "Do you want to hear some of her music?"

"Maybe later. But I already have, you know. Very talented." He winked at Rob. They had heard her already, it was true. I had taken a bath earlier and plugged the cassette recorder into the outlet on the landing so I could listen to her as I soaked, filling the upstairs landing with the dissonant sounds of anarcho-girl punk rock.

"She likes Ella Fitzgerald," I said.

"Good for her. There are some good male singers, too, you know, from that era. You should try them."

"Like Frank," Rob said in a deep American accent, and we laughed.

"Yes, like ol' blue eyes."

We didn't tease him about Frank being an American Republican.

"And she likes Nina Simone and Billie Holiday, too." These were singers Al had introduced me to, and I wondered why they weren't in my father's jazz collection.

"Very moving," he said, adding, "Heartbreaking."

It was easy, though sad, to talk with my dad, but not with my mum. But at least we had an unspoken truce: she said nothing about my hair and unshaved legs and choice of clothes and veganism—rolling her eyes and sighing instead.

"He promised he would never leave me," she said to Kate, one day, and Kate relayed this to me, worried that my mother wouldn't be able to take care of Sarah when the time came.

My mother had always appeared childlike in the relationship with my father, and now she was about to be left alone, in a strange place, with no friends, and a sixteen-year-old daughter to take care of.

And so my father asked Robert, only twenty but already a man of principle, to move to Devon from Andover when the time came, leaving behind his job and his girlfriend to take care of Mum and Sarah, putting on hold any thoughts of college. I felt indignant on his behalf, but Robert, who worshipped our father, seemed fine with it, so I said nothing. Years later, I learned that he was happy to join them, that he was ready to leave Hampshire, that it wasn't a sacrifice at all. But my own ideas of freedom had become the barometer I used to measure everything, and I could not imagine having to give anything up for anybody, even as I felt alienated from just about everyone in my family, from Al, and even from my Greenham friends.

THERE WERE ONLY three women at the fire when I got back to camp, and one of them was Lucy. A fine drizzle hung in the air, almost not moving, and the fire sizzled weakly. Everything was damp—my clothes, my face, my hair, the chair I sat on. I looked around, and all I saw was the mud and the mess of food and crockery in the kitchen area, the filthy tables and chairs we called our living room.

Lucy asked me about my visit home, and I told her numbly what was going on. She sat up tall and told me I needed to find a home. She told me I couldn't possibly put my roots down at Greenham Common because it wasn't secure, it was always changing, I couldn't rely on anyone to truly be there for me, and so I would need somewhere safe I could retreat to and grieve when my father finally died. Lucy was older than me and a social worker. She also had a very authoritative manner, and I was grateful to be told what to do. But I felt disillusioned. I thought Greenham was the answer to all my dreams—a community of loving women who were there for each other as we saved the planet from war and each other from violence. Yet I already knew that I wouldn't find the support I needed there, from Little Jane's comments, asking whether he had died yet, the indifference some of my "sisters" had shown toward my plight, my private sense of guilt for loving a man, my own father, as I did.

Al had two other lovers to attend to, so I couldn't ask her to take me in, and anyway I knew that I wanted to be in nature, where I could lie on the sweet-smelling grass and look at the branches touching the sky, where the moon could lull me to sleep, where I wouldn't have to speak to anyone. So on my next visit to Hannah's in Bath to sign on the dole, I looked in the local paper for rentals in the nearby countryside. I found an ad for a room in a fifteenth-century cottage attached to an old mill and in the courtyard of a working dairy farm ten miles out of town.

I borrowed Hannah's boyfriend's hat, a kind of felt fedora, to hide my hair, took the train to Trowbridge, and hitched the last three miles to Stowford Mill Cottage. Val, the tenant, liked that I had studied at Bath University and that I was a Greenham woman and would be away a lot of the time. She liked me even more after I decided to show who I really was and took off my hat. She told me after I had moved into my tiny, perfect room, overlooking the stream running right below the window, the disused weir, and the adjoining cottage's English country garden, that she didn't trust people who wore hats, and that if I hadn't taken off mine, she wouldn't have offered me the room.

Two weeks after meeting Val, I moved into the cottage, driven there by Jane, one of my radiated friends, on November fifth, Guy Fawkes night. As we sped across the country from Al's flat in Birmingham, where we had picked up my few belongings, it felt auspicious to be accompanied the entire way by small golden bonfires nestled in fields and gardens, firework displays illuminating the night sky.

My dad didn't approve of celebrating burning someone at the stake for wanting to blow up the Houses of Parliament, but he loved the ritual of walking down the lane from our home to the Macnamaras' field to stand around the bonfire and watch the small firework display. "I'd blow Parliament up myself now, if I didn't have you lot to take care of," he said as the whole family, bundled up in scarves and hats and wellington boots, huddled around a huge pile of wood that held an effigy made of old sweaters, jeans, and socks, waiting to go up in smoke.

"We should burn an effigy of Edward Heath. But don't tell the Macnamaras that," he said, winking at me, aware, I'm sure, of how much I loved how radical he was. I made treacle toffee, my dad's favourite, banging it hard with a rolling pin to create small enough pieces to eat, then wrapped each piece in wax paper to hand to unsuspecting neighbours. It was sweet, dark, and delicious if you knew how to eat it right—which meant sucking, not chewing and risking losing a filling. My dad took a few, put some in his pocket and one into his mouth.

In the Macnamaras' field, I felt safe as we stood in small groups before the bonfire, murmuring quietly as English people do, hearing my dad's deep, calm voice coming from the group next to mine. A neighbour came to each group, handing out sparklers and lighting them, their white fizz illuminating our smiling faces. We stood back to watch the firework display—Catherine Wheels, Roman Candles, and a few small rockets that fizzled across the star-spun sky. This was our autumn ritual, our coming together through the crunch of fallen leaves to gather before the fire, in anticipation of winter, faces aglow. Walking back to the house behind my parents, my father's lit cigarette bounced up and down in the blackness.

Now, on this Guy Fawkes night, my mind went spinning back to memory after memory with each bonfire and firework display Jane and I passed until we arrived in the stone courtyard and parked in front of my tiny stone cottage in the darkness.

"It's adorable," Jane said, and it really was.

I spent ten quiet days in my new home. I registered for the dole in Trowbridge, developed a routine for hitching to the local shops and back, and discovered country walks across lush meadows, where Jersey cows with huge brown eyes and long eyelashes chewed the cud, looking up lazily as I passed. I called my family every day from the phone box in the hallway of the main farmhouse, where the farmer, Phil, and his pregnant, freckled wife, Cathy, were bringing up their blonde toddler. Cathy was a permanent smiling fixture in the oversize country kitchen, and I worried that she could hear my phone conversations. I had yet to meet the tenants in the other half of the farmhouse, or those in the white cottages up the hill, but I got the feeling there was a community here, and I wondered how I would fit in.

My mother and I talked more often than we had for years as the coins clanked one by one into the machine. I told her about my new cottage and my new black kitten, Molly, rescued from a squat near Lucy's place in London. She told me she was relieved I had a home. She told me, "He is fine, he's the same, there's no need to come home."

And then there was a reason: Kate called to tell me the doctor had said our father had two weeks left to live.

I hitched a lift from right outside the farm, and a kind man, around my father's age, drove me further than he'd been going, all the way to Exeter. At the train station he pressed money into my hand, insisting I take it to pay my fare. Gazing out of the window at the happy families on the winding stretch of beach as the train snaked its way along the south coast of Devon, I thought of the men who had come to my aid in recent weeks as I made my journey back to my father. They had been kinder to me than many a Greenham woman, and I wondered if men were really that bad, after all. As I watched a young father bend down to pick up a child who had fallen over on the beach, I felt a twinge of guilt for wanting my dad to read such radical writers as Andrea Dworkin, and then a horrible thought caught in my throat and made me feel nauseous: with my recent espousal of radical feminism, did my dad think I didn't love him? On my last visit home, my mother had said that being a lesbian was about hating men and I told her, it's not that, it's about loving women. But was that what they both really thought? My mind was still spinning in a riot of confusion and sadness when I arrived in the hippie market town of Totnes, debarked the train, and stood with my thumb out at the side of the road leading finally to Stoke Fleming.

In the new family home, the five of us spent two sad, tense weeks together, taking it in turn to spend time with my father to give my mother a short reprieve to take a shower, eat a meal, or have a cup of tea.

She sat beside him on the bed almost constantly, stroking his forehead, holding him in her arms, silently weeping where he couldn't see.

The day after I arrived, my father called me into his bedroom, where he was sitting up in bed, his brow furrowed in pain, and asked me to play my guitar to him. "It will help distract me. You always played so beautifully."

I went to Sarah's room to borrow her guitar and, even though I hadn't touched mine in years, when I tuned Sarah's I missed my guitar's soft resonance and felt bad that I hadn't kept up my playing so that I could perform for my father now. I walked back into the bedroom almost ashamed, and nervous, too. I started with an easy Spanish ballad, then did the best I could from memory of John Williams' "Cavatina." As I struggled to remember the notes, I regretted that Martin had stopped me playing guitar, but looking up, I saw that my father was enjoying it anyway. His eyes were closed and he was smiling, which emboldened me to play louder, with more confidence. I got all the way through "Cavatina" without a hitch, and when I finished he clapped, gently, then put his fingers to his temples.

"Do you have a headache? Shall I try and massage it?" I asked shyly.

He opened his deep expressive eyes and nodded. I sat next to him and massaged his temples, his skin papery and hot beneath my fingers. There was not much touching in my family, and I felt awkward to be touching him and hopeful that I could relieve the pain. When I was done, I sat on the bed and simply held his hand. He said that his body felt as if he had spiders crawling under his skin.

My father had an agreement with the doctor that once it got too painful, the doctor would administer a drug to speed the process along. This shouldn't have been a surprise to me, given my dad's membership of Exit, but it came as a shock. I did my best to see it as a reasonable thing to do, when the pain was so great, when the end was so near anyway, but I was tripped up by fantastical thoughts, *What if he lives for longer than anyone expects? What if he starts to get better? What if they find a cure?*

Meanwhile, thanks to the morphine, my father dreamed of beautiful gardens, and joked, "If that's heaven, I'm fine with going there." We knew it was a joke because our dad did not believe in God or heaven, but I hoped there was a beautiful garden waiting for him nonetheless, where he could be free of pain and enjoy the birds and rivers and flowers and blue sky, none of which he would ever see again, now that it was November, the air cool and the trees shaken loose of their leaves, preparing for the long night of winter. I really didn't know what to think and just did as we all ended up doing, honouring our father's wishes, weeping in private, and trying to hold it together for Sarah.

After we had been together a week, my father gave us each something special. When it was my turn, I sat on the edge of the bed, and he handed me some wooden rosary beads that had attached to them a St. Christopher's and a small metal cross, both with stains, possibly blood. I knew it might be blood because these were the rosary beads that a dying German soldier had given to my grandfather in the trenches during World War I as he bled to death in young Arthur's terrified arms. I felt so honoured I could barely speak. I was proud of my grandfather for sending back the medals he received after his war service, unopened, keeping instead this painful reminder of the brutality of that war on the young, untrained men who fought it. It meant the world to me, a peace activist, the political child, my father's rebel daughter.

After almost two weeks together taking care of my father, cooking him meals, keeping him company, watching TV with him, and waiting in the unfamiliar living room downstairs when the doctor or nurse came to see him, we decided that we should each take a break. Kate was missing her husband, John, and without my Greenham friends I felt like a bee that had lost its hive. We agreed that I should go first, and, instead of returning to the camp or to my new cottage, where I knew no one, I arranged to visit the lovely Sally, the animal rights activist who had lived at Porton Down with Zee before they moved to Greenham, and was my only Greenham friend who regularly called to see how I was. She had just moved to a village in Dorset, about a hundred miles away.

The morning I was set to leave, I went into my father's room to tell him goodbye, and he said, "In God's name, what are you wearing? You look like the back end of a bus."

I was wearing my favourite pale grey overalls that were loose and comfortable and made me feel safe from the eyes of men. I left his room quietly wounded. He called me back upstairs, took my hand, and apologized. I didn't know which was worse, the insult, or the apology. I was not used to seeing tears of regret in his eyes. I said it's okay, even though I felt devastated. I wanted him to be proud of me no matter what I was wearing. And to me, to Al, and to my Greenham friends, I had a super cool look, and I wanted him to see that, too. I kissed him goodbye and told him I'd be back tomorrow.


JUST SEEING SALLY'S bright Mohican as the bus pulled into the station brought relief; I didn't feel abnormal anymore, I felt at home. I wondered if we would sleep in the same bed tonight, if she would hold me, and if we would even make love as we had once or twice before.

Back at her stone cottage, we ate dinner with her flatmate at the wooden kitchen table, the soft yellow light of the woodstove dancing on the walls, as Sally listened quietly to me talk about the past two weeks. She was rolling the last spliff for the night before we headed off to bed, when there was a knock at the door. She opened it to find a policeman standing there.

"Is Stephanie Davies here?" he asked. "Her family is trying to reach her."

"That's me," I said.

"Your father is very sick. You need to go home immediately," he said.

I asked him how he found me, and he said that the local police station had received a call from my sister begging them to deliver a message to this address. I wondered how Kate knew which police station to call, then realized, abruptly, that I didn't leave an address and Sally didn't have a phone, so it must have taken Kate time to find me, and things could be even worse by now. It was eleven at night, and the trains and buses would not be running.

"I have to hitch," I said to Sally.

"That's not safe," she said.

"Let me see what I can do," the policeman said, and he went outside briefly, and then returned. "Miss Davies, we have just got permission from HQ to drive you home. We'll take you to your father."

And so I found myself in the back of a police car, its siren wailing as it crossed southwest England, a policewoman in the passenger seat handing me cigarette after cigarette as I smoked and looked at the night sky, the yellow-lit roundabouts, the silhouettes of the trees on the distant hills, the roads getting narrower and narrower as we got farther and farther away from the city of Exeter and closer to the rural hills of the South Hams rolling down to the tumultuous sea. The police officers were kind and thoughtful and the driver drove as fast as he could, putting on his siren to race around the roundabouts at the edges of towns. The policewoman gently asked me questions, but I gave one-word answers, so she stopped. I accepted her cigarettes with gratitude, wondering if they knew I was a Greenham woman. I was so used to the police being my enemy, and yet here they were, going out of their way for me. I realized that just like the men who helped get me back from France and home to Devon, they would be just as kind if they knew I was a Greenham woman, that tonight we were all just human beings. Losing a father is one of the most dreadful moments in anyone's life, and I could see they felt for me. I appreciated their kindness, but had no words to express it.

Two hours later, we pulled up the drive to the family home and I spilled through the front door.

"Why didn't you leave a number?" Kate said in greeting.

"I only left this morning," I said.

"Well, he decided to go tonight. It took me hours to find you," she said as she turned to walk purposefully out of the house toward the police car. I felt guilty for putting her to such trouble and also cared for, and this almost made me weep. Though I didn't know it now, Kate was to become, as we grew older, the person who understood me the most— my indispensable ally, my biggest champion, my closest of friends.

"How is he?"

"He's in a coma. I'm going to thank the police officers."

I was numb to the tips of my fingers. Would I never hear his comforting voice again?

Mother was coming down the stairs, her face white. "He decided to go this evening. He didn't know you were going away for the night."

"But I told him this morning when I said goodbye."

"Well, he didn't understand it, somehow. He thought you'd be back. And he didn't want to wait any longer. When I told him you weren't here, he said, 'Tell Stephie I love her.'"


ALL FOUR OF us sat at my father's bedside, watching him breathe. Sarah was asleep, or not, in the adjoining room. When at last he let out his last breath, everyone was weeping, sobbing uncontrollably.

Everyone but me. I could not feel my body. I could not feel my face. I was completely numb and was terrified to feel a thing because I didn't understand why he chose this night, this time, when I was not around.

"Cry, Stephanie! Cry! Why don't you cry?" my mother screamed at me.

IT WOULD BE thirty years before I summoned the courage to ask Kate what happened while I was racing across the countryside in the police car, desperate to see my dad one last time. She told me he met with each of them, in turn, and he told Kate that she had been a wonderful daughter. She said to him that she was going to have a baby, even though she wasn't even pregnant, because she wanted to give him a parting gift, and didn't know what else to say—a gift that my mother would take away from him almost immediately by telling him Kate wasn't actually pregnant yet. He said to her, too, "Tell Stephie I love her," the five small words I have treasured over the decades, struggling nonetheless to let go of the feeling of rejection from that devastating night, wondering why he didn't wait for me.

I would eventually find a sense of peace, with the help of a skilled therapist in Brooklyn and the teachings of the Buddhist poet, monk, and peace activist, Thich Nhat Hanh. I told Kate I had lived for thirty years with a terror of the power of needles, that my wife knew to switch off the radio whenever the word *euthanasia* came on, and how I took to heart the doctor's instructions to our family that we were to speak of this to nobody, interpreting this as a great family secret, and seeing the doctor as a criminal covering his tracks for a deadly, ill-advised act requested by a depressed and desperate man. Kate would lift that misperception from my shoulders in one miraculous transatlantic conversation.

"That doctor is one of my greatest heroes," she said. "He visited our father at home every day, and they talked for hours. He grew to like him and respect him and they developed a friendship. He took him seriously. He risked his license and reputation to help our dad die a painless, dignified death. He deserves a medal."

ANYONE WHO HAS lost someone close to them will understand how we felt when my father eventually let go and left us for good. They will know about the silences, the weeping, the yawning gulf that opens up inside the chest as you wake in the mornings and, with a jolt to the heart, suddenly remember what has happened, a gulf that threatens never to close. They will know what it is like to see a loved one take their last breath, the silence that descends, the strange relief, the unnerving sense of calm that comes before the flurry of emotion and activity, the weeping, the sobbing, the arranging of the funeral.

How would I fit into my family without his understanding winks, his quiet encouragement, his wise words, his gentle guidance? Much as I rebelled against his old-fashioned perceptions of what women should be and do, he was the only one in the family who understood why I lived at a peace camp outside a United States military base; he was the one who, when I was sixteen, turned the car around and drove away from the dentist when I told him I didn't want braces on my teeth to straighten them in the American way, saying, "If you don't want them, don't get them. You're beautiful just as you are." Random, comforting memories of his constant, calming presence visited me.

But death had stolen him, and now I would never gain his approval for trying to change the world as he wanted to change the world. I would never get to show him as the years passed how I matured, how I came to replace a radical ideology with one of kindness, how my hatred of men would shift to a love for all humanity, how I would find lasting love with a woman in New York he would have spent hours talking with about the wrongs of the world and how to put them right. Nor would he have the chance to hear about how much I had been harassed, put down, and discriminated against for being a woman, a lesbian, and a Greenham woman; he would not hear how I brought a courtroom to its feet, cheering and clapping; he would never have the chance to listen to my experiences and perhaps change from them, too. But my shift began here, with his dying, his final gift, perhaps, starting me on the journey that brought me back from the radical brink, ready to reconnect with the possibility of goodness in all human beings.

# Chapter Seventeen

## "EVER FALLEN IN LOVE (WITH SOMEONE YOU SHOULDN'T'VE)?" THE BUZZCOCKS

A FEW DAYS before my father's funeral, I arrived at Al's in the early evening and stood on her doorstep, my body frozen in shock, my mind filled with images of my father's lone coffin in a dark, unfamiliar church in Dartmouth waiting for the trip to the graveyard in St. Mary Bourne, and my grieving family weeping in an equally unfamiliar house. But my heart was hopeful as Al opened the door, a bouquet of roses in her hand, and took me into her arms, kissing me on the lips. I thought the flowers were for my father, but when I tumbled into the living room I saw she had placed candles all around and romantic music was playing.

She handed me a glass of wine and I sat down on the sofa, taking sips from the glass, tasting nothing. I watched Al in the kitchen as she prepared our evening meal, singing along enthusiastically to the music. I had called her with the news, so she knew my father was dead, but she didn't once ask about him or the family or me, and I could find no words to begin a conversation about it all. When it was time to eat, I sat at the table and picked at the edges of the chickpea curry she had made me, wondering why she had chosen my dad's favourite music, Ella, to listen to. When we went to bed she wanted to make love, and for the first time I pulled away from her. She turned her back to me, and I slept, shivering in my own arms.

I woke up wanting to cry, but found that I was covered in a thick, soft, gelatinous cloud that made me unable to reach or touch anything around me or breathe deeply enough to let the sobs even take shape. I wondered if I would suffocate. I got up to find Al in the kitchen making coffee. She turned to kiss me, then told me about her meeting with Zephyr that morning, the song that was forming in her head, and the concert she was performing at in a week's time. It was as if nothing extraordinary had happened at all, and I wondered for a moment if I was making a big deal out of nothing by feeling sad and numb. Then I wondered if I would ever feel anything ever again.

"Al, will you come to the funeral with me?" I asked. It was the first time I had said the word "funeral" out loud, and I almost had to cough the word out into the room. It was also the first time I had asked Al for anything.

She handed me a cup of coffee, the soya milk curdling ominously in the mug, and we both sat down on the sofa. "You're leaving tomorrow, right?" she said.

"Yes, I am going in the afternoon. The funeral's the next day."

"Sorry, I can't. Got too much on," she said. "And maybe you should go today instead? It's not really working out, you've clearly got a lot to deal with, and I've got stuff to do. Maybe I can come to the farm right afterwards if you like? Romantic walks in the moonlight?"

She took my face in her hands to kiss me on the lips, and I pulled away. She put her coffee cup down and stood up, frowning, "You've got to think about life, Steph." She took my hand in hers to pull me up. "We're alive, we're young, we're in love."

I pulled my hand away, stood up, and walked quietly into the bedroom. The tears had reached my shoulders and were lodged there, gripping onto me in tight knots of grief. I knew Al was being unkind. I knew she was being unfair. But I was terrified of losing her. So I didn't say a word and just started packing.

I arrived at the funeral in a convoy of dark cars from Andover, where we'd spent the night at the home of Bruce, the student my father had taken under his wing a few years earlier, all five of us slept in the same room, somehow, crammed together in one big bundle of grief, my mother clinging on to me as she slept. Seeing the spire of St. Peter's church as we drove down Andover hill into St. Mary Bourne, I thought: my dad never went to church, yet here he was now, waiting for us all. We walked together through the iron gate and over the ancient flagstones leading to the arched church doorway—the last time he was in this doorway, I remembered with a jolt, was when Kate got married, radiant in her long white dress and with flowers in her hair, my father proudly at her side as he prepared to accompany her down the aisle. Now the doorway was filled with family members from up north—my dad's only sister, from Accrington, and her family, our cousins, aunts, and uncles from my mum's side, waiting to walk behind us down the aisle before we took our seats at the front of the church. The pews were packed with Testbourne teachers and students, caretakers and dinner ladies, as well as villagers and dad's university friends. One of his teachers, Pat Kettle, gave the eulogy, banging his hand on the coffin as he spelled out each letter of the school motto, INTEGRITY, to expound upon my dad's qualities. I flinched each time he hit it and wanted him to stop. Afterwards in the graveyard, it was a blur of handshakes, hugs, kisses, and weeping. I wondered if Cluny was there, or even Martin—then suddenly his mother was in front of me, taking me in a warm embrace. We both wept as she held me, and I wondered if she would ever forgive me for abandoning her son and what she must think of my Mohican, which I had flattened to fit in as best I could.

THE NEXT DAY, I returned to Stowford Farm and found that my flatmate, Val, had gone to Australia for a month and might not return. So I was alone and glad of it. But I was not as solitary as I would have liked because my cottage faced onto a cobblestone courtyard frequently travelled by the young, blond farmer with his sporty moustache and the stocky, red-haired farmhand, both of whom waved at me whenever they saw me at the kitchen window washing dishes. I sat in the window seat of the miniscule living room, the fire crackling at my side, and every day around noon, I watched two ducks waddle across the courtyard from different directions, meet in the middle to face each other for half an hour, then waddle off to their separate destinations, as if they were a quarrelling couple trying to work things out, but never could.

It did occur to me—and I might have taken it as a sign—that Al and I might never work things out either, yet even though Al did not come to visit and did not call or return my calls, I could not entertain the idea that I might never see her again. I was so benumbed that late one night, I wrote in my notebook: *I deserve to be raped. I deserve to be hit. I deserve to suffer.* I didn't know why I wrote these things, and I stared at the words in disgust and confusion, digging my fingernails into my palms, trying to break through the thick cloud that refused to let go, trying to feel something besides guilt. I felt responsible, somehow, for my father's death.

Didn't he start to get ill just after I left for Greenham, just as soon as I embraced radical feminism? Did an umbilical cord sever that grey day at Greenham when I refused to go back to the life he hoped for me—to be a successful lawyer or journalist who could support the Greenham women, rather than being one myself? By cutting that cord, did I drain the life from him? I wondered if Al sensed something terrifying in the feelings that threatened to overwhelm me last time I saw her, perhaps she feared being overwhelmed herself, and saw the true me, someone evil, cruel, selfish. Perhaps the pain and humiliation of violence could shock me back into life. Perhaps rape was something I deserved for the upheavals I had caused as I struggled to free myself from male power.

At least I had found a sanctuary here at the farm. I walked for hours on public footpaths through paddocks and meadows, along winding, gurgling streams, past stone cottages, brick mansions, and through jostling herds of bullocks and sweet-tempered Jersey cows—without meeting a single other person. I found a tree next to the river in the farmer's field, hidden from view, whose trunk was curved in exactly the right way to hold me in an embrace over the steady flow of water, and I stood there for hours watching the light reflecting on the water's surface, the waving water weeds, the occasional shadow of a fish gliding far below. On the way to the pub in St. Mary Bourne, my father and I sometimes stopped on the bridge to gaze down at the lush green grasses waving at us from the waters. He would never walk again to the pub, never look down at the water, never again smile at me. I wanted to fall like a leaf into the stream below.

I walked early in the morning or late in the afternoon, hoping to avoid the hippies who occupied the West Wing of the farmhouse, the farmer and his wife in the East Wing, and the farmer's mother with her headscarf tied under her chin and green wellington boots who lived next door to me in the adjoining cottage.

I would have left the house less often if the payphone hadn't been located in the lobby of the main farmhouse and I hadn't been obsessed with Al. I crossed the courtyard several times a day to call her, my head down, trying to hide my red-rimmed eyes under my long fringe. I dialled

Al's number and listened to the interminable ring ring, imagining the click of her picking it up and her deep voice at the end of the line, but it never happened. I agonized over why she wasn't calling: was she not well, had her phone been cut off, did she lose my number? The more she didn't call the more desperate I became. More than once a note appeared on my doorstep, delivered by one of the hippies or Cathy, and my heart leapt. But they were messages that Sally had called, not Al. I was disappointed and at the same time comforted that Sally was thinking of me—but I didn't call her back. Grief for my father was superseded by despair over Al, and I wouldn't have known what to say to Sally about any of it. I was inconsolable.

I called Al's friend—and now mine—Ming de Nasty, a photographer. Ming told me she had seen Al just the week before and had taken pictures of her in concert.

"Her phone just rings and rings," I said. "Is it broken?"

"She just called me last night. She's a strange one, that Al."

I was given a reprieve from my obsessing the following night when I heard a knock at the door and opened it to a smiling woman wearing thick-rimmed glasses. She put her hand out to shake mine.

"I'm Annette," she said. "I live in the farmhouse. We're all going to the pub. Want to come?"

I had been eating a baked potato and reading Adrienne Rich by the fire, and did not want to go. But over Annette's shoulder I could see the hippies climbing into their battered cars and one of them, a young woman with long straight hair, waved to me. I didn't want to be rude, so I put on my boots and followed Annette to her van. As she drove us to the village of Bradford-on-Avon, I learned that she was a printer and had a workshop in the barn, and I felt a bit of interest in seeing her work.

At the pub, we joined her friends who had found seats round the roaring fireplace. She asked me what I wanted to drink, and went to the bar to tell the red-haired farmhand, who was getting the first round. When he returned from the bar, he handed me my pint and said his name was Jimmy.

"Val told us about your dad," he said in a Scottish accent. "I'm really sorry."

"Thanks." I took a sip of my beer and, looking at their earnest faces glowing in the orange light of the flames, I started to feel glad I had come.

I BEGAN VISITING Annette in her studio, Jimmy in his cottage, and the hippies in their living room, where they smoked joints and drank beer around a huge fireplace in which they burned logs as big as tree trunks. They were all kind and funny, and interested in my Greenham stories. I told my new friends the radiation story, but that's all it was—a story, and quite a good one that elicited surprise, shock, and admiration. When I told it, my heart fluttered and I felt nauseous, but the reactions of my audience made me feel heroic, and the uncomfortable feelings soon faded.

One wintry morning, Jimmy knocked on my door and asked if I'd like him to show me around. I glanced over his shoulder and saw that the sky was a piercing blue as the sunshine danced on the frosted landscape. I scrambled into my boots and coat, wrapped a thick scarf around my neck, stepped out in the crisp air, and took a deep breath, which as I breathed out immediately formed a cloud.

"Lovely," I managed, but what I thought was my father wouldn't see days like this again, and I would never again hold Al's hand proudly as we walked together in the sunshine.

Jimmy took me on a route I would never have found without him—up a steep hill and along a single-track road, where we met a farmer on his tractor and had to squash into the prickly hedgerows while the tractor squeezed past, the driver waving as he did so, nodding at Jimmy in recognition. Then down an equally steep hill, this time along a dark, narrow path formed by the hooves of cows, who had walked the same path, Jimmy told me, for decades. Then along a flat plain, the river winding through its centre like a curving spine. We clambered over a wooden stile and walked confidently through a herd of brown bullocks, who looked as if they were frowning at us, nothing like the soft gaze of the Jerseys at our farm. But they let us pass, as Jimmy said and I knew they would, from my walks in my childhood village. We climbed a steep hill at the end of the plain and made our way through a copse of gnarled, ancient trees until we reached a ridge.

I turned to look back down at the landscape we had left, turning now from white to green and brown as the sun melted the last remnants of the frost, the bullocks like pieces in a fuzzy felt landscape, stuck onto a bucolic scene by a child's hand. I followed Jimmy along a dirt lane under a canopy of leafless trees, shards of sunlight spotlighting the ground around us, highlighting piles of dried leaves, twisted roots, the occasional grey squirrel scampering past. The haunting cry of rooks flying above us in black circles, flapping as they settled together on the topmost branches of distant trees, took me back to my St. Mary Bourne walks along our country lanes.

Jimmy didn't talk much, except to point out a landmark hill in the distance, or to say who lived in a particular stone cottage with thick white smoke pouring out of its chimney, or to tell me that the red squirrels had almost all gone now, thanks to the arrival of the grey ones. I enjoyed his talk and also his silence and his comfort with my own. We climbed on protruding flints up the side of a flint wall next to the garden of a mansion and peered at the manicured lawns beneath us, giggling in case we were seen. I hauled myself up onto the rounded top of the wall and sat there awhile.

"What can they possibly do to me?" I said as Jimmy encouraged me to come down. "They won't have armed guards."

"No, but they might have vicious guard dogs. Just don't jump down and get us both in trouble. You're not at Greenham now."

I gazed at a white gazebo standing in the centre of the lawn in front of me, regal, elegant, and empty. I imagined parties and laughter and dancing on lazy evenings in the height of summer. I sighed as I lowered myself down, the scene disappearing behind the stone wall in front of my face.

When we got home, I realized we had walked for five hours and I was ravenous. I invited Jimmy to join me for lunch and served a leek and potato soup I'd already made and a thick peasant bread warmed in the oven. We ate from our laps by the fire in the living room. As we ate, he told me how at night, sometimes, he got out of bed and walked into the barn and snuggled up between the cows to feel their warmth as they huddled together as one. Even though I was vegan and felt sorry that the cows were there at all, Jimmy's love of nature and the farm animals was palpable, and I felt a strong affinity for him. The white cloud seemed to have lifted somewhat, and I began to look forward to seeing him.

Then Christmas was upon me, and I had to accept the fact that Al was not going to show up and spend it with me. I didn't want to risk an argument with my mother in Devon about what I was not doing with my life, so I gratefully accepted an invitation from the Goth Greenham couple, Trish and Trina, to spend the holiday with them in Manchester, but was even more grateful when this first Christmas without my father was over and I could regain the solitude of my cottage, the black sky hiding my thoughts, the only sounds to disturb my grief the crackling fire and the lowing of the dairy cows.

But I didn't quite return home to full solitude because my mother had decided to visit on New Year's Eve. As she pulled up outside the cottage in the red Mitsubishi car my father had bought just months before he died, a small spattering of snow was falling, quickly turning to sleet, not settling. As she got out of the car she looked as if she had lost weight, appearing childlike as she clumsily picked up her bags, locked the door of the car, dropped her keys, picked them up, and made her way to my heavy wooden door, where I was standing in my thick woollen socks. We hugged, awkwardly, and I took her coat and led her into the living room where flames were dancing in the hearth, creating a small arc of warmth, not quite enough to heat the miniscule room.

As we huddled close to the fireplace, Molly in my lap, and drank tea, my mother told me about Sarah's new school (she was making friends), Robert's new girlfriend (she disapproved), Kate's job as a teacher in Cambridge (it was going wonderfully). I didn't have to worry about what to say about myself because she didn't ask me anything, and so I nodded and listened and gazed at the fire and missed my father until it was time for dinner and we headed off to the pub, where Jimmy, Annette, and the two hippie couples were waiting for us by the roaring fire to eat a New Year's pub dinner.

My mother disapproved of my vegan meal of roast potatoes and vegetables. "You're too skinny, you need protein, you need calcium. You'll end up with osteoporosis when you get to my age," she said as she tucked into her lamb with mint sauce.

She chatted with my new friends about the farm, clotted cream, and the weather, my friends drinking more pints of dark beer as my mother drank more glasses of red wine, talking animatedly, as she did so, about my father's achievements as a headmaster, a father, a husband. I knew she was grieving and I thought I should be glad she could even talk about him, but each mention of his name sent a knife through my heart.

The conversation had turned to favourite films when all of a sudden my mother turned to me and screeched, in a sing-song voice, "I hate men!" I looked at my new friends' startled faces, feeling just as startled myself. "That should be your motto, you know, from *Kiss Me Kate*, the musical. 'I hate men'!" She sang a few lines from the song loudly, laughing gleefully at me.

I didn't know how to stop her.

"Because she's a lesbian," my mother added, looking at my new friends, to clarify.

I hadn't told them yet, because I was afraid that would make them not like me. I glanced at Jimmy, who was looking away.

I didn't want him to think I hated him, so I said, quietly, "I don't hate men, Mum, it's not about that, you know it isn't," then shrank into the white cloud that had been waiting for me all along.

Annette winked at me, turned to my mother, and asked cheerfully, "What kind of art do you like?"

The conversation continued as if nothing weird had happened. Nobody spurned me, nobody turned away, nobody seemed to care that I was a lesbian or that my mother thought I hated men. So I remained hopeful they were all still my friends. We got home before midnight and drank champagne in the hippie household until the clock chimed twelve times, and we all kissed and embraced before my mother and I headed unsteadily across the courtyard back to the cottage through the light sleet.

I had barely spoken all evening. As my mother made her way up the narrow steep staircase to Val's room, she turned to me and said, "I don't know that you can have ever loved your father, you know, being a lesbian."

Years later, I would realize my mother was lashing out at everyone and everything in her grief, like a wounded lioness, but the shock was so great I felt there was no choice but to take complete refuge in the white cloud, to forget my small forays back into the world. Before I fell asleep, I opened the window to let in the sharp, cold air, the night scents, and the light of the falling sleet. I imagined myself drifting above the cottage, my mother, and the farm, floating away past the moon and the stars, into nothingness.

But then immediately after I waved her off the next day—nervous at finding her way, a crumpled map open at her side—I heard a knock and opened the door to find Jimmy, short and stocky in boots and a thick sweater, his ginger hair partially covered by a woollen bobble hat, a walking stick in his hand.


MY ATTEMPTS TO reach Al had dwindled to once a week phone calls. I knew the phone would just ring, but I couldn't help myself. I felt there had been a gross injustice, but instead of being angry about it, I wanted to right it by making her see the error of her ways and come back to me. I called Ming, and when she suggested I go and see Zephyr, the other half of On the Rag, I travelled to Moseley the very next day. Zephyr invited me to sit on embroidered Indian cushions in her sunny living room, poured me herbal tea, and got right to the point.

"Al has no sense of reality." She looked me in the eye. "We slept together more than a year ago, and she still insists we will end up together one day. Even though I have a boyfriend, even though I have told her a million times I am not interested, that I am more straight than gay. She doesn't listen to reason. She's not a good person to depend on."

"She told me never to rely on her," I said, wondering if this pain was my due for not listening to her in the first place. "But, you know, I had no idea, that my dad would die," my voice faltered. "And that I would . . ."

"That you'd want her to behave like a normal person?"

I was startled at the criticism and also refreshed by Zephyr's directness, a quality I knew Al loved about her—and, presumably, my inability to express myself clearly was one of the things she didn't like so much about me.

"She's living a fantasy rock star life," Zephyr said.

*Was I just a groupie?* I wondered. I had fallen for the captain of the football team, and now the person I worshipped was a punk rock singer in a band. Did I like to be an audience? Did their fame make me feel as if I were someone special, too?

"I'm sorry to say this because she is my friend and I do love her, but really you're better off without her."

We moved on to other topics—Greenham, my court case, the farm, her days at Yellow Gate, her latest song. By the time I left, Zephyr and I were fast friends, and I saw Zephyr as a bright star and everyone else, including Al, as orbiting planets, lucky to be caught in her field. Maybe Al was not such a big deal after all.


STILL, THE WHITE cloud followed me everywhere all winter, making it difficult to feel, touch, taste, or smell anything. Finally, I visited a doctor and explained my condition in her sterile office, hoping she could offer me a pill, or at least some understanding.

She leaned forward in her chair and patted me on the knee. "You know at times like this, I find the best solution is to have a glass of sherry. Why not get yourself a bottle when you leave here today and have just one glass a night, and see if that helps?"

I was surprised and pleased to have such an easy prescription. That night, I poured a glass and sipped the sweet, thick drink as I sat alone by the fire. This was my mother's favourite drink as she prepared dinner at home, while I sat on the stairs playing my guitar to her, and my father lay resting, no doubt in pain, in the adjoining living room. I broke down in heaving sobs. The next day, I gave the sherry to Annette.

I tried a homeopath, a small, cheerful woman who lived in an elegant townhouse in Bath and who asked me things like whether I liked thunderstorms (I loved them); whether I liked hot or cold food (hot); and my favourite time of day (twilight, as the sun sets, the sky turns pink, and everything, including magic, feels possible). She scribbled down comments as I spoke, and at the end of our session told me that homeopathy worked on the physical, emotional, and spiritual planes.

I nodded.

She talked about energy and nature and spirit and handed me a paper envelope containing a cluster of sugar coated pills I had to put under my tongue and let dissolve, just once. I took the pills that night, rolling the tiny balls under my tongue, hopefully. When I fell asleep that night, I dreamed of a court case where my mother and I were on trial. The judge was yelling and banging his mallet, the members of the jury were shrieking and arguing, and my mother and I were rising toward the ceiling, above the fray, holding each other, disappearing through the high domed roof, which parted as we rose and floated into the bright blue sky.

I woke up abruptly and bent over to look out of the window, as I always did. The sky seemed bluer than usual, the rushing water was clearer than usual, the grass was a bright, bright green, and I saw, for the first time, the snowdrops that were already appearing, white harbingers of colour to come, the daffodils, crocuses, and primroses just days away. I dug my nails into my palm and it hurt, so I stopped. The water in the bathtub was fresh, and the soap smelled delightful. My morning coffee was strong, sweet, and just right, jolting me awake with the welcome rush of caffeine. I was back in the world.

# Chapter Eighteen
## "DON'T GIVE UP" PETER GABRIEL AND KATE BUSH

WHEN THE LETTER finally appeared from the solicitor, in March, summoning me and my co-defendants to appear at Reading Crown Court on charges of criminal damage to two fences at AWRE (Atomic Weapons Research Establishment) Aldermaston, I was taken aback by who it was addressed to: Stephanie Bell.

I sat on the stone step to my cottage and wondered who this Stephanie Bell was. I could remember every detail of what she had done that night, but it was as if I were remembering a particularly memorable film, and the Stephanie of the film was an entirely different person from me. She was someone with a father, a girlfriend, a community, and a driving purpose to save the world from war. Now, I had a part-time job at the Feminist Archive at Bath University, I rarely went to Greenham, and the only woman I still saw from that night at Aldermaston was Zee. And that was only because when my flatmate, Val, decided to stay in Australia, Penny from Blue Gate moved in, and she and Zee had become lovers. But they lived mostly at Blue Gate, visiting the cottage mainly to sign on the dole, and when Zee came, she and I never talked about the fact that we may have been radiated, she never mentioned the monk that she feared was chasing her through the centuries, and neither of us discussed that the scientists had told us we might develop cancer in twenty years.

The tests we'd had at the NRPB said we hadn't been contaminated, but we didn't believe them. Why would we believe a government agency testing us for radiation when we'd broken into another government agency that should not have exposed us to radiation? We'd started to do our own investigations with journalists and scientists more than willing to help, but then my father had become gravely ill, I'd moved to the farm, and all thoughts of tests and radiation and preparing for court had taken a back seat, while Zee, Jane, Karen, and Maggie scattered into their disparate lives. Between us we let the whole thing drop, because it was too terrifying, because we didn't know what to do next, because we didn't really want to know if we'd been radiated, and because I couldn't think about me dying in some hypothetical future when my dad really was dying, right then.

Sometimes I'd half-wake in the middle of the night with my heart and mind racing like galloping horses as I worried about whether my body was riddled with radiation, but when I woke up in the morning, it felt like a bad dream, and I'd go about my day as if nothing had happened. But now I had a letter from the lawyer making it all very real, and I couldn't ignore it any more.

I went back into the cottage and rifled through the top drawer of the writing table I'd inherited from Val and found a crumpled note with the name "Trevor Brown, Councillor" on it. This was the Newbury Councillor who was fired from Aldermaston for rocking the boat about safety concerns—something about the workers breathing in too much plutonium, I couldn't quite remember exactly.

I wrote to him, he called right back, and a week later, I was standing on a quiet road in front of Trevor Brown's suburban home on the outskirts of Newbury. I looked around and thought about the time I went to rescue Grace from her abusive husband in Wigan, which was the last time I had been on a cul-de-sac like this, perfect homes with pristine lawns edged with narrow, identical flower beds. It was thanks to Grace, in great part, that I had freed myself of Martin. I wondered how she was doing, if she had ever found a safe place to live, or if she ended up going back to her abusive husband, like so many women do. That was exactly a year ago, and today I was unrecognizable, even to myself, about to meet a Councillor about possibly being exposed to radiation after breaking into England's premier atomic weapons research establishment, and facing time in jail.

A man with silver hair and beard, a tweed jacket, and metal-rimmed glasses opened the door before I had time to press the doorbell. We had that awkward moment English people often have when we meet, not knowing whether to shake hands or not, bobbing from side to side a little, our arms loose before us. Our bodies decided not to shake hands after all, but Mr. Brown put his hand on my shoulder as he guided me into the living room.

I looked down at the cream, plush carpet and at my boots, which seemed enormous in this tidy setting. "Shall I take them off?"

"No, no need at all." He ushered me to sit on the leather sofa, and I was grateful, because my boots took ages to unlace.

He took his place opposite me in an armchair next to a glass-topped table with tea and biscuits laid out for us. I took a digestive biscuit, feeling a sliver of guilt because it wasn't vegan, and watched as he carefully poured tea from the teapot into a china cup on a saucer. He had laid press cuttings on the table in front of us, pushing back a framed photograph of a smiling woman to make room. The formality of the afternoon tea, the press clippings, and the excitement of meeting with someone to discuss something political and meaningful made me think about my teenage conversations with Cluny about apartheid, except she used rustic mugs made by local potters and eschewed saucers altogether. Perhaps she, too, was sitting down to tea right now, in her white cottage, just fifteen miles away.

Mr. Brown was probably around my dad's age. He was wearing a tie, which was slightly askew, and I imagined that he had just got back from a Council meeting.

"It started in the early sixties," he began, leaning back, forming a triangle with his forefingers and bringing the tips to his chin as he continued. "That's when I started at Aldermaston, and I knew right away that we weren't handling the plutonium correctly, but my superiors weren't interested in what I had to say about it." He leaned back and took a sip of tea.

I took out a pen and notebook and started taking notes as fast as I could.

"When I was promoted to Senior Industrial Chemist in the early seventies, I saw it as my chance to implement more stringent safety measures at last, but again, I met a brick wall. I wanted an independent expert to assess health and safety, but Aldermaston did an internal investigation instead, concluding that everything was in such good order that they actually got rid of some safety staff and put people who didn't agree with me over me. I said the investigation was a sham. That's when they got intimidating."

He stopped to take another sip of tea.

"By now I was a Liberal Councillor, and they decided to make it as difficult as they could for me to go to meetings on work time, when beforehand that hadn't been a problem. Colleagues refused to work with me. I started getting late night phone calls telling me to drop this nonsense. Cars would follow me home, sometimes, I am sure of it. That's when my wife started to get sick. With worry."

He glanced from the photograph on the table beside him to another in a gold-rimmed frame on the wall of a pretty woman in a wedding dress, a younger, handsome Trevor all suited up at her side.

"It sounds like Karen Silkwood in America," I said, referring to the nuclear power plant worker in Oklahoma who died in 1976 under mysterious circumstances after speaking out about health and safety concerns.

"I felt like Karen Silkwood," he said. "And like her, I feared for my life. I would sit in my car in a lay-by on my way home, shaking, trying to compose myself before I walked through the front door. I got nervous when I saw car headlights behind me, thinking of how she died in that car crash on her way to speak to a *New York Times* reporter. You don't want to mess with the nuclear industry, you really don't. But I felt a moral responsibility toward my constituents, some of whom worked at Aldermaston, and so I kept going. The following year, they unexpectedly agreed to do tests for atmospheric contamination and the results were just as I expected. Three workers had three to four times the permitted levels of plutonium in their lungs, and many more had a far higher exposure than was permitted under international regulations. So in 1978 the whole place was closed down."

"You got the whole place closed down?" I wished my father could see me now, scribbling down the story of this principled man, just like a journalist, just like a lawyer preparing a case.

He smiled. "Yes, after a government inquiry led by Sir Edward Pochin took place. He ended up agreeing with most of my findings and made safety recommendations that would cost millions of pounds and several years to implement. When I spoke with the NRPB—you know them, right?"

It was my turn to smile, albeit with a pang of panic in my chest. "Yes, they tested us last June. I actually brought the results to show you. But please finish your story first."

"Great," he said. "Until this inquiry, I had no idea—nobody at Aldermaston even knew—that international guidelines on the safe handling of plutonium existed. There was even a booklet that, if I'd only known about it, I could have used to back up my concerns all those years. I mean, our workers were getting exposed to plutonium in the same way miners in uranium mines in Namibia were getting exposed. No concern for safety."

"Namibia?" I said, remembering images I had seen of miners in South Africa and Namibia—the beaten down, exhausted faces, the strong backs, the total lack of recourse to justice in any way, shape, or form.

"Yes, that's where a lot of our uranium comes from. Aldermaston enriches it and makes it into plutonium here. Then they make bombs and test them in Nevada."

I let out a long breath. "I was a big anti-apartheid activist at university," I said to explain my sigh. "I know a lot about Namibia."

"Good for you," he said, and I wondered how someone so nice, with such apparently progressive views, and a Liberal Councillor, to boot, could have worked for so long in the nuclear weapons industry. "I couldn't do anything for the people in Namibia, of course," he added, apologetically.

I leaned forward and picked up one of the photocopied articles on the table before me. Staring at me was a photograph of a serious looking Trevor Brown gazing directly, almost accusingly, at the camera, a sheaf of documents in his hands. It was from *Woman Magazine*, May 1984, less than a year earlier. I skimmed over the text, which covered the story he had just told me, and my eyes landed on a quote from Mr. Brown in the last paragraph. "My wife died last May and one can only speculate to what extent worry affected her."

I glanced at her picture on the table. "I am sorry about your wife."

"As far as I am concerned, they killed her," he said. "The BBC devoted a Panorama and a Newsnight documentary to it. I was told not to talk to the press, and I said something very bland on Newsnight—something to the effect that Aldermaston had allowed secrecy to interfere with safety. This was hardly news, it was something I'd said publicly before, as a Councillor, and in other interviews. After that I was told I wasn't needed at Aldermaston anymore."

Mr. Brown gazed out of the window as a silence draped over us.

"You got justice for the workers," I said, finally.

"Yes, I did," he said. "Though it was too late for Ken Cummins. He is a worker who died of colon cancer not too long ago."

"And your wife?" I was being bold, but my dad had just died, so I felt I could ask this kind of thing.

"She died from stress, fear, and intimidation," he replied, without missing a beat.

We sat in a silence filled with the absence of Mrs. Brown.

"Do you think we could have been exposed to radiation?" I asked at long last.

Mr. Brown took a deep breath, and in one long exhale he was back in the room. "Tell me what happened." He leaned forward attentively.

I described the bin bags with radiation stickers on them, the clicking Geiger counters, the police blackmailing us into confessing to breaking in, the tests at the NRPB. I recalled the conversations with the scientists in Manchester and London and their ominous predictions for our health had we been exposed.

When I was finished, Mr. Brown said, "We buried drums of radioactive waste in different plots around the base. So it's possible that this is why the area you crawled through was restricted. Plutonium is likely found only inside the buildings, and uranium is only dangerous when mined—hence the contamination of workers in Namibia. So I don't think it likely you were exposed to anything life-threatening. Did you think to get a sample of the grass to test?"

"Yes, we tried," I said. "We went back a week later because Greenpeace told us to. There was a lot more security, though, so we couldn't get in. But that wouldn't have helped anyway. The grass had been mown down to the ground."

Mr. Brown raised one eyebrow, just like my father used to when he was sceptical. "Let me see your tests."

I handed him the Measurement Report from the NRPB, and he scanned it quickly. It was all scientific language with numbers and long scientific words, and I hadn't understood much of it. The only thing I understood from the report was, "There is no evidence to suggest that the persons, or the clothing examined, are contaminated with radionuclides."

"It seems to be good news. Except . . . this is not my field of expertise. My field was waste disposal and safety management. But I wonder why they didn't look for alpha-emitting radionuclides; that's the way you look for plutonium." He noticed my alarmed expression. "But, either way, I think it very unlikely that you would have been contaminated by alpha-emitting radionuclides in the time that you were inside the perimeter fence."

I didn't feel reassured.

Before I left I had one last question. "Mr. Brown, would you be willing to appear in court as a witness?" I held my breath, imagining the gasp of surprise from the jury as a former safety officer from Aldermaston took the stand on our behalf. But he was shaking his head before I had even finished the sentence.

"No, not that," he said. "I have had my fill of Aldermaston. And my case is still before the European Court of Human Rights. I have to focus on that."

I HITCHED TO Blue Gate, where I knew no one by the fire but Zee. The next day, we got a lift to a narrow Victorian building on a busy London street. We climbed the steep stairs to the offices of Fisher, Meredith, and Partners, where a surprisingly young, bespectacled woman in a smart blue suit introduced herself to us as Janet Hickman, our lawyer. Sitting at a polished mahogany table behind her in the conference room were Maggie, Karen, and Jane. We all hugged and laughed.

"You're still glowing," Maggie said.

"You can turn the lights off now, Janet. Just plug us into the wall," Zee said.

We dissolved in hysterical laughter. Janet, our lawyer, though, was not smiling. She was looking at her watch, and I remembered that she was offering us her services for free.

"OK ladies," she said, still standing, "I've looked over the charges and I've looked into the different defences we can use. First of all, are you all still comfortable defending yourselves in court?"

We looked at each other and nodded in unison.

"There are several 'lawful excuses' within the Criminal Damage Act you can use," Janet continued. "You have the right to use force if you believe you are preventing a greater crime; you can damage property in order to protect property belonging to yourself or another. These are defences that have been used successfully—and unsuccessfully—by a lot of Greenham women. In the instance of Aldermaston, the crime being committed was that of, for example, creating weapons that will kill people. But there are other possible crimes, too. It might be a good idea for each of you to think back to why you did it, and turn that into your defence."

Zee and I looked at each other and giggled after an awkward silence. The others soon followed.

"What's so funny?" I could see we were annoying Janet.

"We didn't really think about why we were going in," Zee said.

"We actually were headed to Abingdon to spray paint the planes and took a wrong turning," I added.

"We had no idea Aldermaston made nuclear weapons," Karen said.

"We just knew it did something bad," Maggie added.

"Well, I hope that's not the defence you're planning to present in court." Janet pulled out a chair, sat down, and leaned forward, turning from one to the other of us as she spoke, looking directly into our eyes. "Each of you will need to find a compelling reason that propelled you to take such dire risks. Compelling enough that you risked arrest and radiation. Compelling enough that you want to stand up and have your day in court. You need to come across as so passionate that you are even doing this without the help of a barrister because you want to speak for yourselves."

"We've learned a lot about Aldermaston since," I said quickly and firmly, sitting up straight, not smiling now. "We know exactly what we are going to say."

The others looked at me quizzically.

"I just met with Trevor Brown, the former safety scientist at Aldermaston, who was forced out for speaking out about safety concerns," I continued. "I just have to discuss with the others how his story fits into our defence."

I was a journalist yesterday. Today I was a lawyer. Why not? It didn't seem that hard. And perhaps something of Trevor Brown was rubbing off on me. I felt Janet wasn't taking us seriously, that she thought we were hopeless because we laughed so much. But I could be very, very serious when I wanted to be. Now that Mr. Brown had told me about the link with Namibia I felt as if I had something truly important to say.

"Well, that's great. Use what you've learned and build your case around that. It's the only chance you've got of winning." Janet took a deep breath. "The stakes are higher than I expected. The authorities have been giving longer sentences recently, and some women got nine months just last week, when a few months ago they'd have got a week, at most, or even a fine. We have to prepare for the worst-case scenario— nine months in jail." It's just what Detective Osland had said.

None of us was smiling now.


I SPENT THE next six weeks on the phone in the farmhouse lobby, talking with scientists, anti-apartheid and Greenpeace activists, academics, journalists. Sitting at the writing table by the living room fireplace, I scoured through the papers that Trevor Brown had given me and hand-wrote pages of notes, whittling them down into concise arguments. I stood in front of the mirror in the bathroom and talked out loud to convince myself of my case. I wrote to Duncan Campbell, the *New Statesman* journalist well known for his knowledge of the country's nuclear industry, but he declined to help because he'd taken a year off to "organize his papers." I received long letters from Janet explaining the process in court, with sub-headings such as "Self Defence" and "Lawful Excuse" and "Duress and Necessity" along with photocopies from books on criminal law, outlining how we were entitled to use reasonable force if the threat was imminent, to defend ourselves or a stranger, and a copy of Section 3 of the Criminal Law Act of 1967, which was central to my defence, and of the Genocide Act, important for the others.

I did my best to understand it all and to understand the order in which we should give evidence about the facts and when to mention the laws we were using in our defence. It was complex and exhilarating. Janet had sent a transcript of our conversations with the detectives Trevor Osland and Gareth Williams, and I exclaimed in indignation as I crossed out quotes and added in my own, correcting their lies.

I went over the tiny print of the legal documentation she sent with a highlighter pen, incorporating what I found into my notes until I could easily explain what the Criminal Law Act and the Criminal Damage Act allowed and didn't allow.

I still went to work at the Feminist Archive at Bath University three days a week, but I was preoccupied, and my colleagues, finding the whole thing exciting, were happy to help me practise my defence. I met with Hannah and her Mum, Mari, who knew everyone in the anti-apartheid world and who put me in touch with the Namibia Support Group. I fell asleep exhausted every night, my small black cat, Molly, with her almond eyes, stretched out next to me in the bed, the window open, the sounds of the rushing water lulling us to sleep.

One night, the night of a full moon, I opened the window wide and looked at the landscape below, the trees forming dark shadows on the lawn, an electric stillness enveloping the flowers, bushes, and stars, the whole universe captured in the moon's piercing gaze. I felt part of the landscape, part of the sky. I moved my mattress onto the floor so that I could lie in the moon's silver light, letting my body absorb its intense energy, and drifted to sleep to dream of gardens of gnome-like chattering scientists sitting atop flowers, smiling to each other in a Technicolor garden where giant-size trees edged frothing, racing rapids.

THEN THEY ARRIVED. Maggie, Jane, Zee, and Karen, of course, but several more friends from Blue Gate, too—Penny and Sally and Elena and Lucy and Trish and Trina—all here to give their support and also looking for an adventure, taking a day out in the country. My heart was filled with happiness to see them stepping into my new life with their laughter and irreverence, for my farm friends to see that I really did have a life beyond the sad, solitary one they saw me living in my cottage. My Blue Gate friends looked as if they belonged on the farm with their sensible boots, practical jackets, and no-nonsense expressions, as if they were budding farmers themselves—except most of them were vegan and exclaimed in horror when I showed them the calves in their stalls, separated from their mothers so that the mothers would hear their cries and produce more milk. We tiptoed into the stalls, one after the other, for the tiny calves on their long unsteady legs to latch onto our hands and suck, suck, suck, their entire bodies shivering in the sole pursuit of milk, comfort, their mothers.

At lunchtime, I led Blue Gate proudly across the fields to the nearby castle, skipping at the head of a playful tribe of striding, giggling women. When we got there we ran around and played hide and seek and laughed and posed for photographs, flashes of colour darting through the ruins. We bundled, laughing, into the pub for lunch, ordering pints all round and Ploughman's lunches, some without cheese or butter, garnering alarmed looks from the locals at our loudness, our appearance, our number, and especially from the publican, who looked at me askance from under furrowed eyebrows. Jimmy was at the bar, deep in conversation with the publican, and he didn't wave back when I waved enthusiastically at him. After lunch, my co-defendants and I left the others playing at the castle and made our way back to the farmhouse, where we sat on a chequered blanket on the lawn in the farmhouse's walled garden and got down to work. The sun had come out and the April flowers were in full bloom.

"Joan Ruddock has agreed to be my expert witness," Karen said. "To talk about the risk of radiation to the local community. Since you are focusing on the animals, Zee, she can speak for you, too."

"That's amazing," I said. Joan Ruddock was the head of the Campaign for Nuclear Disarmament and was later to become a Labour Member of Parliament. "I am sure we can get press if she is there."

"Since we can't have Trevor Brown in person," Jane said. "I can use the media clippings you sent, Steph, to talk about the lack of attention to security and safety, to highlight the fact that the place isn't secure."

"I've got someone from the Namibia Support Group who says she can get a representative from SWAPO, the South West Africa People's Organization, to come and speak about how Aldermaston is in breach of international law," I said. "And she says we may get a telegram of support from the United Nations."

As we pored over our documents, I took notes to help bring our separate cases into one coherent whole. We exclaimed together at the inaccuracies of the police interview transcripts that Janet had sent, and reconstructed the night's interrogations in all their absurdity.

"They blackmailed us," Karen said. "They said if we didn't confess to cutting the fence then Aldermaston was going to deny we went in, and we wouldn't be able to get tests or medical treatment if we needed it. We have to find a way to fit that in."

"Do we have a date yet?" Maggie asked.

They all turned to me because I was our liaison to Janet. I shook my head. "In her last letter, Janet told me that because Reading deals with all the Heathrow cases of drug smuggling and things like that, cases like ours can get pushed down and down the list. She thinks we may have to wait until the summer."

"I don't want to go to prison in the summer," Zee wailed.

"I don't want to go to prison at all," I said, stroking Molly, who was sitting in my lap, wondering who would look after her if it came to this.

I looked up to see Jimmy walking across the courtyard and put up my hand to wave to him. I was sure he saw me, but he turned his back and kept walking.


THE SUN WAS fading by the time we were done. Everyone arrived back from the castle, giggling, doing cartwheels, holding hands. Penny, Trish, and Trina disappeared into the cottage, and reappeared a couple of hours later carrying plates piled high with baked potatoes and a vegetable curry. Blue Gate sat in a happy circle in Cathy's walled garden, accompanied by the sounds of birds and the occasional lowing cow. Every now and then, Cathy, her husband, Phil, or one of the hippies walked by, waving at us over the wall, and we all waved back. We drank beer and ate, and discussed the latest news from Greenham: who had been arrested, who was sleeping with whom, the specifics of our case. And we talked about the upcoming walk in May across Salisbury Plain, which was criss-crossed with seams of magical energy called ley lines. Military bases had sprung up on this special tract of land, and women planned to walk across their shooting ranges and camp out at sacred sites, like Silbury Hill, along the way.

Sally asked if I was coming and I told her I had to work, but would come at the end, for Stonehenge.

The next morning, as I waved them all goodbye, I felt filled with light, happier than I had in months. Our case was taking shape, I no longer missed Blue Gate because Blue Gate had come to see me, and my two worlds were joining together. It was a Saturday, and I was sitting on the grass in the meadow just across the courtyard from my cottage, Molly in my lap, when Jimmy strode over and stood over me, red in the face. I could smell alcohol.

"What's up with you and your fucking dyke friends?" he yelled.

"What are you talking about?" I tucked Molly closer to me.

"Marching into the pub like you own it, taking it over like it's yours."

"We just came for a drink. And why didn't you wave back when I waved at you?"

"You think I wanted to be associated with you bunch of perverts?"

"Really?" I was genuinely shocked. "But you knew . . ."

"Kissing and holding hands and not wearing bras. I doubt you'll ever be allowed back there again. You were a disgrace."

"We were only doing what you do every day," I said. "Having a drink and having lunch. I don't remember kissing anyone." I paused, emboldened by the image of my lovely friends swarming around the pub, making it ours. "I wish I had, though. Really give everyone something to think about."

"You fucking pervert. You sick, fucking pervert." He moved closer to me, and I quickly picked Molly up and scrambled to my feet. I was towering over him as he spat in my face before he strode off toward his cottage. "You sick, fucking pervert."

I ran back to my cottage, put Molly inside, then followed Jimmy to his house, my heart pounding in my chest. I banged on the door once, twice, three times before it opened. He was standing there shirtless, his body as red as his face.

"How dare you come and speak to me like that. I thought we were friends, I have been nothing but nice to you, and now you show you're just as bad as the rest of them."

He stepped toward me and pushed me, hard. I staggered backwards, falling to the ground. I jumped up and glared at him in horror.

"Are you really doing this to me? You're all the fucking same!" I yelled as he slammed the door.

I walked back to my cottage, shaking, my heart pounding, and decided I needed a drink. I was afraid to leave Molly alone in case Jimmy did something bad to her, so, for the first time since I had come here, I locked the door to my cottage, before making my way across the same fields I had run through with my friends just the day before. It was getting dark, and I imagined Jimmy following me, but I felt no fear. Let him just try, I thought in my fury. I marched into the pub, its bright lights startling me for a moment, and suddenly I felt as if all eyes were on me.

"A pint of bitter, please," I said.

"No you don't," the publican said. "You're banned. You and the whole lot of you beer-swilling dykes showing your tits off and frightening my customers."

"Frightening your customers?" I looked around at the usual array of farmhands and local workers, strong ruddy-faced men with thick, grimy hands. "You're frightened of a bunch of women?"

I turned on my heel and strode out, crossed the road, climbed over the barbed wire fence, and marched home through the field of cows, the words to the Poison Girls' "(I'm Not A) Real Woman" drumming in my head.

> I'm not a real woman, I don't aim to please
> Or twinkle my knickers or garter my knees
> The nails on my fingers are tattered and torn
> I have had dirty hands since the day I was born

I sang the chorus as loud as I could in the twilight, attempting Vi's husky, deep London accent. Her voice was full of mischief and laughter, but mine was rocked by indignation and sorrow:

> I'm generous I'm mean
> I'm a law unto myself
> I just laugh at everything you say
> Don't be surprised
> If I don't look into your eyes
> My eyes are on a million miles away

I stopped suddenly and collapsed on the ground in tears. The song reminded me of Al, and I wished she were with me now to stand up to these mean locals, to take on Jimmy and the bartender, to proudly take my hand and walk with me through the fields. I loved to walk to this pub from the farm, it was a place I had relied on to sit and watch the sun go down as I drank a pint and smoked a roll-up alone, thinking of my dad, and how much he enjoyed his local pub. Now I had nowhere to go.

I thought I'd found community, but instead I'd found the same thing we had experienced in Newbury—men terrified of strong women, bullies taking it out on young women who just wanted to be a bit different. Only this time I had nobody to comfort me, to make me laugh. By the time I got home I was sobbing uncontrollably, and I couldn't tell if it was anger or sorrow. I picked up Molly and held her comforting, jet-black body in my arms, my tears dampening her fur. She nuzzled against my cheek, purring madly, and I managed a smile. I wanted to call my dad and tell him what had happened, ask him to come down and have a word with the publican and Jimmy, put it all to rights. That made me sob even more. I looked into Molly's yellow eyes.

"I won't let anything happen to you," I said. "I won't let him near you."

# Chapter Nineteen
## "RIDE A WHITE SWAN" T. REX

I TOLD EVERYONE who was willing to listen to me what had happened—Cathy, the hippies, even the postman whom I caught off-guard as he spilled the mail onto the large table in the farmhouse lobby.

"He pushed you to the ground?" the quiet, elderly postman said kindly in his thick Wiltshire accent, a shocked expression on his face.

"Yes. So if you see him near me, please look out for me."

I felt as if the more people I told, the safer I would be. I strode into Cathy's kitchen and asked her to ask Phil to fire Jimmy, but she didn't think he would—it's my word against Jimmy's, she said, and couldn't we just resolve it? I called my brother, Robert, who was a long way away in Devon, but whose shock at what happened made me feel loved and protected. He offered to come and stay, and I told him I could handle it and that I had a lot of support around me, but I just needed to tell him. I popped into the hippies' living room, and they vowed to protect me against Jimmy and even offered to come and sleep in my house whenever Penny was away, but I didn't want them to go out of their way, and I wanted to feel safe to live in my own home again without locking the door.

After lunch, I walked into Annette's print studio and told her the whole story from start to finish. She put down her tools, boiled the kettle as I talked, and poured us two cups of instant coffee, adding Coffee-Mate and stirring it vigorously with a spoon before sitting opposite me, staring at me intently.

"You have to do something to reclaim your space," she said. "I'll help you."

Annette was not "cosmic" as we liked to put it—she didn't believe, as I did, that there were ghosts living in the passageway between my cottage and the mill. Walking back to my cottage in the evenings, I often heard a man and woman arguing, loud music playing in the background.

Annette said it was the water carrying the sounds from upriver where a couple must be arguing, but Penny thought it was ghosts, and I preferred Penny's version. So I was surprised to hear Annette use language like "reclaiming space."

"Sage?" I asked. "A ceremony?"

Annette laughed and shook her head. "Beer!"

That evening, she turned up with two six packs, and we sat on the doorstep, watching the sun set in the distance. The two quarrelling ducks were late today and met in the evening instead of at lunchtime. We imagined their conversation as they stood facing each other a few feet in front of us, before they turned their backs on each other and walked in opposite directions. The feral cats slunk past, looking for crumbs, and I held Molly tight in my lap. We could hear Penny, who had returned from Greenham that day, humming in the kitchen as she made us dinner. We were determined to eat on the doorstep, no matter how cold it got.

"We're reclaiming the space," Annette said, raising her bottle in the air. "We'll eat here, we'll drink here, we'll listen to music here."

Penny squeezed between us and sat next to us on a wooden stool she had brought with her, the one we used to sit by the fire when we stoked it.

"I'm going to create a circle of silver light around the house," she said, smiling.

Annette burst out laughing, but I was all ears.

"I'm going to create an energy circle that will protect the house from male aggression. He won't dare step over it."

"You do it your way, Pen," Annette said, snorting. "I'll do it mine. Bottoms up." And we clinked our beer bottles and laughed.

We drank beer and ate dinner on our laps, then sipped herbal tea and smoked roll-ups until long after the sun had set. Penny dragged the speakers from the living room into the hallway to face the front door so that we could listen to David Bowie, Joan Armatrading, Luther Vandross, all my favourites. When the Au Pairs' "It's Obvious" came on, Penny and I jumped up and danced around in the courtyard yelling out "We're Equal But Different!" over and over again every time the chorus came on. We didn't care who saw us, but there was nobody to see, really, only the cats, the ducks, and the cows in the distance.

"This is Stephanie's space, and Penny's too, it's a strong woman's space, and woe betide any man who violates it," Annette cried into the dark, slurring her words.

"Cheers to that," I said, and we lifted our bottles like the three musketeers and clinked again.


THE NEXT MORNING, I was washing dishes in the kitchen when Jimmy walked by the front of my cottage. He didn't look my way and took a perfect arc around the house, as if held back by an invisible circular wall. Penny walked in behind me. She had been watching from the living room window seat.

"See?" she said.


SATURDAY MAY 4, 1985, was a full moon, a special full moon, apparently, one that the Green Gate women said could switch the tide of violence, bring women's energy back to the fore, and help create a gentler, safer planet. The days before the full moon, hundreds of women were going to walk across Salisbury Plain, before descending upon Stonehenge to "reclaim the space," visiting several sacred pagan sites along the way, including the breast-shaped site of Silbury Hill and neighbouring Avebury, with its own platoon of mysterious standing stones. They were hoping to tap into the ley lines of powerful energy that criss-crossed the plain, waiting to be connected to and understood. The plain was also home to the occasional crop circle and UFO sighting. Many of us at Greenham thought it was no coincidence that the British military had chosen to practise so many of its war games here. They developed weapons at Porton Down and carried out military exercises all across Salisbury Plain, including dropping bombs, many of which remained unexploded. They commandeered low-flying warplanes and whirring helicopters, which flew over the countryside. We thought that the military energy was attracted to the pagan, life-loving energy pulsing along our sacred ley lines—either to suppress it or tap into it, we were not sure which.

Mary, one of my colleagues from the Feminist Archive, drove us through the thatched-roof villages dotted along the high-hedged country roads that led from Bath to Stonehenge. She was older than I, and very small, with a hunched back from a spine disease that she said left her in pain most of the time. Despite this, she was endlessly cheerful, smiling in excitement at the adventure ahead, while I pictured my mother standing at the edge of the garden waving her fist at the helicopters from Salisbury Plain as they flew over St. Mary Bourne, yelling, "Go home, stop playing war games, stop terrorizing us!" We used to take family visitors to Stonehenge, and we kids would lie on the stones and pretend to sacrifice each other, or do mock ceremonies, then chase each other around the stones. But you couldn't touch the stones anymore; you could only view them from afar, to protect them from damage.

We arrived in the car park nestled at the foot of Stonehenge, and my heart quickened as I saw dozens of familiar-looking women milling about, putting up tents, parking cars, building fires, embracing. Penny, Sally, Zee, Lucy, and Elena had created a Blue Gate fire pit, and I ran to them and kissed each in turn on the lips, hugging them close.

"Steph's here," Lucy cried. "No need for flashlights anymore."

"Ha ha," I said, drily, glancing at Zee. The radiation jokes were running a bit thin. "You know it wears off after a while. You'll just see a dull glow wherever I have been from now on."

Trish and Trina, with their matching jet-black hair, were here, too, and, true to form, were bent over a large cooking pot. They each kissed me before turning back to their cuisine.

"No time to chat, making dinner for you all," Trina said in her Liverpudlian accent, and I smiled, so happy to be with my Greenham family again as we all sat together and ate the lentil and vegetable stew.

Small fire pits were dotted around us, with groups of women gathered around each one, the powerful silhouette of Stonehenge towering on the hill above us. I felt as if we had been transported back in time and were a merry band of Druids, pagans, and wiccans gathering for a full moon ceremony. Nobody really knows why Stonehenge was created, or by whom—but we all knew it was one of our most sacred ancient sites and that it was designed to observe the heavens, predict eclipses, and celebrate equinoxes and solstices, aligning the earth with the heavens much like its global sisters at Chichen Itza in Mexico, Angkor Wat in Cambodia, and Macchu Pichu in Peru. Now, it was run by English Heritage as a tourist attraction, and the modern-day wiccans, Druids, and pagans who wished to worship here were not allowed near the stones, with the whole site now surrounded by chain link fencing. We all knew about the famous Stonehenge Free Festival that happened every June, when thousands of "travellers"—nomadic hippies—descended upon the stones for several days of music, dancing, and drugs—and were tolerated by the authorities. Now, one hundred Greenham women were here, planning to break in and spend the night next to the stones. We didn't have permission, and we didn't know how we would be received.

"How was the walk over Salisbury Plain? Was anyone arrested?" I was thinking of the live firing ranges.

"No," Sally said. "We walked right across and stopped them doing their war games for the afternoon. They just waited for us to finish and let us go on our way."

"Strange," I said.

"Starhawk thinks they left us alone because of the ceremony we did last night on top of Silbury Hill," Sally said. "She's an American witch, and she led this totally weird ceremony. Some of us were into it. But *we* weren't."

"No, we weren't," Lucy said emphatically. "She kept bossing us all about. So we had a meeting this morning and decided that for Stonehenge, we each do our own thing. No overall ceremony led by anyone."

"Starhawk says the energy is very strong at Stonehenge and we have to be careful," Sally said, as she put a roll-up to her lips.

"We decided yesterday that her real name is Edna or Mavis," Lucy said.

I laughed and asked, "Where is she?" I had her books *The Spiral Dance* and *Dreaming the Dark,* and I imagined a tall, striding wild-haired woman, the grass and trees parting in reverence before her.

"She's up at the stones doing a ceremony to stop it raining tomorrow night so we can experience 'the full energy of the moon,'" Elena said.

"Gosh, I wish we had her on family holidays," I said.

Our conversation was interrupted by an outburst of hysterical laughter at the fire pit next to ours. Not wanting to miss out on a good laugh, we quieted down to listen. A heavy-set woman with a smiling face, long, wild, red hair, black loose clothes, and a rascally laugh was holding a toilet roll high in the air.

"We bless this toilet roll with our female energy," she said in a mock serious voice, passing it to her left, asking each woman to hold it before passing it along.

Women closed their eyes, blessed the toilet roll, and stifled giggles as they passed it along. When it arrived back to the red-haired woman, she stood tall facing Stonehenge, holding the toilet roll above her head in both hands.

"We honour our ancestors, living and dead, the Druids and matriarchs and pagans and Celts and Saxons and Arthur and Merlin and those who built Stonehenge and all those who did not have toilet paper!" she boomed. "We bless this roll and vow to use it as the sacred object it now is!"

Everyone was laughing. I liked the look of the red-haired woman and turned to Elena and asked, "Who's that?"

"Shula, from Green Gate," she said. "She's new. Not really a Green Gate type if you know what I mean, though I think she's pretty cosmic in her own way."

"Yes, she astrally projects all the time, apparently," Penny said.

"And the toilet roll?" I asked.

"You needed to be on Silbury Hill last night," Penny said. "Starhawk's ceremony. Then you'd get it."

I'd missed the humour, the laughter, the communal eating, the dirty fingernails, the big boots, the warm smiles, the hospitality. My colleague, Mary, had fitted right in, laughing along, carefully setting up her tent with help from Elena and Sally, chatting to women on either side of her at the fire pit. I knew she was in pain, because she always was, and I hoped she would be okay sleeping on her thin mattress on the ground.

Friday arrived clear and bright, not a cloud in the sky. A small woman in a bright pink anorak, tied unflatteringly around her chin despite the lack of rain, and with a few wisps of curly brown hair poking out, walked to our fire and smiled to us all, bowing with her hands in prayer. I smiled back and she moved on to the next fire.

"Starhawk," Lucy hissed in my ear.

"She made it sunny," I said, and Lucy looked at me quizzically.

She couldn't tell if I was being ironic or not. Neither could I. But I was a bit disappointed that Starhawk wasn't six feet tall, wearing leather sandals, and with birds nesting in her waist-length hair.

WHEN EVENING CAME, we made our move. One hundred women, armed with bolt cutters, bottles of water, and sleeping bags swarmed through the chain link fencing, dark splotches bobbing and weaving up the hill toward the majestic stones. Mary was not strong enough to throw her sleeping bag over the fence, so I threw it for her, along with mine. We crawled under the fence, our faces, elbows, and knees pressed against the earth, and as I emerged on the other side, I jumped up, picked up both sleeping bags, shook off the memory of Aldermaston that flashed through my mind, then ran laughing and hooting toward the stones. Looking behind me, I saw the uniforms following us—police officers, this time, not soldiers, and they were walking, not running, with not a gun to be seen.

We arrived at the stones and dispersed, like horses let loose after a night in the barn, drifting this way and that in freedom. In the distance, the full moon was slowly appearing on the horizon, heavy, orange, and huge in the clear night sky. Below us, a line of cars wove along the A303, like toys, and I wondered if the drivers could see us dancing, playing, and celebrating, if they, too, were entranced by the auburn moon, or if they saw only the road in front of them and the headlights behind, as they made their way to brightly lit kitchens and curtained living rooms blocking out the magic of the moon.

Women were gathering in the centre of the stones, lighting incense, sitting on the ground, closing their eyes in prayer. Starhawk was among them. She had taken off her anorak hood and let her thick hair fall loose, her face shining. Behind her, Sally and Elena played leapfrog. Mary sat quietly next to a stone that was lying flat on the ground, stroking it gently. I heard the distant sound of a guitar and soft singing. We were each in our own magical worlds, connected to each other by the electricity in the air, the shimmering stars that appeared brighter and brighter as dusk ushered in the dark expectant night, watched over by our sister moon. I walked quietly around the entire circle of stones, watching my friends and fellow activists play, pray, and dance. One small group was singing one of my favourite Greenham songs, "Sister Moon watch over me/Your friend I'll always be/Sister Moon watch over me/Until we are free."

As I stepped out beyond the inner circle, I met another circle—of police officers. But there were only a handful, interspersed at quite a distance from each other, and they did not seem the least bit worried by what we were doing. I walked up behind two who were standing together, surprised to discover that they were whispering. They must have been captivated, too.

At last, I plucked up the courage to walk up to one of the stones. I had been dying to touch one, but I felt silly doing it. I looked around and nobody was watching—everyone was doing her own thing, and nothing I did would seem unusual anyway. I looked up to see the stone looming high above me, its shadow falling softly on the luminous ground, the stars and the now bright white moon shining in the sky above. I put out both hands, palms outstretched ahead of me, and placed them on the stone. A deep humming, a dark vibration, electrified my hands. I breathed in deeply, relaxed, and let the energy enter me, dark and light, powerful and creative. It was male energy at Stonehenge, one of the Green Gate women had said earlier, Silbury Hill was female and Stonehenge was male. But what I felt transcended gender, time, and space. What I felt was the pulsing of the universe, the breathing of the oceans, the life force that gives and gives and gives.

When at last I was ready to sleep, I found Mary, Sally, and Elena already in their sleeping bags, which they had placed in a row facing the glowing full moon, the stones at our backs. Mary was staring peacefully at the massive sky enveloping us. I fell asleep to the sound of distant laughter, the strumming of a guitar, the lilting of a flute.

"EXCUSE ME LADIES." A male voice startled me from the deepest sleep I'd ever experienced. I opened my eyes to see a red-haired, freckle-faced police officer bending over me. "The site would like to open up," he said, cheerfully. "If you wouldn't mind leaving now?"

I sat up slowly, remembering the times the police had dragged us by our armpits, yelled at us, called us names.

"Of course," I said politely and looked around to see his colleagues gently waking my friends, who were quietly and obediently standing up, rolling up their sleeping bags, and getting ready to make their way back down the hill. I nudged Mary awake, and she sat up, stretched, yawned, and looked around her, an expression of utter alarm on her face.

"What is it?" I asked, worried.

"My back," she said, putting her hand behind her to touch her slight hump. "I can't feel any pain. For the first time in my life, I don't feel any pain."

As for me, I felt as though I had enough life-giving energy to tide me through the court case and way, way beyond.

# Chapter Twenty

## "YOU CAN'T KILL THE SPIRIT" NAOMI LITTLEBEAR MORENA

THE DAY BEFORE our court case, Zee stood to welcome me as I arrived at Blue Gate.

"We're not staying here," she said. "Shula has made a new gate for us close to Green. Black Gate."

I burst out laughing. "My goodness, that's cheery."

"She's a Goth," Zee offered as I followed her through the woods from Blue to Green, where we took a right and found Black Gate's fire, nestled in the woods, surrounded by tents that had already been put up for us. I was touched. It was very private, giving us space to think and rest after our days in court, with no traffic, no police officers, no soldiers, and no visitors.

Shula smiled as I approached, and I noticed how deep her hazel eyes were. She gave me a bear hug, then turned to stir a large pot of vegetable stew. "Ready for dinner?"

Sally was here and took my hand as I sat at the fire and leaned my head to rest on hers. Lucy was here, too, because she was my McKenzie friend. When you defend yourself in court without a barrister, you are allowed to take somebody in the dock with you for moral support, and they are called McKenzie friends. I had asked Lucy because she was clever and made me laugh. So instead of five of us in the dock tomorrow, there would be ten.

My other co-defendants Karen, Maggie, and Jane emerged from an evening walk in the woods, and we embraced before sitting down to dinner around the smouldering fire. My heart was pounding, and it was hard to swallow my food because I knew this might very well be my last week of freedom for a while. But I did my best, if only to please Shula, who seemed intent on making sure we all got fed.

"Did you hear about the Stonehenge festival?" I asked.

Just three weeks after our transformative night among the stones, hundreds of people had arrived at Stonehenge in a convoy of battered cars and caravans for the annual free music festival. They were immediately attacked by police with what some journalists described as the most brutal police behaviour they had ever seen, in what came to be known as the "Battle of the Beanfield." Travellers, hippies, and musicians, adults and children alike, had been beaten, harassed, and chased off, and a local earl, so indignant about the horrors he had witnessed, had let them take refuge on his neighbouring land.

Everyone nodded.

"How come they were so nice to us?" I asked.

"Because we are women," Zee said.

"That doesn't make any sense. You always say we get beaten up and attacked *because* we are women. And there were women at the festival anyway. You can't have it both ways."

"You'll never see me going both ways," she said, with a mischievous grin.

"It's because of Starhawk," Sally said.

"Because we were there to do something spiritual and quiet and energetic, to go with the flow of the energy," Shula said. "Because the police were bewitched."

"They certainly acted it." I nodded.


AFTER DINNER, EVERYONE left the five of us at the fire to discuss our strategy one last time. We didn't drink beer or smoke pot, talked for a while, then dispersed to our separate tents. I fell asleep to the sound of someone strumming a guitar at the fire and women talking in low murmurs. I felt like Frodo Baggins the night before he left Rivendell for Mordor, the elves playing their instruments softly in the trees. My thoughts drifted back to Stonehenge, and I pictured fairies possessing the police officers as they watched us dancing and singing and sleeping among the stones, whispering in their ears that they should protect us, then blowing away all memories of the night from their minds the next day as easily as if they were blowing the seeds from a dandelion head, leaving a dreamscape, a scent, a hint of strangeness in its place. I hoped the fairies would be with me tomorrow.

EARLY THE NEXT morning, Jane drove us all to Reading at her usual helter-skelter pace, a convoy of battered, multi-coloured cars and VW vans filled with more than fifty women in close pursuit. I read through my notes one more time, scribbling in the margins, taking deep breaths, trying to memorize parts of my closing speech, even though that moment might be days away. Reading was a big city, and we swirled around the roundabouts, past multi-storey car parks and huge supermarkets, where ordinary people were doing ordinary things like shopping, going to work, or taking their children to school. We arrived as a pack in front of the majestic Crown Court building with its sweeping front steps and bundled out, singing loud Greenham songs, turning disapproving heads on the busy pavement. The June sky was a bright blue, the sun promising to warm us into a beautiful summer's day. I thought of my cat, Molly, at the farm and hoped that Annette would let her out to play in the sunshine as well as feed her; I thought of nine months in prison, and butterflies leaped from my stomach and into my throat.

THE FIVE OF us presented ourselves at the front desk, our McKenzie friends at our sides, while the rest of our supporters squeezed into the viewing gallery, laughing, singing, and filling it to the brim. A serious-looking policewoman searched our bags, then nodded to us to go through to the waiting area, where an equally serious-looking court official led all ten of us into the dock. Within minutes, the judge appeared—an elderly man in a big white wig. The prosecution lawyer, a sharp-featured, middle-aged man in a black suit, whispered something to the judge as he sat down to face us from his perch. I looked up at the ceiling and at the wood panelling on the walls, and wished there were windows. Was it really me sitting here? I glanced at the notes in front of me and my false name stared back at me. It's Stephanie Bell. Not me, not really me at all.

Then the judge banged his mallet and the prosecution lawyer, his assistant, and the stenographer stood up. It was just like on television. They turned to us and I realized that we were supposed to stand too. I did it, reluctantly, remembering how my family would refuse to stand for the national anthem at village pantomimes, and the others followed.

"You each have the right to refuse three jurors," the judge said in a colourless, upper-class accent, peering at us over his wire-rimmed glasses. "Just put your hand up to let us know if you want somebody removed from the jury. Are you ready?"

I glanced at the others and we nodded. I thought we were supposed to say, "Yes, Your Honour," but I couldn't quite bring myself to do it.

A line of men and women appeared single file from the doorway to the right of the judge and walked slowly before us. I pointed to the first man to indicate I didn't want him on the jury. He turned around and walked out of the room. Zee pointed to the next man. Maggie pointed to the next. The second man I pointed to had a big beard, a checked shirt, a warm face, and smiling eyes, and I hesitated as I pointed to him. He looked like a peace activist. But we had agreed. We would accept all women and refuse all men. But when twelve women were left standing before the ten of us, I glanced at their faces and was not reassured. There were quite a few "blue rinses"—older women with white blue hair who looked as if they staffed tearooms and historic homes and jumble sales and voted Conservative. There were a couple of younger women in smart skirt suits, who looked like bank clerks, and who didn't look as if they had smiled in a while. There was one hippie-looking woman, with long hair and a flowing skirt and peasant top, a teacher perhaps, who seemed to sneak me a smile. But it may have been the light, and she didn't catch my eye again, so I wondered if I had made this up. I also wondered if our strategy was a good idea after all, but it was too late now. We had the image we wanted, and I had to admit it was quite powerful: a male judge and male prosecutor, ten female defendants, dozens of female supporters, and twelve female members of the jury.

WHEN THE JURY was settled, the judge turned to us and said, "Let me hear from each of you."

I stepped forward. "When I was a teenager, I saw footage on TV of the Soweto Uprising in South Africa, when innocent children were gunned down for protesting because they were not allowed to have school lessons in their own language. When I was at university, I chaired

Bath University's Anti-Apartheid Group for three years. We picketed Barclays Bank asking them to disinvest in South Africa because Nelson Mandela and other anti-apartheid leaders were calling on the world to stop investing in South Africa. I went on demonstrations; I learned all I could about the evils of this system that enslaved an entire population because of their race."

The jury members' faces were drawing a blank. They must have been wondering what this had to do with Aldermaston. Maybe they didn't even know what apartheid was or where South Africa was. Perhaps I had started in the wrong place and needed to speed up.

"Aldermaston uses plutonium to make its nuclear weapons," I said. "They get the uranium they need to make it illegally from Namibia, which is occupied by apartheid South Africa. Illegally because there is a United Nations embargo against trading with Namibia. I have a telegram here, from the United Nations, supporting our action because it highlights the fact that Aldermaston is breaking international law."

The prosecutor stood up and faced me. He was all in black, wearing a white wig over his black hair. "Do you admit to criminally damaging the fence at Aldermaston on the night of June 12th, 1984?"

"I admit to breaking into Aldermaston," I said. "To try to prevent the greater crime of violating international law."

A burst of applause filled the court room, women's voices whooping loudly.

"That is all I have to ask," he said as he sat down and turned his back to us. I felt a bit disappointed. I wanted to say more. But I knew I would get my chance when I summed up.

The next day, I presented my expert witness, a tall Namibian man with a serious voice who held the entire courtroom in his thrall. He talked about the dire conditions under which uranium miners worked in his country, the importance of international solidarity to bring apartheid down, and how much SWAPO (the South West Africa People's Organization) appreciated our action. I was not really sure that was the argument to convince the stony-faced jury, who may well think of SWAPO as nothing more than a guerrilla army. I wondered if the telegram from Guyana's Ambassador to the United Nations, Noel G. Sinclair, who was also President of the UN Council on Namibia, would mean anything to them.

My heart surged with pride as I read the two pages out loud. "The United Nations Council has learned with great satisfaction of the actions taken by a group of women activists to ensure respect for Decree No. 1 for the Protection of the Natural Resources of Namibia . . . endorsed by the General Assembly in 1974. The Council commends this demonstration of concern for the natural resources of Namibia and for the interests of the rightful owners of those resources. The Council hopes that such actions would increase the awareness of international public opinion, especially in countries whose corporations are involved in the illegal exploitation of Namibia's natural resources . . ."

I sat down, feeling flushed, wishing I could tell my dad I had the support of an ambassador at the United Nations. He would have been proud.


WHEN IT WAS her turn to speak, Karen said that her actions were motivated by a desire to prevent genocide being done in her name. Her expert witness was Joan Ruddock, the head of the Campaign for Nuclear Disarmament and quite a famous figure. She looked a bit like the jurors in her smart suit, coiffed hair, and immaculate makeup, and I hoped this would help the jurors look at us in a kinder light.

"Aldermaston is leaking radiation into the surrounding community," Joan said. "Affecting the workers, families living nearby, and the animals."

Another wave of cheering filled the court room, and Joan shuffled uncomfortably, before she continued to cite evidence in support of her statement.

Then Zee talked about the impact of nuclear material on the animals and birds who flew, burrowed, and scurried through the base, with no awareness of the dangers awaiting them inside, where grass looked like grass and trees looked like trees, animals who had no way of knowing that some may have been riddled with radiation, damaging their health, cutting their lives short.

Then Jane got up to speak. "What if we were terrorists? What if we wanted to make our own bomb? If five untrained women can enter a base containing plutonium and uranium undetected, who else can? Who else has?"

I could see that this had caught the jurors' attention.

THE FOLLOWING DAY, we heard from the prosecution witnesses. When a Ministry of Defence constable from Aldermaston took the stand, I asked him what time he had checked the fence and what time he had found the hole.

"I first checked the fence at two am," he said. "Then at five am, when I checked again, I found a two-foot square hole."

"So between two am and five am nobody checked the fence? Anyone could have got in during those three hours?" I asked.

He shrugged.

I turned to the jury. "This is how these dangerous nuclear weapons are being protected." I turned back to him. "Were you in touch with Detective Osland at any point during the night?"

"Yes. He called the base to confirm that there was a hole in the fence," he said, shuffling on the stand.

"What time was that?" I asked.

"Around six am," came the reply.

When Detective Sergeant Trevor Osland took the stand, I had just one thing to clear up.

"Constable Watts has just told us that you contacted him at six am to confirm that there were holes in the fence," I said. "Do you recall that conversation?"

Osland smirked and nodded.

"You interviewed me at seven am, an hour later. During that interview, you told me that Aldermaston said there were no holes in the fence. Do you recall that?"

Osland smirked and nodded again.

"Why did you lie to us?" I said.

"You told *us* lies," he said. "You denied cutting the fence. So I don't see any harm in telling a couple of porky pies myself."

A gasp of astonishment flashed across the room, catching us all in its wake, defendants, jurors, prosecutor alike.

"You told lies?" I said, incredulous that he would admit it.

I swore I saw him wink at his detective partner, Gareth Williams, before he nodded again.

"You knew that we were worried about being radiated," I said. "And you lied to us to try and get us to admit to cutting the fence. You said that if we didn't admit to it, we couldn't get tested because Aldermaston was denying there were any holes in the fence."

I faced the jury, shaking my head in disbelief. Some of them were looking alarmed. Women in the viewing gallery started chanting, "Porky Pies, Porky Pies, the pig he told some porky pies."

"Silence," the judge called out, but he looked perturbed himself.

"How can we take the prosecution seriously, when one of its key witnesses admits to lying? Especially about something so crucial—not just to your case." I looked at the prosecutor. "But to our health. We thought we had been exposed to radiation and might need testing and treatment."

"That's as may be, Miss Bell," the judge said, and for a moment I forgot he was addressing me and looked around wondering who Miss Bell was, cringing at the word "Miss." "But it doesn't take away from the fact that you have all admitted to cutting the fence, which is the criminal act here."

A collective groan of disbelief came from the body of women in the viewing gallery. "Only doing my job" was one of the songs we often sang at police officers as they dragged us away. A new version popped up in the viewing gallery, "Lying on the job," until, again, the exasperated judge intervened, and the singing died down.

One by one, the remainder of the guards, police officers, and Aldermaston representatives took to the stand and read aloud the statements that we had all seen and disagreed with. When it was our turn to cross-examine them, we did it boldly and indignantly.

"Is Aldermaston really secure if it took three hours for the hole to be discovered?"

"Why didn't Aldermaston offer us its full body scanner when the NRPB said that would have been the most appropriate test at the time?"

"How do we know you are not lying, since your colleague Trevor Osland seems to think lying is OK?"

But in the end, none of this mattered. We had cut two fences, we had committed criminal damage, and even though the Criminal Defence Act allowed us to commit a crime to prevent a greater crime, the jury's faces told me they were not buying it.

Day Four, the day before we were sentenced, was my birthday. I didn't tell anyone because I didn't see anything to celebrate. I was sure we would be found guilty and go to prison. But I also felt proud of what we were doing. In the afternoon, I stood up tall and made my final speech.

"If you care about a peaceful world, if you care about the future of your children, if you care about this beautiful planet, if you care about justice for people living under apartheid, then you will understand that what we did was nothing compared to the crimes being committed by Aldermaston, right under your noses. I am from St. Mary Bourne, a village not far from here." I trembled a little as I remembered I had given a false name and wondered if I would be found out. "And I think we live in a beautiful part of the world. But it is covered in scars. Greenham, Aldermaston, Salisbury Plain, Porton Down, Abingdon, there are so many. We are riddled with places focused on trying to kill people, and as they do that, they are also killing us. And the people of Namibia, thousands of miles away. I may have been radiated. If I was, I may get cancer in twenty years. But the thing is—so may the workers and the community living around Aldermaston." I realized I was taking Jane and Karen's arguments, when I was supposed to focus on my own. I glanced at them, and they nodded encouragingly. "All we are asking is that you look at the five of us and realize we are not so different from you. We may dress differently and live differently, but we are women who care about life and children and the planet, and we are sick of the war and destruction that our government is developing right under our noses. We know we are right morally. But we are also right legally. We committed a so-called crime to prevent some far greater crimes. It was the only option left to us."

I sat down. I felt flushed in the face and turned to Lucy who was beaming. It took a few moments before I realized that the entire viewing gallery had broken into applause. This was my birthday gift. I glanced over and saw Zephyr, smiling and waving, whistling a loud wolf whistle through her fingers. I saw Hannah grinning and I waved to her—I didn't know they were coming, they must have just arrived today. I was touched. I imagined my father sitting quietly at the back, behind the rowdy women, the only man in support, smiling with pride.

That night, our last before sentencing, we sat around the fire pit congratulating each other, making radiation jokes, and gulping down our fear at what was to come. I admitted that it was my birthday and everyone sang Happy Birthday, Shula made an impromptu cake out of biscuits and jam, and I fell asleep feeling loved, then woke up to a bright sunny morning, the kind of morning you don't want to go to prison.

As I walked up the steps to the court through the throngs of cheering women and into the dock once more, it was hard to keep myself from shaking. But I also felt powerful, because I got to say what I wanted to say, I got to talk about apartheid and war and violence and peace in a British court of law. I had been moved by my friends' passionate speeches explaining why they were here, too, and even though we were really here because we took a wrong turning one bright moonlit night, we were also here because we had a shared vision for how the world could be, and this court case had given us the chance to articulate it. If we were sent to prison, then so be it. I was no longer afraid.

The jury members walked in one by one, their heads down, not a single one giving me eye contact. The foreman, or forewoman, I should say, stood up when the judge asked her what verdict the jury had come to. She was wearing a white jacket and navy slacks, her thin hair pulled back tightly in a bun, her lips a bright red, and without a moment's hesitation, in a loud brittle voice, she responded, "Guilty."

Silence enveloped the room as if a giant cobweb had fallen from the ceiling and softly immobilized us all. I was holding Lucy's hand with my left hand, Zee's with my right. Zee was trembling and so was I.

The judge called the prosecutor over and whispered something in his ear. We glanced at each other. All I could think of was a nine months' sentence, the precedent for our case. I worried about my cat, Molly.

"Ladies, please stand," the judge said.

We didn't like being called ladies, but we stood anyway.

"Upon consideration of the evidence presented before this court today, the jury has decided you are guilty on two counts of criminal damage in the early hours of the 12th of June, 1984. It is my job to offer a punishment to fit the crime. You are not the first Greenham women who have appeared in my court, and I am sure you will not be the last. I am familiar with your crusade to end nuclear war, to use breaking down fences and trespassing as a form of protest against the manufacture or deployment of nuclear weapons. And while I do not share your views on what makes us safe, or your approach to expressing those views, I must say I have been moved by your testimony, your diligence, and your commitment to your cause. In particular, I must say I absolutely agree that apartheid is heinous, and I think it quite important that you have brought Aldermaston's link to Namibia to light. However, the court is not the place to pursue this finding—and ruling on international law does not fall within my purview here at the Crown Court. So while I can laud your reasons, your careful defence, and your choice of expert witnesses, I cannot let this sway my decision. You committed a crime and you must be punished."

I turned to Lucy, feeling flushed with happiness that he had said he was against apartheid and confused that he was not accepting our defences.

The judge took a deep breath. "I therefore sentence you all to a two-year conditional discharge."

I lost all sensation and clasped more tightly onto Zee and Lucy's hands, but could not feel them. Two years! I turned to Zee, my face contorted in horror. She was grinning.

"Conditional discharge," she said.

I had no idea what that meant, but it must have been good because everyone around me in the dock was laughing and crying, the women in the viewing gallery were whooping and keening, and a song took hold across the courtroom until we were all swaying and singing one of our old favourites: "Old and strong/She goes on and on and on/You can't kill the spirit/She is like a mountain . . ." and on and on and on we sang, the song lifting my spirits and carrying me out of the dock as if I were on a wave.

I WAS EXHAUSTED to the core. I felt like a piece of paper that could blow away in the wind, and when Zephyr took me in her arms in a hug of delight on the court building steps I clung onto her tightly, afraid I might float over the rooftops. There were women all around me cheering and singing and hugging each other, hugging us. I smiled at Zee, who was standing next to me, and I could see she was as wiped out as I was. I was desperate to retreat to my cottage, see nobody for weeks, walk in the woods in the sunshine, dangle my feet in the river, lie at night in the moonlight, Molly at my side, and gaze at the stars.

"Want to go home?" Zephyr said, as if she could read my mind. "Want me to come?"

"Thanks." I was surprised. "But I thought you had a concert this weekend."

This was the first time I had thought about Al the whole week. I felt nothing.

"I moved things around. I thought you might need me."

And so, after I hugged my exhausted co-defendants, Zephyr and I set off for the train to Trowbridge.

ZEPHYR STAYED WITH me for a week, and I was happy for the company, but more than anything I wanted to tell my dad about my victory—that peace and women's groups across the country had agreed to pay our fines and that *Peace News* was writing an article about our case. The realization that he was not here to tell, and never would be, hollowed out my chest, created dark rings under my eyes, drew in my cheeks, and made my head heavy.

ZEPHYR DID HER best to keep me afloat. She cooked us meals and took long walks with me across the meadows and through the grounds of the castle. She sang and played her saxophone, wrote music, and laughed at the ducks, while I sat on the grass and stroked Molly, stood in the arc of my favourite tree hanging over the flowing river, gazing forlornly into the depths, and attempted to read Adrienne Rich and Audre Lorde poetry on my doorstep. We visited the calves in the stalls, who we knew had just been separated from their mothers, and it broke our hearts. We vowed not to eat a cream tea, though we were both bursting to try one. We drank coffee with Cathy in her kitchen, had tea with Annette in her studio, and sipped beer with the hippies in their living room, and they all fell in love with Zephyr's enthusiastic, fun-loving nature. I felt like a mushroom in the shade of a bright blossoming tree as I sat quietly at her side, speaking only when I had to, my mind a million miles away inventing conversations with my dad, seeing the crease of his eyes as he broke into a smile.

I craved nighttime, when I could drink in the soft night air through my open bedroom window, filling me with hope, life, and comfort. I slept deeply and woke with nightmares filled with clanking prison doors, unfriendly guards, scowling judges, and sneering unfriendly Greenham women shoving me toward angry police officers. Sometimes my father was the judge, and he didn't recognize me or smile at me when I waved crazily at him, ecstatic that he was still alive. I tried to cry out, "It's me, it's Stephanie," but nothing came out, and he turned his back and walked away. I woke in a sweat, grabbed my notebook, and jotted down every dream, every nightmare, looking for meaning, hoping to expunge the dread and darkness gripping me. I wondered if I needed to see the homeopath again. I wondered if this time nature would heal me on her own if I could just slow down and listen for long enough.

I REFUSED TO weep. I called my mother and she told me about Sarah's school and Robert's new job and her own grief, and I said very little, even though I was bursting to tell all. I let her know that I was not going to prison and that we had a two-year conditional discharge. She gasped at the thought of her daughter having a sentence at all, even if it was conditional, even if it was not in her real name, even if, after two years, it would no longer exist. A child of war, throughout my life my mother imagined the worst whenever any of us did something so simple as drive a car, take a plane, or leave the house.

"You'd better keep out of trouble for the next two years if you can possibly manage it," she said, adding, "Which I highly doubt."

I wanted her to say she was proud of me. I wanted her to say that my father would have been proud of me. I thought about asking to talk to Robert and Sarah, but then I thought they were too young, and they had enough on their plates readjusting to life in a strange town without our father and away from their friends. I didn't call my older sister, Kate, because I knew she disapproved of what we had done because she was afraid, like my father had been, for my safety. So I kept my terrors, my adventures, and my victories to myself.

When I came back from the phone call, Zephyr was in the kitchen making crepes filled with vegetables and herbs from Cathy's garden. She tilted her head and looked at me quizzically. "What's going on?"

I shrugged. "Nothing."

"Oh no, I'm not having that 'nothing' business," she said, matter-of-factly. "After dinner, we're going to walk to the pub and you are going to tell all."

"I'm banned from the pub," I said, on the verge of tears.

"Ha! We'll see about that."

After dinner, which we ate on our laps on the doorstep facing the courtyard, we walked across the meadow and up the hill and Zephyr sat me down firmly on a bench in the pub grounds, facing the castle and the setting sun.

"Pint of bitter?" she asked, and I nodded.

Five minutes later, she arrived, two pints in her hands.

"They have never seen me before," she said. "Why on earth wouldn't they serve me?"

I smiled, sipped my bitter, and started to relax. I turned to Zephyr and told her I missed my dad, that I wanted to tell him what had happened, that I felt no connection to my family, that I was having nightmares, and that I felt alone. She took my hand and nodded. I could see she understood and I let out a sigh.

The next morning, Zephyr and I woke up at five so we could watch the sunrise from the castle grounds. We walked silently hand in hand in the hushed predawn light across the flower-filled meadow, and before we climbed the steep slope to the castle, we stopped on the narrow bridge over the gurgling brook, let go of each other's hands, and sat down to watch the water dance over the water weeds and stones. I faced upstream and marvelled at how, after all the upheaval that had happened in one year, I'd come to be here in this place of beauty. Zephyr faced the opposite direction, watching the water weave its way into the future.

"It's because you're a Cancer and I'm an Aries," she said as we walked away. "You are all emotion and attachment and home and history. I am all about the future and movement and new things."

I wished I had Zephyr's lightness of step, her interminable curiosity, her singing like that of the elves.

"You're sensitive," she said, taking my hand as we headed toward the castle. "Smell that?"

"Wild garlic." We pushed our noses up against the tall plants with their small white flowers, breathing in their sweet scent.

"You care deeply and you feel deeply, and I love that about you. You're a loyal friend, you're clever, you're passionate, you're strong, you're caring. You did an amazing summing up, you even got the judge to agree that it's wrong to use uranium from Namibia."

"Why are you saying such nice things to me?" I could barely stand how nice she was being.

"Because you seem to have disappeared."

We had reached the castle grounds, and we were out of breath. We'd missed the sunrise, but we hadn't missed the bright early light, the twinkling dew on the ground, the dawn chorus of the morning birds.

"And I know exactly how to bring you back."

I looked at her sceptically.

"I'm going to teach you to sing."

I took a deep breath and looked up to the sky. I felt shy about how my voice would sound. I didn't want Zephyr to hear it.

"Hold your stomach. And breathe as deeply as you can into it. We want your voice to come from there."

I did as she said and started to feel calmer.

"Now, breathe in as far as you can and follow me." She let out a loud, "Ya Helo!"

I did as she said, and the loudest sound I had ever made came out of my mouth. I burst into laughter. "That was me?"

"It's all in the breathing. Ok, we're going to do a duet. It's a Czech cow-calling song. Here's your part."

She sang "Ya Helo Ya Helo" and I repeated it, marvelling at the sound coming out of my mouth.

"Now this bit," she said and sang the whole verse. I didn't understand the words, but it didn't matter, the sounds were easy to make.

We sang it together, one round after the other until I got it.

"OK, can you do it on your own now?" she asked.

"I'll have a go." I was totally into it now.

"OK, so don't be distracted by what I do."

I sang and she harmonized, and then we laughed and laughed and laughed.

Zephyr turned me toward her and took both my hands. "Look at you. You're all filled with Stephness again."

I could tell. My cheeks felt flushed, my heart was racing; the energy that flowed through Stonehenge so fiercely, and nature so gently, was pulsing through my veins.

"I've got a great idea." I grabbed her hand.

We ran down the hill, climbed through the fence, and made our way half way across the meadow, where I stopped us both in our tracks. I pulled Zephyr toward the barbed wire fence that wound along the edge of the river and pointed to the herd of cows on the hill in the distance.

"Ready?" I said.

She laughed and nodded. We let go of each other's hands and belted out the cow calling song in magnificent harmony, the fear and darkness leaving me with every exhale, the promise of life and fun and love filling me with every inhale. I lifted my eyes to see birds darting across the bright blue sky, heard the river flowing—the scent of the trees, grass, and flowers filled me to bursting. And then it happened.

There was a bustling, a snorting, a stamping of hooves. I looked straight ahead and there before us, trotting to the fence, where they stared at us in wonder, was the herd of brown dark-eyed bullocks, jostling and vying with each other to get closest to the sounds coming from the two tall women dancing and laughing on the edge of the river.

# Epilogue

## "#WHERESTHELOVE" THE BLACK EYED PEAS + THE WORLD (VIDEO)

"THERE'S A BUNCH of cops with machine guns in front of the supermarket," I say, unleashing the dogs and shutting the door to the apartment behind me. "And all along the street. Why do they need machine guns?"

"It's the beginning of the police state," Bea says, handing me a coffee.

And we really think it is. Today is January 20, 2017, it's the day that President Barack Obama leaves office, and a misogynistic white supremacist takes his place. We try not to say his name, as if he is Voldemort or an evil spirit.

"I spoke to some of the people attending the inauguration," I say, squeezing between half-filled boxes of our belongings to get to the balcony for a better view of the police with their guns and the groups of people in Make America Great Again hats streaming to the Washington Mall. "There aren't half as many as for Obama's inauguration, and they all seem a bit sad."

"What on earth did you find to say to them?" My wife, Bea, is American and this shift in politics has hit her hard, not least because she's been working for Obama for the past few years as the head of the Department of Justice's Office on Violence Against Women, a job she loves and now must leave.

"One of them said she thought he was going to support her transgender daughter," I say.

"Where the hell did she get that idea?"

"Another said he doesn't mean what he says about women and immigrants."

"So why does he say it then?"

"Another just wanted to say hello to the dogs and asked about their names."

I reach out to stroke Emma, who looks like a stocky German shepherd, but is a mix of all kinds of wonderful breeds. The Trump supporter hadn't heard of her namesake Emma Peel, the high-kicking secret agent in *The Avengers,* but I explained anyway. She recognized the pitbull in my boy dog, Jean-Luc, and had heard of the *Star Trek* captain he was named after.

"Dogs can always bring people together," I say, but you can also use dogs to hunt people, and that's the kind of history I fear is unfolding in Washington right now.

I'd smiled at two men wearing Standing Rock T-shirts who were incongruously caught up with the people headed to the Washington Mall. I talked to the supporters because I needed to remind myself that the people who elected him are human beings, too, and I want to think that they have been manipulated. That there must be a reason they did what they did that doesn't mean they are all racists and homophobes and hate women and immigrants and don't care about our climate, which is at breaking point. One woman said, "You're afraid of Trump. I'm afraid of Hillary." I told her I'm not a big Clinton fan, though maybe for different reasons. That I wanted Bernie to be the Democratic candidate and she said, "Bernie? Sure, we could have lived with Bernie."

I say all this, but I can't quite connect with how much I care. Many of my friends have been privately weeping and publicly ranting about their fears that fascism has found its way to the White House. I'm just going through the motions. My own private tragedy is unfolding, and it's far bigger than any of this. Kate, my older sister and my hero, is dying of cancer in England.

As soon as we've packed up Bea's apartment in Washington, as soon as we've moved back to Brooklyn tomorrow while tens of thousands of women are marching on Washington, I'm taking a flight to England so that I can sit at Kate's side and hold her hand.

Kate was always the first person I called when anything happened—good or bad. I called her to commiserate when Trump was elected and she said, "God, and I thought *we* were stupid." She was furious about Brexit. "I was in the village shop and a customer in front of me said how happy he was about the result. And in the very next breath he said he was moving to Spain in a couple of weeks."

She's the one I called when Bea and I tried to drive across the Mexican border with our dogs and got caught in a post-hurricane flood emergency. She's the one I called from a phone box from outside the hospital in London where my friend Clive had just died of AIDS. She's the one I called from the airport before almost every flight to help me trust the pilot and the air traffic controllers and face down my claustrophobia and get on the plane. She's the one I called every time I had a success or a challenge at my job in New York with Doctors Without Borders/ Médecins Sans Frontières, whenever I needed approval or support, or just to talk about our father, what his loss meant to us, and how best to handle our difficult relationships with our mother. She accepted the twins as her new nephews immediately, the two young Polish boys who lived on our block in Williamsburg, Brooklyn, who suffered a violent home, and who became part of our family. Kate was always my biggest champion and closest friend, and now it feels as if I am losing a piece of my soul.

"We all married well," she once said of us four siblings. "But you married the best."

Which made me laugh, because I had married a woman, which seems normal these days, but it really wasn't when we did it in San Francisco in 2008, in that small window of opportunity when they made it legal before Proposition 8 banned it again statewide. It was her way of saying how much she accepted my relationship with Bea. At our wedding reception in the village hall in St. Mary Bourne six months later, I wore my younger sister Sarah's dramatic red bodice and full white wedding skirt, and Bea wore a black suit with a flowing Adam Ant shirt beneath. The wedding party walked single file across fields of bluebells and sheep from the pub where we were staying to the recreation ground where I used to play football with Rob, getting funny sideways looks from the people watching the cricket match, where the men in white against the green of the pitch made the perfect backdrop for wedding party photographs. The Morris Dancers in the village square, with their bells and flags and sticks, threw me up in the air and kissed me on both cheeks over and over as part of the dance routine. And later, my siblings and I danced, as we always did when we got together, to Sister Sledge's "We Are Family." Then Kate and Rob and Sarah recited a twenty-verse poem they had written called "The Dynamic Duo," teasing me for my attachment to causes throughout my childhood and adult life—from the anti-apartheid movement to animal rights to peace to feminism to LGBTQ rights.

> Super Steph lived in the attic
> With posters all over the walls
> It's hard being "right on" in Hampshire
> But that didn't stop her at all
>
> Her beanie hat covered in badges
> With cuts on her Super Steph knees
> Determined to save all around her
> She started by just hugging trees . . .

They talked about how I was destined to meet Bea, my American soul mate, who worked for the New York City Gay and Lesbian Anti-Violence Project when I met her.

> Bea was equally driven
> By subway she went day and night
> Tackling cruelty in every borough
> Determined to fight the good fight
>
> Superman, Batman, and Robin
> All wore special cloaks you will find
> Bea Wonder patrolled New York City
> With dreadlocks flowing behind . . .

She'd developed those dreadlocks in Israel when she spent a year there on a moshav in her early twenties at the same time I was at Greenham. She almost came to the camp on her way home through Heathrow, but decided to keep going instead because she had too big a rug to carry and was tired. We always wonder what would have happened if she hadn't bought a rug in Istanbul. If she would have come to Blue Gate, or if she'd have gone to Yellow with the rest of the Americans, if I would have dared to speak to her, if we would have fallen in love and had an extra ten years together.

In the poem, my siblings talked about Bea's one day working for Obama, and took credit when she was offered the job.

"See, we wrote it in the poem, and now it's happened!" Kate exclaimed. "Watch out for what I write next." She couldn't have been prouder, and that is all I wanted, all any of us wanted—Rob, Sarah, Kate's three amazing kids, her husband. "Dad would have been so proud of you," she said more than once, knowing how much it meant for me to hear that. And even when she didn't understand, she supported me, like when I started *A Queer Tribe* magazine in Brighton in the 1990s; and when I worked for Thich Nhat Hanh's monks and nuns in the woods of upstate New York and learned about mindfulness and engaged Buddhism, while Bea went to Washington, DC to work for Obama, even though Kate worried about us living apart. Kate, with the brightest of energy, the sun we orbited around, the one everyone turned to when she walked into a room, expectant and delighted, Kate, who was going to show us all how to grow old without losing our light, our fire, our humour.

I have collapsed on the kitchen floor again and Emma is right there, like she always is, licking the salty tears from my face, Bea looking helplessly on.

WHEN I WALK the dogs the next morning, the crowd of despondent white families going to the Presidential inauguration has been replaced with crowds of laughing black, brown, and white women and children with brightly coloured signs, many wearing identical pink hats, on their way to the women's march.

"Why pink?" I say in disgust when I get home. "Pink is such a girlie colour. Why not flaming red for rage or purple and white and green for the suffragettes?"

"This is America," Bea says. "We haven't heard of the suffragettes or care about anything that happened more than twenty years ago. Anyway, they are pussy hats."

A sea of women wearing hats to represent their vaginas—some pink, some brown—in response to a presidential candidate talking on camera about "grabbing women by the pussy." I hate the term, I hate that we are letting this person define our response—but is it any different from reclaiming the word queer or fag or dyke, which I've done with gusto? I think of Judy Chicago's *Dinner Party*, which I first heard about when I was at Greenham. It was a large installation of plates at a dinner party, with a vagina at each setting, each representing a famous woman. I remember Lucy saying, "I'm sure Virginia Wolf would be delighted to learn she is going to be remembered for her vagina."

Perhaps it's empowering for young women to reclaim this word, to wear these hats proudly with thousands of other women at a time when everything seems to be going backwards for us after years of progress. I feel like a prude, out of touch, and old. Mostly I am filled with rage but it's not the same rage that everyone else is feeling. I don't have the energy to reach a state of anger about what's happening to my adopted country. I am raging against the injustice of what is happening to Kate. I'm not planning on attending the march even though it is literally on my doorstep.

I'm pretty sure Lucy won't be attending the march in London, either. The last time I saw her, she was living with a parrot in a flat in London and gave us burnt toast for breakfast. She was working as a social worker with the elderly and immigrants, had written a book about mental health, and spent her time working, raising money for small charities, visiting her son, and having rambling conversations with her intellectual friends about literature, children, and the state of the world. I wonder what she thinks of the pussy hats, and if she's boycotting the march in true Lucy style because she believes social change happens in the kitchen, community centre, school, and hospital, in the daily kindnesses that weave together our social fabric, and because she thinks large marches and movements get hijacked by big egos and others' agendas. Last we spoke, she told me she had grown tired of marches and movements and didn't believe they really effected much change. I actually like them, for the reminder that I'm not alone and for the collective energy, which can lift me like a kite. I can even get excited by a baseball match in a bar if there are enough people excited by it, even though I don't know the rules. And nothing brings me more joy than the collective energy of the World Cup every four years. But today I don't care.

"Let's just go for ten minutes before we drive." It's lunchtime and Bea is standing at the door with both dogs leashed up. "They need a walk anyway, we can just go and look."

We've packed all we can to take with us and the movers will follow with the rest next week.

"I haven't got a sign," I say. "If I go, I want a sign saying 'Smash the Patriarchy.'"

But all of the cardboard has been used up to pack our books and kitchen things and everything else, and we can't find a marker.

I shrug and follow her onto the streets. We walk along 2nd Street NE to the entrance to Union Station, a magnificent building whose triumphal arcs are disgorging trainfuls of happy, shouting, laughing, colourful women. It reminds me of Greenham—the handmade signs, the hand-knitted hats (though here they are all the same); the smiles, the children, the press, the smattering of male supporters, the chill in the air.

WE WALK PAST two smiling cops wearing pink pussy hats, yellow flowers in their buttonholes, guns on their hips. There are homemade signs everywhere. "Make America Not Racist for the First Time." "I Have Decided to Stick With Love." "Love Trumps Hate." "Black Lives Matter." "Make America Kind Again." "Bridges Not Walls." "Make Facts Great Again." "Trans Rights Now." "Stop Making Shit Up." Then a boy walks by with a sign that says, "What Do We Want? Evidence Based Science. When Do We Want It? After Peer Review."

I like this one a lot. I work for a scientific organization now, even though I can't add up and didn't study science. I arrange events and write for the Drugs for Neglected Diseases *initiative*, a not-for-profit drug development agency created by Doctors Without Borders/ Médecins Sans Frontières with its Nobel Peace Prize money. We make drugs for neglected diseases that affect people in faraway places who are too poor to constitute a "market" for the pharmaceutical industry— diseases few people have heard of like sleeping sickness and Chagas and leishmaniasis—oh, and paediatric HIV, a disease people have heard of, but most research for HIV has been into drugs for adults, with hardly any focus on the little ones—so we work on that, too.

"Let's walk a bit farther," I say, and we join the river of women and girls as it winds along the wide paths leading past the Supreme Court Building and down to the Mall.

And that's when I see her. A young girl, maybe eleven years old, and she's carrying my message "Smash the Patriarchy." I laugh for the first time in weeks.

"Can we have a photograph?" I turn to her parents, two women, who nod.

"Can I put it on social media?" I ask. They nod again, and smiling, we part, as I watch the girl happily chanting as she swings her placard in the air.

"Wow, I wish I had known what the patriarchy was at her age," I say. "She had my banner."

For some reason this makes me inordinately happy.

As we walk, women stop to greet the dogs, we take photos of their banners, it's all smiles and chants and laughter, a colourful antidote to yesterday's grey skies and grey crowds. We have hope, it seems, not despair. Like we had at Greenham, when faced with nuclear war, we had humour and hope and love. And we helped make change happen. I visited Blue Gate recently, with Bea, and we walked along winding paths in the woods, meeting the occasional dogwalker or family out for a stroll. It's no longer a military base, it's open common land bustling with birdsong and wildlife, with informational signs telling the history of the base, including photographs of Greenham women protesting. It was peaceful and ordinary, no wild women crouched around fires, eyes ablaze; no piles of food and plates posing as a kitchen; no soldiers with guns standing to attention behind mesh fencing; no police officers guarding the front gates; no battered old vehicles doubling up as a room for the night. We read on a flyer that you would soon be able to visit the watch towers—without having to climb through tunnels and risking arrest—and that a café and event space called The Greenham Watchtower would be opening in the near future. The cruise missiles are long gone from the United Kingdom. If we could get rid of them, surely we can endure, and get rid of, this new American president.

I wonder if the rest of my Greenham friends are marching today. We were out of touch for the longest time after I moved to New York, but slowly, one by one, I found some of them on social media, and stayed in touch that way. Zee lives off-grid in a cottage in the Scottish Highlands, on two acres of land populated with rescue goats, cats, dogs, and chickens. She's a psychic medium, plants herbs, and posts pleas on social media for help rescuing or housing abused animals. Is there a march in Scotland, and would she even go if there was? She was on a different plane from the rest of us—radical, spiritual, truly with the fairies—and always willing to take risks others wouldn't. If anyone was climbing a bridge to hang a banner or dig through a tunnel to invade a facility, Zee was the kind of fearless person to be at the helm, laughing, taunting, challenging. Zephyr now lives in a Berlin suburb with her husband and two sons, teaching music. She has a home with a garden large enough to raise chickens and grow tomatoes and spinach and squash as well as herbs for her famous tisanes. And she still sings sometimes, recording lilting lullabies or strident anthems, playing her banjo or saxophone, bringing her passion and creativity to the world as best she can. Is she marching with her boys and her husband, yelling slogans in German, making up songs that catch the crowd in waves, like she did at Greenham?

We all lost touch with Elena, my fragile crush, who often seemed just inches away from disaster, with her later brushes with drugs, crime, the wrong girlfriend. Is she still alive, is she happy, is she marching in the north of England with a loving girlfriend or wife, does she have children, as she always wanted? I know Ming is marching today in Birmingham. Later, she will tell me how flat it all felt, especially in contrast to a Black Lives Matter demonstration she attended weeks later that inspired her as much as the anti-nuclear and queer marches of the eighties used to, attracting people of all ages and genders and races and ending with a peaceful sit-down and sing-a-long outside the police station in the city centre. She photographed much of it, she's a well-established photographer now, her favourite projects are of queers and women and working-class people and activists, and she has held exciting outdoor exhibits with images of people projected onto bridges and walls, like the French photographer JR. I found Al on social media not long ago and hesitated and decided not to contact her. She still has a red Mohican. She has a new name and works as a strongman in a travelling circus in Europe. Did she join a merry band of circus performers and entertain the crowds at the women's march in Barcelona, Paris, or Rome?

Gentle Penny left Greenham when she fell in love with a male, anarcho-punk, animal rights activist in Bristol, and became a hunt saboteur and defender of innocent and much-loved animals like badgers and hedgehogs. I wonder if she's marching or if she's given up on the human race with its power politics, violence, and unkindness. I wouldn't blame her. When you've looked a terrified fox cub in the eye, when you've rescued tiny puppies from a crowded puppy mill, when you've seen the inside of a facility testing products for humans on animals, and when so few other people seem to care, you need all the energy you've got. Shula was unaware the marches were even happening. She was embarking on a period of her own monumental change, studying in Bristol and Ireland to become a spiritual therapist, while in the midst of leaving a happy twenty-year marriage with a man to start an exciting new relationship with a woman. As for Sally, she spent this momentous day lying on a beach in Thailand with her partner, Ruth, watching the global marches on their phones, exclaiming at the size and scope of the demonstrations taking place all across the globe from Australia to France to Alaska to Nigeria to India—lifted by the energy, smiling at the young faces, liking our posts on social media. She almost wished she was there, she told me later, because she was livid about the American election, the backwards slide, the greed, the racism, the disrespect shown to women and the planet. But she travels every winter to escape the English gloom, somewhere warm with sea, sand, and good food, returning reinvigorated to the alternative health practice in Sussex she runs with Ruth, where she teaches families how to cook nutritious food, how to escape, as she puts it, the pharmaceutical grip on health care.

THE ENERGY OF the march, this massive crowd of women, has unexpectedly brought my Greenham friends back into sharp focus—all of us thrown together for an intense experience that was so life-changing for me and connected me deeply to these women, wherever they are and whatever they are doing. That's what it all comes down to in the end: it's not giving in to despair, it's not letting the patriarchy's madnesses define your own relationship to life. It's love and happiness and music and kindness and community and fairies and funny slogans and protecting animals and marvelling at the wonders of nature and doing what we can to make change for the good wherever we are and to whomever is around us. And from time to time, a demonstration or occupation or movement emerges as a collective expression of our anger, our hope, our vision— like the Chartists, the Suffragettes, and the civil rights movement; like

Occupy Wall Street and Black Lives Matter; like Extinction Rebellion and the Chilean Lastesis collective—with its viral feminist anthem—yet to come.

I LOOK AROUND and see thousands of shining faces looking toward the sun, people emanating kindness and justice, and I have a glimmer of hope that perhaps, just perhaps, there are enough of us. Everyone here has a story, just like mine, a trajectory that took them through a rich and complicated life and landed them here, at this demonstration, for this moment of collective connectedness, meaning, purpose, power, and belonging, for this expression of public love that stretches across the globe to nourish us as we weave back into our individual lives, ready for the days ahead.

# Acknowledgements

I want to thank my sister Kate for championing the book in its early drafts and for being the heart and soul of our family, missed beyond words; my sister Sarah for reading the final draft to find Americanisms I didn't know I had in me; my brother, Robert, for playing football, cricket, and snooker with me at a time when girls were supposed to play with dolls; my mum, Pam, for her humor and feistiness and who blessed the book's publication despite what I say about her; my dad, Bob, for imbuing me with his passion for social justice; and my nephew and nieces Tom, Alice, Rosie, Alicia, Annie, Charlie, and Nell, who may now know a bit more about our family and why we are the way we are.

I have so much gratitude to Claudia Wilde at Bedazzled Ink for believing in *Other Girls Like Me* and to C.A. Casey and Liz Gibson for their upbeat energy and for making the publishing process fun and easy. Great thanks, too, to Beverly Donofrio for starting this all off in her memoir class in Woodstock and for her incisive and ruthless editing skills—and to all the members of that class, especially the two Alices, David, Al, Margot, and Denise, whose writing and comments on my own taught me so much. I also want to thank Christabel Gurney of the Anti-Apartheid Movement Archives, Tim Murphy, Pete Fender, Gem Stone, Nick Leather, Isobel Carter, Mary Donovan, Aaron Sinift, and Caroline Hardman—and the Impress Prize for New Writers for shortlisting the book in 2018.

Thank you to friends who read early drafts of the book and gave me encouragement—Marc Boone, Chris Nadori, Julia Pittorino, Christophe Vigier, Heather Joyce, Debbie Scanlon, Michelle Chiu, Sophie Delaunay, Ian Pryce, Rosie Hopkins, Bridget Currie, Gillian Jagger, Alice Schechter, Carrie, Mike, and Marley Pradieu, and my mother-in-law, Austra Hanson; Jason Nguyen for creating my website (and for so much more); and my Greenham friends Lizzie Spring, Sally Galloway, Penny Thornton, Shula Roscoe, and Xak A Roo for fact-checking the book and who, along with many others, gave me a host of adventures told and untold. Special thanks to Ming de Nasty, photographer extraordinaire, for the photograph she took at Stowford Farm that captures the era so perfectly and that now graces the cover. Thank you to Lorna Chiu, Barbara Kancelbaum, Verna Gillis, Sebastian Junger, Ann Limb, and Frances Weil for their ongoing encouragement and advice.

Much love to my New York family for their support, always: Hamza Giaffar, Tollevin Williams, Jason Nguyen, Marc Boone, Rachel Cohen, Carrie, Mike, Marley, and Elijah Pradieu, and our wonderful "sons" Dominic and Damian Bielak. Writing the book is inextricably bound with my dogs, Emma and Jean-Luc, who lay by my side as I wrote. Finally, I want to thank my wife and life partner, Bea Hanson, who keeps my feet on the ground and my heart in the stars.

Stephanie Davies is a writer who worked for many years in communications for Doctors Without Borders/Médecins Sans Frontières in the United States. A UK native, Stephanie moved to New York in 1991, where she taught English Composition at Long Island University in Brooklyn and led research trips to Cuba. Before moving to New York, she co-edited a grassroots LGBTQ magazine in Brighton called *A Queer Tribe*. Stephanie earned a teaching degree from Aberystwyth University in Wales and a BA in European Studies from Bath University, England. She grew up in St. Mary Bourne, a small village in Hampshire. Today, Stephanie divides her time between Brooklyn and the Hudson Valley, New York where she lives with her wife, Bea, and rescue dog, Emma.